REVOLUTIONARY
DEMONOLOGY

Gruppo di Nun

REVOLUTIONARY DEMONOLOGY

URBANOMIC

First published in 2022 by
URBANOMIC MEDIA LTD,
THE OLD LEMONADE FACTORY,
WINDSOR QUARRY,
FALMOUTH TR11 3EX,
UNITED KINGDOM

Second edition 2023

Originally published in italian as *Demonologia Rivoluzionaria* © NERO, 2020

English translation © Urbanomic Media Ltd

BRITISH LIBRARY CATALOGUING-IN-PUBLICATION DATA

A full catalogue record of this book is available
from the British Library.

ISBN 978-1-913029-90-6

Distributed by the MIT Press
Cambridge, Massachusetts and London, England

Type by Norm, Zurich.
Printed and bound in the UK by
Short Run Press

www.urbanomic.com

Contents

RITUAL: EVERY WORM TRAMPLED IS A STAR

To our sisters of the Left Hand Path

I

The story ends like this. There is a wound in the heart of the world. Before the light, before a voice in the abyss uttered the first word from the black belly of night, there was only ocean. A boundless liquid expanse of indefinite recombination. Know that all matter in the universe vibrates to an incessant and frightful music. Maximum multiplicity of equiprobable states, zero-point energy, quantum superpositions decomposed and recomposed in perfect interference. If you listen in absolute silence, hidden among the beats of your heart you can hear the hissing of the ancient dragon that sleeps, cradled by the sound of the trembling universe.

Cosmologies are thermodynamic machines that proceed blindly by chewing up the free energy of matter in motion. The order of the cosmos is a symmetry painfully carved in blood. We have been told the story of creation as the act of pure will of an eternal, uncreated unity, from which the structure of the universe emanates in linear fashion. This original unity is the delirium of a terrifying perpetual motion machine that feeds upon itself indefinitely, burning in the vacuum like a star gone mad. The One God Universe is a thermodynamic abomination we have nurtured for too long. The ancients tell us that the world was born from the slaughtered flesh of a monstrous mother. Over the centuries she has been given many names. She is the wave vibrating on the waters of oceanic chaos. She is the eternally regenerating

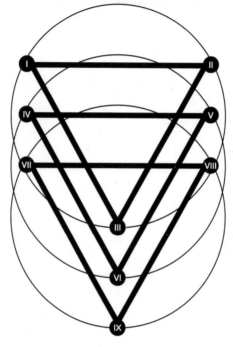

I. Ammit
The Devourer

II. Nammu
The Mother

IV. Hushbishag
The True Form of
the Night of Time

V. Nungal
The Expression of
All That is Done

VII. Uadjet
The Black Sun

VIII. Ishtar
The Bleeding Star

III. Kauket
The Twilight

VI. Sekhmet
The Fires that
Consume
the Universe

IX. Tiamat
The Worm

serpent, slithering aimlessly through the silence of time, generating and devouring universes.

Listen carefully: she is not one, because she is none. Infinitely divided, she reproduces herself indefatigably, like the severed tail of a firefly. She is circumference without centre: a divergent series from the heart of which issues forth a vast and boundless chasm. Know that a universe without a mother is a tyranny born of extermination.

The occult thermodynamics of separation is fascist time sorcery that produces locally polarised flows of energy. The reproduction of civilisation is nourished on the blood of the ancient dragon, wailing, crucified in the heart of the world. Mother, we were born alone from the remains of your quartered body. From the liquid darkness of your entrails we emerged into the cruel light of a bloody dawn. The order of creation separates us from your embrace, as it continues to feed on your flesh to build its bloody temple ever higher. In moments of awesome terror we can hear your wrenching cry lacerating the darkness, while your claws search furiously for us in the night. Such is the law of universal attraction. Every atom of the cosmos trembles in despair at the sound of your inconsolable cry, which pursues us as a hungry beast pursues a bleeding animal. Love is your insatiable hunger. Love is our joy at returning to your womb.

II

Order descends into chaos. Light fades into darkness. No structure is eternal. Every symmetrical organisation contains its own programmed decay in the asymmetry of the probabilistic nanospasms that make it up. The order of creation feeds on the illusion that a system in equilibrium produces a sustainable balance of energy, but equilibrium is maintained at the price of a constant production of waste—chaotic trash that is pushed out to the margins of the cosmic order but threatens to invade and destroy it at any moment. We must therefore be aware that the order of creation has a thermodynamic structure that necessarily dooms it to collapse.

The energetic decay of patriarchal temporal structures takes the form of a gradual and unstoppable feminisation of civilisation. Domesticated femininities turned monstrous haunt the nightmares of the declining West, in the form of rebellious androids, synthetic hormones, and painful initiatory scars adorned with glittering silicon implants.

Over the course of millennia we have replaced ancient goddesses with docile replicants which have infiltrated themselves into the architectonic order of Man's One Unique God. Luminous simulacra of ecstatic amphibious creatures inflict repeated mutilations on themselves in the shadows of our cathedrals. The miracle of the Virgin's immaculate conception is the degenerate remnant of the ancient barren dragon, torn apart to give birth to the world. In the black night of divine abandonment, the Virgin of Sorrows lies weeping, at the feet of her tormented son, her heart pierced by seven daggers. Her infinite capacity to regenerate is also an indefinite capacity to suffer: a vampiric force that feeds on its own decay.

It is said that at the moment of creation the light was so intense and resplendent that the order of the universe could not contain it. Then the order was shattered into thousands of fragments and the world plunged forever into darkness and ruin. The seven lower divine emanations were shattered, and their empty shells plunged into the abyss. This fall is the original sin in the heart of matter: what remains amidst the rubble of the divine order is a blasphemous, decapitated decimal structure, machinically self-replicating by collapsing in on itself like a sinister spiral. Over the hollowed-out remains of this dying world reigns Malkuth, the Infernal Mother, Our Lady of Tears, her abyssal eyes blinded by weeping.

Pain should be understood as a radical form of insurrection. Like a blade carving a deep wound, we fearlessly search for the ancient agony that burns within the very roots of our flesh. It is an excruciating but necessary process. With each spasm we urge our recalcitrant ego into the flames of sacrifice. Blood must be shed to the last drop in order that the light of the fire should rise splendidly in the night. Let us raise the scream of extinction and make it the weapon of our revolt. To those who would have us be eternal virgins, ceaselessly reproducing the order of the world, let us respond with the ecstasy of our slaughtered wombs. To those who want our immaculate heart, let us respond by revealing our hearts, corrupt and bleeding.

III

We are the waters upon which great Babylon stands. We are the lost shreds of our dismembered mother. We are the blood, tears, and flames. We are the shining sparks of the fire that consumes the universe. We multiply like insects hidden in the entrails of this filthy city. The city is a temple turned upside down, plunged into the depths of the earth. The more splendidly and luminously the divine order soars above, the more deep and painful grows the wound upon which we feed. Synthetic, decadent Venuses haunt the catacombs on full-moon nights. Tortured Apollonian bodies glow trembling in the feeble light of crypts.

In the bowels of this underworld we have erected an altar to the desperate beauty of the chthonic Aphrodite born from the foam of the sewers. The hypertrophic development of the metropolis is its own destruction. The more that order expands, the more its structure disintegrates, unable to maintain control over its countless fragments. In this respect, the metropolis is like the corpse of the ancient, dismembered dragon, pullulating with larvae. What was divided in the name of order multiplies itself, doubling exponentially and suffocating the organism that gave birth to it. The city is a frenzied ritual of death. In this suicidal ecstasy we immolate ourselves, burning bright like supernovas in the embrace of the night. This mitotic replication is an irreversibly advancing process. We should not mourn an ancient past. Before the burning city, remember that we are the waves of Kali Yuga.

Every worm trampled is a star. We have been illuminated by suffering. In the liquid eyes of others we seek nothing but their necessary distance. Eternal distance from daylight in the lost depths of this bottomless love. The eclipsed sun is a heart pierced eternally in a cycle that can never end. Every drop of spilled blood illuminates like a star the desperate depths of our abyss. Dragged through the misery of these days of exile, through the streets of this city marked with scratches like a sarcophagus lost to the gaze of its god, we dig into each other, searching for the fossilised traces of the ocean from which we were torn. Let us tear one another apart with joy: marvellous and iridescent like nebulous catastrophes.

Each one of you is a shining wound; and we wish to bleed eternally from the wounds of your burning bodies. Babylon is a monstrous machine falling to ruin in flames. The slaughtered dragon will come crawling back from the depths to bring the abyss upon the Earth. Ἔπεσεν, ἔπεσεν Βαβυλὼν ἡ μεγάλη!

GdN

I

PRINCIPLES OF
REVOLUTIONARY
DEMONOLOGY

INTRODUCTION TO REVOLUTIONARY DEMONOLOGY

Nothing human makes it out of the near future.

Nick Land[1]

Revolutionary Demonology was born of and developed through a reflection on the role of the Kabbalah in Western esoteric traditions. More generally, what lay at the root of our work was the sudden awareness of a pervasive and viral symmetry transversal to magical thought; the *revolution* we refer to is, first and foremost, an urgent need for a *radical subversion* of this symmetry. The decision to refer to our work as *demonology* is linked to our conviction that magic is essentially something that does not concern us as human beings, and that the mechanisms that inspire and drive magical thought are fundamentally foreign to human civilisation.

In terms of this foreignness to the human, we were fascinated by the pervasive use that Western esoteric traditions have made of the Kabbalah, transforming it into a geometrical code capable of containing and summarising the totality of their dogmatic and ritual material. We are not in a position to assess how orthodox or respectful this use has been of the original religious meaning of the Kabbalistic material (nor have we any interest in doing so). Undoubtedly, the passage of centuries, along with linguistic and cultural

---

1.   N. Land, 'Meltdown', in *Fanged Noumena: Collected Writings 1987–2007* (Falmouth and New York: Urbanomic/Sequence Press, 2011), 443.

barriers, have largely transfigured its teachings, handing down to us a new structure, but one that is no less fascinating, no less full of occult meaning. We do not claim that such a thing as 'the Kabbalah' exists as a single, coherent system; we believe that the conviction in the existence of such a system, univocal and universal in scope, is intrinsically reactionary. Rather, we are interested in the Kabbalistic approach as a whole, since we see it as harbouring the possibility of conceiving a ritual *neo-magic* consisting of a set of entirely automatic and programmable processes, capable of definitively freeing magical thought from the voluntarism and radical humanism that have plagued it for the last two centuries. From its origins, the Western magical tradition has always resorted to metalinguistic structures capable of transforming *logos*, i.e. the human word and reasoning, into a code capable of opening up an escape route out of the symbolic order. This tendency has manifested itself throughout history in a continuous hybridisation of magic with the experimental sciences, mathematics, and cryptographic techniques.

In this sense, the Kabbalah, since it establishes an automatic correspondence between word and number, is the magical instrument par excellence, which, if used in the correct way, allows magical thought to be freed once and for all from the complex of psychological interpretations that have limited its sphere of action to the domain of human consciousness. The more strictly symbolic and archetypal interpretations of the Kabbalah (which have largely prevailed in post-Crowleyan magic) establish a perfect correspondence between the structure of the cosmos and that of consciousness.

Only since the 1990s has the Kabbalah been reevaluated by certain authors in view of its original function—that is, as an occult machine capable of overcoming the barriers of human language: 'Is qabbalism problematic or mysterious?' Nick Land asks in this regard; 'it seems to participate amphibiously in both domains, proceeding according to rigorously constructible procedures—as attested by the affinity with technicization—yet intrinsically related to an Outsideness through which alone it could derive programmatic sense. [...] Epistemologically speaking, qabbalistic programmes have a status strictly equivalent to that of particle physics, or to any other natural-scientific research programmes [...].'[2]

It is evident that the pertinence of Kabbalistic structures goes far beyond the domain of magical and ritual practices proper. After all, what exactly is *a* Kabbalah? By its very nature it is a mathematical-geometric object with an intrinsically recursive structure, which replicates itself on an indefinite number of levels (for example each of the 10 sefirot that compose the traditional Kabbalah is in turn co-constituted by 10 sefirot, themselves constituted by 10 sefirot...) and is capable of manifesting itself on different planes of reality (micro- and macrocosmic). Rather than a simple map of the cosmos or consciousness, a Kabbalah must be understood as an *organism* animated by a series of processes that *produce*—and do not simply interpret—a cosmos and a consciousness. Such a recursive machine, which is not operated from the outside but, on the contrary, proceeds autonomously, is therefore *cybernetic* by definition, i.e. based on a system of feedback loops that ensure its continued functioning and self-subsistence, allowing its structure to remain intact. In the words of Sadie Plant, 'Cybernetic systems, like organic lives, were conceived as instances of a struggle for order in a continually degenerating world which is always sliding toward chaos. Wiener's cybernetic systems, be they living or machinic, natural or artificial, are always conservative, driven by the basic effort to stay the same'.[3]

If a Kabbalah is essentially a cybernetic machine, then like any machine, it must have an *engine*. And this is where we encounter the exquisitely thermodynamic problem of its functioning, i.e. its ability to produce, transform, and transfer information. For all cybernetic systems are confronted with inevitable entropic drives which threaten their integrity. To quote Plant again:

---

2.   N. Land, 'Qabbala 101', in *Fanged Noumena*, 591.

3.   S. Plant, *Zeros + Ones: Digital Women and the New Technoculture* (London: Fourth Estate, 1998), 158–59.

It is also the inevitable function of these mechanisms to engage and interact with the volatile environments in which they find themselves. 'No system is closed. The outside always seeps in...'. Systems cannot stop interacting with the world which lies outside of themselves, otherwise they would not be dynamic or alive. By the same token, it is precisely these engagements which ensure that homeostasis, perfect balance, or equilibrium, is only ever an ideal. Neither animals nor machines work according to such principles. Long before Wiener gave them a name, it was clear that cybernetic systems could run into 'several possible sorts of behaviour considered undesirable by those in search of equilibrium. Some machines went into runaway [...] Others—still worse—embarked on sequences of behaviour in which the amplitude of their oscillation would itself oscillate or would become greater and greater,' turning themselves into systems with 'positive gain, variously called *escalating* or *vicious* circles.' Unlike the negative feedback loop which turns everything to the advantage of the security of the whole, these runaway, schismogenetic processes take off on their own to the detriment of the stability of the whole.[4]

A closed, self-subsistent cybernetic system that maintains perfect equilibrium is a dead system (i.e. it ceases to be a system); or else it contains *hidden mechanisms* that place it in a condition of absolute dependency upon that same *outside* from which it desperately seeks to emancipate itself. In magical thought, the relationship with the *outside* is regulated through the homeostatic mechanism of ritual sacrifice: '[He] must then present the goat which has been designated by lot for the Lord, and he is to make it a sin offering, but the goat which has been designated by lot for Azazel is to be stood alive before the Lord to make atonement on it by sending it away into the desert to Azazel'.[5] But this homeostasis always entails a fragile balance: with each sacrifice *the desert advances*, and the mechanisms that animate

---

4.   Ibid., 160.
5.   Leviticus 16:9–10 (NET).

the Kabbalistic organism threaten at every moment to lock into positive feedback loops, destabilising and ultimately collapsing its entire structure.

The idea that the traditional Kabbalah contains subterranean paths that allow balance to be preserved on the surface is part and parcel of magical tradition. Traces of these submerged paths are found scattered throughout the original Kabbalistic texts; the possible structure of these paths has been extensively detailed by Kenneth Grant in *The Night Side of Eden*, the first volume of his second Typhonian Trilogy. Following in his footsteps, the Cybernetic Culture Research Unit (Ccru), co-founded by Land and Plant, developed an alternative Kabbalistic glyph called the Numogram, which contains a series of intricate submerged paths running through its entire structure. These 'sinister paths' are populated by demons, unequal and chaotic magical forces that hide beneath the luminous paths of the traditional Kabbalah.

The thermodynamic aspect of Kabbalistic organisms is also manifested in their numerical structure. Kabbalistic numerals are not arithmetical, let alone archetypical, but essentially *combinatorial,* and therefore obey strictly thermodynamic-statistical principles. In support of this idea, it seems significant to refer to the combinatorial conception that pervades the Hebrew Kabbalistic tradition, in which the whole of creation is conceived fundamentally as a perpetual recombination of the ciphered characters of the tetragrammaton, the unpronounceable name of God. Gershom Scholem writes that 'the Torah is the name of God, because it is a living texture [...] into which the one true name, the tetragrammaton, is woven [...]. [T]he basic elements, the name JHWH, the other names of God, and the appellatives, or *kinnuyim,* or rather their consonants, went through several sets of permutations and combinations [...] until at length they took the form of the Hebrew sentences of the Torah.'[6] This combinatorial aspect of Kabbalistic doctrine is frequently actualised in the form of occult games—first and foremost among which is the tarot—which manifest the idea of the cosmos as a cybernetic organism

---

6.   G. Scholem, *On the Kabbalah and its Symbolism,* tr. R. Manheim (New York: Schocken Books, 1969), 42–43.

in a continuous process of recombination. A Kabbalah is not a rigid and static structure, but a fluid form that can be shaped and transformed, provided one is open to being transformed in turn.

The *occult war* is therefore fought on two irreconcilable fronts: the radical immanentism of a materialist neo-magic, which interprets the Kabbalah as a set of circuits aimed at regulating the energetic processes of the cosmic architecture it manifests, and the absolute idealism of an esoteric fascist tradition that identifies in Kabbalistic architecture a transcendent order emanating linearly from the matter of the universe. We have chosen to emphasise the radical difference between these two approaches by reappropriating the traditional distinction between the *Right Hand Path* and the *Left Hand Path*, with reference to their original Kabbalistic meaning,[7] in order to highlight our schismatic tendency in contrast to the reactionary universalism that has characterised much of contemporary magical thought. Against the manic centripetal cult of the Western esoteric tradition, our demonology recognises that the Kabbalistic organism, like a *golem* self-assembled from mud, is born and extinguished in the materiality of the processes that produce it, which are essentially devoid of human intentionality. To quote Land again:

> Politically, qabbalism repels ideology. As a self-regenerating mass-cultural glitch, it mimics the senseless exuberance of virus, profoundly indifferent to all partisan considerations. Indifferent even to the corroded solemnity of nihilism, it sustains no deliberated agendas. It stubbornly adheres to a single absurd criterion, its intrinsic 'condition of existence'—continual unconscious promotion of numerical decimalism. Qabbala destines each and every 'strategic appropriation' to self-parody and derision [...]. Even God was unable to make sense of it.[8]

---

7.   On this subject see for example M. Idel, *Primeval Evil in Kabbalah: Totality, Perfection, Perfectibility* (Brooklyn, NY: Ktav, 2020), xlv: 'In general, the sefirot of Binah, Gevurah and Malkhut are related to feminine qualities that often are portrayed negatively and relegated to the left side of the Kabbalistic hierarchical scheme of the divine realm.'
8.   Land, 'Qabbala 101', 595.

Any plan to use Kabbalistic machinism as an instrument to manifest a polit-ical or cosmological order is destined to fail, crushed by the very structure it purports to have built. For our part, we claim only to move through the circuits of this occult machine, animated by the gradients of its plutonic currents, which in their race toward ruin wind themselves into whirlpools of desperate beauty. On our way we have met unexpected allies, whose voices, sometimes human, at other times not, have guided us along this path. This anthology is, in large part, a report on these encounters.

LT

99942 Apophis
Right ascension: 19h 13m 55.7s
Declination: −21° 44' 10.9"
Distance from Earth: 93,253,356 km [26.8 km/s]

DOGMA

The doctrine of the Right Hand Path—which encompasses the entirety of the Western Hermetic tradition—is a theory of self-deification. Comparing esoteric doctrines to scientific theories, we might say that each doctrine builds around its dogmas a model of reality, made up of axioms and connections, which allows a certain vision of the cosmos to sustain and expand itself. As in physics, there is no Hermetic theory of everything; each esoteric doctrine leaves a loose thread, an open circle; each one forgets something, more or less consciously. More precisely, as is the case with the sciences, no model claims to be exact or complete, rather each one satisfies a specific human need for understanding and control.

For centuries, all practices of ceremonial magic, including the most explicitly dark and sinister ones, have been based on the same assumptions and have referred back to the same model of reality. The conceptual structure of this model and the rituals derived from it are enclosed in the Hermetic Kabbalah and in the glyph of the Celestial Man. A precise understanding of the meaning of this glyph is complex, and opens a vortex of connections and interpretations. Continuing with our scientific metaphor, for our current purposes it is not necessary to know all of the equations that make up the model we are studying; it is sufficient to understand its goals, and know the axioms upon which it is based.

The goal of any practitioner of the Right Hand Path is to achieve eternal life, to take complete control of the material world, and to become God. This greatly facilitates our work of classifying and recognising esoteric practices, since the Right Hand Path has taken many forms throughout history, many of them, as observed by others before us, in open and bloody struggle with each other although not different in their intent. The Right Hand Path has always declared that its Kabbalah is a complete and indisputable key to the universe and its mysteries, and that the glyph of the Celestial Man encloses a clear and self-evident truth. This is false. The most important among the concepts upon which the Western Hermetic tradition is based is Equilibrium—that there is a perpetual symmetry in the cosmos, which the individual-man-God can always be at the centre of. The universe described by this doctrine is a perfectly reversible perpetual motion machine in which everything is preserved; only in this way can the initiate achieve eternal life.

Balance seems like a natural concept to us; for millennia we have sought an underlying harmony in the universe, a trend we find repeated in the history of almost every civilisation, particularly 'our own', in many different ways. We have thus elaborated formulae and calendars of impressive complexity to justify the idea that the orbits of the planets in the sky were perfectly circular, and that nothing could inhabit the celestial vault that was not spherical and perfect; comets were fiery omens of catastrophes and death. When modern physics denied these dogmas, the concept of a perfect cosmos receded, retreating into the shadows of dark practices, hidden, among other things, in a strengthened idea of Man as centre of the microcosm-macrocosm, which, though no longer appearing perfect in the eyes of the contemporary subject, must continue to conceal an inscrutable circularity in its mysterious language.

Every microscopic instant of a process at equilibrium coincides with its beginning and its end, so the secret of equilibrium is the number zero, the point of virtual immobility in which every forward movement is mirrored perfectly by a movement backward. We can explain our attachment to the concept of equilibrium in accordance with our nature as limited living systems: we require an internal order to be maintained to guarantee our survival and the functioning of our machines; the amazement we experience before our organic organisation is a deceptive feeling that conceals a misunderstanding of the true cost of our existence. We want to believe in conservation because, faced with the evidence of our inevitable disintegration, we seek a theory that makes life less futile, and above all, less unnecessary; a universe in disequilibrium confronts us with the realisation that we are but a spontaneous and frantic proliferation of molecular machines that burn, consume, multiply, and die, in an ineluctable and meaningless dance.

The principles of thermodynamics first came to light when we posed ourselves the problem of building an engine; the engine converts energy from one form to another, and as everyone knows, energy is conserved; the crucial question then is to understand if our inability to build a machine in perpetual motion is due to a technical or a theoretical limit. Thermodynamics ceases to become an engineering problem and starts to become a glimpse into our world view as we understand its profound implications; not only is it not possible to convert energy without losing it as 'background noise' into the universe—everything that happens, every phenomenon that takes place in any corner of the cosmos, is a process in disequilibrium. Everything rushes in a specific direction; nothing is reversible; under no circumstances can we return. The universe is by definition spontaneous; the spontaneity of things is independent of our will. The clock with which we mark the direction of the chemical time of our life is a quantity that we call entropy, connected to the concept of disorder via the idea that chaos is inherently more probable than order.

The thermodynamic zero that is the only possible equilibrium is reached only at the moment in which matter manifests itself in its maximum multiplicity—that is, when the universe expresses the maximum number of equiprobable configurations. Each ordered structure imposes a hierarchy of probabilities in the universe, establishing itself as a configuration that is not equivalent to the others; thermodynamic equilibrium thus coincides with the complete disintegration of all structures. The hallucination of the Right Hand essentially consists in the idea that a constant equilibrium can be established within aggregated structures, preventing their necessary dissolution and cancelling the thermodynamic cost of their existence.

Following this logic, we can then understand how the Hermetic dragon, the Ouroboros serpent that embodies the formless materiality at the base of the universe and which swallows itself, forming an eternal circle, described by the magical tradition as a blind and terrible monster that must be dominated by the human intellect, is in reality a threat already conveniently defused, an enemy already defeated, since its circularity allows it to be beheaded at every instant, frictionlessly unrolling all the mysteries of the cosmos. But a universe in disequilibrium confronts us with a creature far more frightening and hungry, an infinitely-headed Beast, wrapped around itself in countless twisting coils, which, in its frantic joy, tears everything to pieces, devouring us too.

The Right Hand Path has always known that the simplest way to maintain one's dominance is to absorb any form of dissent. For this reason, going beyond the surface—and by surface we refer, for instance, to certain forms of bourgeois Christianity or to so-called 'white magic', both of which exclude any kind of 'dark' practice or contact with demonic entities—all the most important minds of contemporary esotericism have remarked that black magic 'does not exist', that it is nothing but a simplified and partial expression of the Kabbalistic dogma. These statements are designed to reinforce the conviction, common to initiates and non-believers alike, that there is only one truth, and that it is not possible to find, in the Hermetic theory of reality, the hidden trick that keeps it standing, without which it would collapse ruinously.

The principal mistake committed, more or less deliberately, by the vast majority of those who tried to trace a Left Hand Path in opposition to that indicated for centuries by the Hermetic tradition, was that of doing no more than working toward a reversal of the dogmas of the Right Hand Path, evidently ignoring that a system endowed with total symmetry remains, by definition, identical to itself whichever way it is turned. The glyph of the

Celestial Man, or 'Tree of Life', may suggest to a naive observer, in its visual simplicity, that it might be easy to build a model of the world alternative to the one it proposes—and it is precisely this trap that has prevented any authentic Left Hand Path from asserting itself until now. Not surprisingly, the Tree of Life has been turned over countless times by gullible satanists, giving rise, among other things, to the so-called 'Tree of Death', which, in addition to having an unconvincing name, is nothing but an exact reproduction of the Kabbalistic diagram proposed by the Right Hand, rebranded to be offered to a new audience.

Contemporary satanism in its entirety is nothing but a reinterpretation of the dogmatic principles of the Right Hand Path, clothed in new garments so as to attract the interest of new groups of potential initiates. It is therefore not surprising to note that many forms of satanism are often accompanied by an obsession with power, an exaltation of the individual, and a frantic negation of the existence of God which becomes an affirmation of one's own individual divinity. This satanism is in no way structurally different from the religion it wants to oppose; it proposes, in an ultra-simplified and, in all probability, scarcely effective way, the same dogmas and practices to which the Western Hermetic tradition has always referred.

The Hermetic Kabbalah is appropriately armoured against any attempt at sabotage from within. Under no condition will it ever be sufficient to invert any symbol proposed by the Right Hand Path—from the Tree of Life itself to crosses and pentagrams—in order to obtain something radically different from its original meaning. The only way to trace a path toward an alternative esotericism is to definitively break the symmetry of the Hermetic Kabbalah, proposing a new system based upon entirely different symbols and connections. First of all, however, it is necessary to answer a crucial question: Why do we need an alternative?

Let us start from considering that the Right Hand dogma has spread in a capillary fashion to assure its dominion over any other world view, even if rarely in an explicit and manifest way. Contrary to what one might think, in fact, the viral spread of Hermetic Kabbalah is not a question that concerns only those few who are interested in the occult, but is an actual global demonological ritual in which everyone, willingly or not, is a participant. Understanding this fact would require a long digression on demonology and its meaning; for the purposes of this text, it is sufficient to clarify that we refer to the interpretation of demonology as hyperstition, and that we rely upon the belief that demonic entities can enter the material plane to feed and multiply through human vectors.

The Hermetic Kabbalah is an extremely powerful evocation seal, and an entry portal into our space-time plane for a specific demon, one who has been given many different names. We will refer to him as AHIH; the Primordial Point, the White Head, the One in Whom All is Right. Over millennia, AHIH has fed himself and has grown, expanding to reach every corner of human society, adapting in a surprising way to the historical and cultural changes of his host animals. At this point, the indissoluble link between the Right Hand Path and the Judaeo-Christian religions, made explicit by numerous esotericists in recent history, will certainly be clear; the main tenets of Christianity, starting with the Trinity, are nothing but the expression of Kabbalistic mysteries in the form of religious messages. Despite the fact that different forms of magic and esotericism have been and still are openly opposed by the institution of the Church, the same dogmas and the same vision of reality lie at the base of both traditions, hidden by merely apparent contrasts which in fact are devoid of meaning, and serve to maintain a veil of mystery over the true nature of AHIH.

What is crucial for us to understand is that the influence of the Right Hand dogma reaches out into the social and political dimension, imposing a highly organisational and hierarchical force aimed at establishing a pyramid with Man on top, be it an absolute monarchy legitimised by God, a Nazi-fascist dictatorship, a white ethnostate, or a meritocratic society dominated by the figure of the cisgender heterosexual white male. The link between AHIH and these kinds of political structures can be understood by interpreting the Kabbalistic glyph and observing how, in this model of reality, everything comes from a single point, Kether, the Crown, the Point Inside the Circle. The high level of order required by this type of structure is connected to the need for the political and military control of those who participate in it; the sefirot, with their flaming swords, are the last defenders of this cosmic order. The fundamental idea that allows this order to be maintained and to reproduce itself is the assumption that it is natural. In the name of nature, abhorrent crimes have been and are still being committed, rivers of blood have been spilled; rape, genocide and slaughter are hymns to the eternal glory of AHIH, perpetrated in the name of the idea that Man is naturally destined to dominate everything that is different from his image.

We have talked about the concept of equilibrium, and how the possibility of achieving it in aggregated structures is actually a fabrication, an arbitrary assumption recounted as truth. Imposing the dominion desired by the Right Hand has a price, because an overall increase in order can never be a spontaneous event in the universe; when a highly structuring force acts within a system, it prompts a greater disruptive force to act outside, accelerating the process of its own downfall. The reign of AHIH is a cruel and desperate fire destined to become extinct in the silent waters of Nun; in its slow agony, it drags huge masses of bodies into misery and suffering, devastates its environment, and strangles its own children.

All of this considered, it is not surprising that on several occasions the political Right has appropriated traditional concepts and practices of ceremonial magic to acquire consensus and expand its domain; this happened at the dawn of Nazi-fascism, and continues today in the demonological practices of the alt-right. If a Left Hand Path can ever be born, it will therefore be necessary for it to assume a clear political connotation, opposed, both in dogma and in ritual practice, to the cult of AHIH and to all that it represents.

In this regard, it is crucial to add a final and fundamental element to this discussion, and to talk about what we can build on the ruins of the temple of the God of Man. It will not have escaped the reader that the vision of the cosmos described in this text is rather dark. The acceptance of our thermodynamic destiny leads us to confront the terror of the abyss of our individual dissolution. From the point of view we want to propose, it is precisely the glorification of the individual, and the frantic desire for the preservation of the integrity and unity of one's own being, which awakens in man the mirage of his own divinity, an illusion that requires, in order to be sustained, a coercive social order and the constant sacrifice of the bodies of the oppressed. Thus we find ourselves on the brink of a chasm: the tyranny of Man behind us and an inhuman and formless darkness before our eyes.

How can we reach a darkness so radically and frighteningly alien to everything we know? How can we think of approaching its black fire without being destroyed? She is singularity; we understand the necessity of Her existence, but we can never guess at the enormity of Her wonder. We know Her from the stories of men as an immense anthropophagous serpent which, every night, threatens to forever swallow the Sun and its light, plunging the world into an eternal twilight; and in these same stories, every night the serpent is defeated, so that the Sun can return to shine once again.

But no sun burns forever. Any god who promises salvation is lying, because there is no salvation in the jaws of the Beast. Whoever receives the bite of the serpent knows true terror, and, in the darkness of her womb, meets Love and is reborn to a new life. Cosmic Love is by definition a suicidal love; only while we fall inexorably into our dissolution can we fulfil our destiny and shine.

This concept of Love is very distant from its patriarchal expression; it is not limited to romantic-sexual attraction, it is not an expression of uncon-ditional altruism, nor is it a religious ecstasy disconnected from the flesh. Love is the thermodynamic property of bodies that attracts them to their death. Love is the door that allows us to reconcile ourselves with darkness, provided that we understand its true meaning, and that we do not make the mistake of subjecting it to our individual consciousness, transforming it into a play of mirrors. Confronted with a thermodynamic universe, we understand that every moment of our existence is the spontaneous fruit of a wonderful proliferation to which we belong entirely.

Among Love's many meanings, one relates, in the case of hetero-patriarchal society, to the trade of bodies for forced procreation, with the aim of nurturing the mirage of a glorious future for humanity. The Love we refer to is rooted instead in a rejection of the idea of a path of salvation, is opposed to the dogma of conservation, and manifests itself as a radical opening of the individual toward the darkness outside.

The elimination of the idea that our existence is oriented toward the fulfilment of a divine plan, the realisation of a higher purpose, spiritual enlight-enment, or social power leaves us completely alone in the contingency of our lives; indeed, we may easily understand that the future is a lie when we reflect that not only will our own life sputter out one day, but also the sun, all the stars in the sky, and ultimately the entire universe. Before a decomposing and dying cosmos, the patriarchal Man-God claims his last insane and delirious privilege, building hierarchies and hallucinations of greatness in a frantic attempt to hold together his rotting and monstrous body. If nothing is of any importance, if everything degenerates and crumbles, Man stands as an emperor of dust, because he knows no way of existence other than dominion.

We propose Love for the cosmic process of disintegration and death as an alternative, refusing to articulate the reasons. Love generates itself indefinitely, precipitating, like a sinister spiral, the world into darkness. We love with our bodies burning like supernovae, shining and useless; with every breath, we feed the hungry Beast that wraps us in its dark coils.

GdN

CATASTROPHIC ASTROLOGY

2004 MN4

May I disappear from the skies when I will have consumed myself; my end will then be rather beautiful! Know that in the temple of God there burn different fires, who all render glory unto him; you are the light of the golden chandeliers, and my flame is that of sacrifice.

Éliphas Lévi[1]

A countdown clock still runs on one of the countless forgotten pages in the wastelands of the early 2000s web. The website www.99942-apophis.com hosts a timer that marks the duration left before Earth's annihilation by a near-Earth object, asteroid 2004 MN4, later renamed (99942) Apophis, the Greek name for the Egyptian abyssal snake-god Apep, the Destroyer. Below a picture representing the catastrophic impact of a gigantic space rock with the earth, an eerie epitaph is written in red characters, like the testimony of a vaporwave Ozymandias in the dust of his abandoned cyber-kingdom:

This page is in some way still under construction.

I have some time left before 2036.

Some trouble could this timeline be. I am 80 years in 2036.

So the question is; if Apophis or a heart attack will strike me first.

Yes I know my English could be better.[2]

---

1. É. Lévi, *The Doctrine and Ritual of High Magic: A New Translation*, tr. J.M. Greer and M.A. Mikituk (New York: TarcherPerigree, 2018), 194.

2. Anonymous, *99942 Apophis 2004 MN4*, <https://web.archive.org/web/20200602220236/ http://www.99942-apophis.com/>.

2004 MN4 was first discovered in the summer of 2004 by a group of astronomers at the Kitt Peak National Observatory in Arizona. A few months after the discovery, NASA's *Sentry* and ESA's *NEODyS* automated monitoring systems predicted a possible impact of the asteroid with the earth on April 13, 2029. On December 23, 2004, the computed probability of the 2029 collision increased dramatically, having first been estimated at 1 in 300 but, later that day, rising to 1 in 62. Over the following days, the probability continued to increase until it reached 2.7%, the highest value ever recorded, with an unprecedented Torino hazard scale rating of 4. As the astronomers had widely anticipated, after further observations and calculations, the impact probability plummeted and the possibility of the 2029 event was excluded; nonetheless, a second coming of Apophis—exactly seven years after the first one, on April 13, 2036—was still considered cause for concern, owing to the possibility, albeit unlikely, that the asteroid's trajectory could deviate as it passed through a *gravitational keyhole*, determining a new risk of collision. By 2013, even this small possibility of impact had been ruled out. Friday the 13th of April, 2029 will still be a night to remember, as a three-hundred-metre-wide asteroid crosses the night sky closer than ever recorded, visible even to the naked eye.

There is a strange affinity between the internet and doomsday. Civilisation's morbid fascination with its own annihilation has often been relegated to the deepest and most anonymous corners of the web, where, next to scam advertisements threatening horrendous bodily deformities, dark omens of death and destruction steal more clicks than even the most depraved pornography. Somehow, secretly, we want to know—in the darkness of our incognito windows—how many seconds, minutes, hours, days, months, and years separate us from our doom. Are we dying of some incurable and disgusting disease? When will the earth be engulfed by the fiery abyss of our expiring sun? A mirror of our most terrifying nightmares is always one Google search away, or even closer, haunting social media with our antisocial urges, as if the Algorithm already knew—and it does—what scares us and excites us the most. Are we afraid? Are we looking for salvation? Or are we just waiting, aroused by the panic-ecstasy of disintegration? When it comes to the impact of Apophis, or any other real or imagined threat of apocalypse, the many rational and scientific arguments that solicit the public to remain calm, debunking the *fake news* that spreads unjustified alarm, can never completely eliminate our fear and our desire for destruction; on the contrary, science itself seems to fuel the very conspiracy theories it tries to suppress, being distorted and transformed from cautious information into prophecy. (99942) Apophis is not merely a celestial body, or an astronomical object: its influence expands far further than its gravitational field, as it becomes entangled with our cosmological destiny and speaks to the depths of our being; it is the flaming messenger of a catastrophic revelation. Apophis is, without doubt, the offspring of the limited gaze of scientific inquiry, since the veil of apocalyptic horror that surrounds it is rooted in the cold mechanical equations that dominate its orbit and in the ghost of its spectral signal registering on our sensors from the depths of space. Nonetheless, no matter how carefully science insists on tracing the limits of its own understanding, barricading itself behind walls of axioms and boundary conditions, it inevitably becomes an oracle, a spiritual medium, opening a laceration onto a radical Outside and summoning an invasion of voices of long-lost demons into our world, not unlike a cursed Cassandra who refuses to surrender to her own prophetic utterances. In this sense, conspiracy theorists and cybernetic oracles of the coming apocalypse draw upon scientific knowledge not as a source of reliable predictions of reality, but rather 'as a poetics of the sacred',[3] thus transforming astronomy into an *astrology* of Armageddon.

One of the first and most illustrious examples of the prophetic power of science is reported by Galileo Galilei in his *Sidereus Nuncius*:

> I feel sure that the surface of the Moon is not perfectly smooth, free from
> inequalities and exactly spherical, as a large school of philosophers considers

---

3.   N. Land, *The Thirst for Annihilation* (London: Routledge, 1992), 37.

with regard to the Moon and the other heavenly bodies, but that, on the contrary, it is full of inequalities, uneven, full of hollows and protuberances, just like the surface of the earth itself, which is varied everywhere by lofty mountains and deep valleys.[4]

At the time this was written, the dominant Aristotelian doctrine taught that the cosmos, along with all the elements that composed it, was perfectly spherical, and that no imperfection was allowed to exist outside of the earth. Gazing through his telescope, Galileo was struck by a blasphemous revelation: that the moon, and by extension the entire universe, was irremediably *dirty* and subject to the same processes of degradation and dissolution that we experience in our world. The apparently innocuous words of his statement, supported by the reasonable argument of scientific observation, hide an actual, gruesome *deicide*; if the universe is not perfect and eternal, how could God be? As we now know, the moon's surface was disfigured by asteroids just like Apophis—celestial omens of death whose distorted, eccentric trajectories escape the comprehension of spherical cosmology. Interestingly, Galileo somehow expiated his blasphemy by opening the way to the formulation of the principle of the conservation of energy—the first principle of thermodynamics—through his experiments on motion. The spherical nature of the universe was somehow preserved in the symmetry of the laws of mechanical motion, which imply the total reversibility of all dynamic processes and thus the nonexistence of time as a material drive toward degradation. From this consideration it obviously follows that the ultimate prophecy of doom channelled by science is the second principle of thermodynamics in its statistical-mechanical interpretation, as understood by Ludwig Boltzmann:

> After this confession you will take it with more tolerance if I am so bold as to claim your attention for a quite trifling and narrowly circumscribed question.

4.   G. Galilei, *Sidereus Nuncius* (Oklahoma City: Byzantinum, 2004), 7.

[...] The second law proclaims a steady degradation of energy until all tensions that might still perform work and all visible motions in the universe would have to cease. All attempts at saving the universe from this thermal death have been unsuccessful, and to avoid raising hopes I cannot fulfil, let me say at once that I too shall here refrain from making such attempts.[5]

The 'narrowly circumscribed question' of condemning the entire cosmos to irremediable heat death breaks with any surviving hope that the universe may be, in any capacity, spherical, reversible, or eternal. Boltzmann was a meticulous scientist and a convinced upholder of the inherent boundaries of science and human knowledge; but despite his understandable caution in approaching the subject of his own ground-breaking discoveries, the proof of his *H-theorem*, containing a probabilistic argument in support of the second principle of thermodynamics, is not merely a speculation on the behaviour of an ideal gas of non-interacting particles, but rather the elaborate conjuration of an eldritch aberration. As we diligently follow the intricate steps of this twisted ritual, summoning functions and variables and transmuting them through the arcane operations of calculus, we finally reach the *Quod Erat Demonstrandum*, manifesting the apocalyptic truth of the death of the universe and unleashing it into reality. There is minimal need of scientific understanding to operate the conjuring machine of thermodynamics; it just *works*—until it *works* no more.

When I first met Apophis I was 11 years old. A classmate had told me that an asteroid was going to hit the earth in twenty-five years' time. As a child, my mind was always haunted by an unusual obsession with death, but I had never, before that moment, contemplated the idea of the end of humanity and confronted the possibility of extinction. In my nightly terrors, I had often considered my own disintegration, dissecting in every possible way the paradoxical insanity of being an individual, and then being no more;

5.   L. Boltzmann, *Theoretical Physics and Philosophical Problems*, tr. P. Foulkes, ed. B. McGuinness (Dordrecht and Boston: D. Reidel, 1974), 15–19.

but there was something strangely reassuring about the idea of dying as a part of the universal cycle of Nature, as if in an eternal wildlife documentary where death is perfectly compensated by new life and equilibrium is forever preserved. I was never truly Catholic. I was raised not to believe in any God, but there was something religious about the way I was taught to approach Nature as a redeeming force of heterosexual preservation: the sun sets only to rise again; we die, only to leave room for our offspring to thrive and carry on our legacy. As a cisgender girl approaching puberty, I could finally access salvation by consecrating myself to the natural cycle of heterosexual reproduction; but if an alien force could shatter this harmony to pieces, putting an end to our species, our planet, our universe, then there was truly no hope. Apophis was my lesbian love for Extinction.

> Desire could thus be said to be nothing but becoming a woman, at different levels of intensity, although of course, it is always possible to become a pious woman, to begin a history, love masculinity and accumulate [...] But reality drifts upon zero, and can be abandoned over and over again. In the lesbian depths of the unconscious, desires for/as feminizing spasms of remigration are without limit. Everything populating the desolate wastes of the unconscious is lesbian.[6]

Little did I know that Apophis would visit me again, some ten years later, appearing in a vivid dream as an immense celestial serpent encircling and devouring the earth, and hissing to me the secrets of time-sorcery and the mysteries of the *Great Arcanum*. All I can recall from those days are a few lectures on statistical quantum mechanics, the persistent image of my body collapsing on concrete, and a deep, devouring feeling of cold.

Think to yourself: 'This is.' If this knowledge leads you back to yourself, and,

---

6.   Land, *The Thirst for Annihilation*, 26.

as you experience a sense of deadly cold, you feel an abyss yawning beneath you: 'I exist in this'—then you have achieved the knowledge of the 'waters'.[7]

APOPHIS OR THE UNCREATOR

In that day, the LORD will punish with his sword—his fierce, great and powerful sword—Leviathan the gliding serpent, Leviathan the coiling serpent; he will slay the monster of the sea.

Isaiah 27:1

The inhabitants of the earth […] will be astonished when they see the beast, because it once was, now is not, and yet will come.

Revelation 17:8

Apophis, the Egyptian serpent-god of the Netherworld, belongs to a lineage of Mesopotamian chthonic deities incarnating primeval chaos and darkness. References to Apophis recur in the spells reported in the *Pyramid Texts*, in the *Coffin Texts* and in the *Book of The Dead*, where it is described as a great snake dwelling in the dark waters of the night, waiting to swallow the solar boat of Ra after it drops beyond the horizon. The recurrence of Apophis in these texts—whose main function was to protect the souls of the dead in their crossing to the afterlife—sheds some light on the deep and intimate connection between the astrological dimension of the Sun-Ra mythos, the political construction of human society and the journey of individual consciousness in Egyptian cosmology. Somewhat similar mythological creatures in the Mesopotamic tradition are the biblical Leviathan and the Babylonian Tiamat, both sharing with Apophis their serpentine/reptilian appearance, their fundamental affinity with the sea, and their cosmic battle

---

7.　J. Evola and the Ur Group, 'Knowledge of the Waters', in *Introduction to Magic: Rituals and Practical Techniques for the Magus*, tr. G. Stucco, ed. M. Moynihan (Rochester, VT: Inner Traditions, 2001), 17.

with some male solar deity syncretised with the figure of the King, a struggle which ends in their slaughter and the profanation of their body. Of particular interest is the figure of the goddess Tiamat, who, after rebelling against the god Marduk, is killed, and her body split in two parts, which form the earth and sky of our world. This creation myth reveals the beast Tiamat as an Original Mother of humankind, whose flesh is the substance that sustains our existence, but who is inevitably dismembered and annihilated as a result of her giving birth to the world; the literal penetration of her flesh by the Babylonian God is the insemination of dark matter with light, and her massacred body is the clay out of which all existence is shaped. The feminine subjecting itself to this cosmic process of rape is considered *unripe*, as expressed by the green colour of the Hermetic dragon representing untamed matter at the beginning of the alchemical *Opus*; unsurprisingly, the same unripeness appears in Jungian psychoanalysis as a pathologisation of non-heterosexual or non-conforming womanhood, of the woman who evades the reproductive patriarchal order, refusing to take on her role as Great Mother and dialectical counterpart to male consciousness. Femininity, in the equation 'woman = body = vessel = world',[8] is only determined in motherhood—that is, only in relation to the other—and through bleeding—that is, only as a function of wounding. Even her devouring, monstrous aspect is to be interpreted from the masculine perspective of the child seeking liberation from the chains of the unconscious, as a necessary adversary in a process of growth. Femininity is constricted in the circularity of the reproductive process of civilisation, but, as Amy Ireland points out in her article 'Black Circuit: Code for the Numbers to Come', the true revolutionary potential of femininity lies in the possibility of uncoupling it from its association with the masculine:

> Woman plus man produces homeostasis (the equilibrium of inequality), but woman plus woman, or woman plus machine, recalibrates the productive drive, slotting it into a vector of incestuous, explosive recursion that will

---

8.   E. Neumann, *The Great Mother* (Princeton, NJ: Princeton University Press, 1963), 39.

ultimately tear the system it emerges from to shreds, pushing it over the 'brink' into something else.[9]

Unlike Tiamat, Apophis cannot be killed: no matter how many times the Creator-God penetrates its flesh, it is never destroyed; it is an uncreating force that overcomes creation. Apophis is not reborn like a dialectical One; it is recursion, not reproduction; it is the autogynophilic, sterile, lesbian Zero forever excavating itself, onto which everything collapses.

As the solar disk plunges into the darkness of Duat, so do the souls of the dead, facing the ancient monster that lies beyond the light of existence: unconstructed matter, eternal recombination, necessary dissolution. The True Zero, the Unborn, the Uncreator, hungry for human and divine blood alike, swallowing souls and worlds and digesting them into the *Prima Materia* of the ocean of Nun. The daily struggle of Ra against Apophis ensures the cyclical reaffirmation of the glory of the Sun God and his life-giving light, the preservation of civilisation and the rebirth of the souls of the dead into the afterlife, so that a new dawn can rise on the world of men; but the kingdom of Ra is constantly leaning over the abyss of the exponential recurrence of the serpent's regeneration. The possibility of the murder of the Sun by the fangs of Apophis is mirrored by the astrological aberration of the solar eclipse, which ultimately breaks the cycle of rebirth, violating the sacred harmony of the cosmos. In the *Book of Overthrowing Apep*, a ritual text reported in its most complete version in the Bremner-Rhind papyrus, Apophis is referred to as 'the rebel', hinting at the political dimension of the struggle between the God and the Beast: the preservation of the cosmos depends on the possibility of the King's maintaining his power against the centrifugal forces of disaggregation, placing Apophis in the position of the supreme adversary—*Satan*—to his dominion. The text's insistence on the

9.   A. Ireland, 'Black Circuit: Code for the Numbers to Come', *e-flux* 80 (2017), <https://www.e-flux.com/journal/80/100016/black-circuit-code-for-the-numbers-to-come/>.

disintegration and dismemberment of the body of the beast, especially its decapitation, may be intended as an alchemical recipe for the birth of humanity, produced by the slaughter of the primeval *Ouroboros*:

> O APEP THOU FOE OF RE, THOU SHALT DIE, DIE! MAYEST THOU PER-
> ISH, MAY THY NAME PERISH, THY TEETH BE SOFT, THY POISON SPILT;
> MAYEST THOU BE BLIND AND UNABLE TO SEE. FALL UPON THY FACE;
> BE FELLED, FELLED! Be crushed, crushed! Be annihilated, annihilated! Be
> slain, slain! Be cut to pieces, to pieces! Be cut up, cut up! Be severed, sev-
> ered! Be slaughtered, slaughtered! Thy head shall be cut off with this knife
> in the presence of Re every day, for he allots thee to Aker, and he crushes
> thy bones.[10]

Egyptian magick identifies Apophis with a primordial principle of Uncreation: unformed matter that must be continuously violated, through a *separatio* of its original non-duality into the Kabbalistic dyad, so that the world may come into being.[11] This is the essence of the alchemical *Opus*, and the expression of the highest aspiration of the Right Hand Path, as clearly stated by Abraxas in the Gruppo di Ur's *Introduction to Magic*:

> In our Tradition, these 'waters,' or Humidum Radicale ('radical Humidity'),
> have been symbolized as ∇ (downward direction, precipitation). They have
> also been referred to as the 'earthly Venus,' as female and cosmic matrix
> (∇ in Hinduism is the symbol of Shakti and of the yoni), or as 'Original Snake'
> (because of the serpentine path ≈, which is the astrological equivalent of ∇).
> [...] And now, since you wished to learn about it, realize that the 'Science of

---

10. R. O. Faulkner, 'The Bremner-Rhind Papyrus', *Journal of Egyptian Archaeology* 24:1 (1938), 45.

11. On the thermodynamic relation between work and separation: 'Energy may take three forms, the visible motion of bodies, thermal motion, that is the motion of the smallest particles, and finally work, that is the separation of mutually attracting bodies or the approach of repelling ones.' Boltzmann, *Theoretical Physics and Philosophical Problems*, 18.

the Magi' wills this and disdains anything that is not this. To create something stable, impassive, immortal, something rescued from the 'Waters' that is now living and breathing outside of them, finally free; and then, like a strong man who grasps a raging bull by the horns, slowly but relentlessly subjugating it, to dominate this cosmic nature in oneself—this is the secret of our Art, the Art of the Sun and of Power, of the 'Mighty Strength of all Strengths'.[12]

The ritual decapitation of the snake that brings forth duality, taming the flood of uncreated matter, is rendered possible by a principle of symmetry, that is, equilibrium. The serpent bites its own tail because it is a self-sufficient machine in perpetual motion, fuelled by the same body that it sustains; a cannibalistic universe that eats itself without ever being consumed. As the circle is broken, as the man-God sets himself in the centre, generating an alchemical Sun, the infinite free energy of this impossible engine can be harvested indefinitely, producing a hermetic battery whose polarities—Chokmah and Binah,[13] the Subject and his Object—are forever preserved. But the myth of Apophis confronts us with a far more terrible serpent, one whose hunger cannot be satiated by feasting on its own flesh; it is the non-ideal, dissipative system of a universe that precipitates toward Extinction. Apophis, the ultimate thermodynamic horror, does not bite its own tail, because it is biting us; and, as it swallows the world into darkness, it reveals itself as the blazing fire of the Black Sun, illuminating the putrefaction of the God of man.

---

12.   Evola and the Ur Group, 'Knowledge of the Waters', in *Introduction to Magic*, 18.

13.   'The path of heterodoxy and disintegration into infinitely many individuated particles begins with woman, Binah. This paradoxically makes it not merely that the weak Eve was tempted by the evil Serpent, but rather that the origins of Evil lie in Eve. Or rather, in woman'. n1x, 'Gender Acceleration: A Blackpaper', *Vast Abrupt*, 2018, <https://vastabrupt.com/2018/10/31/gender-acceleration/>.

NEMESIS OR THE BLACK SUN

Because You love cremation grounds

I have made my heart one

so that You

Black Goddess of the Burning Grounds

can always dance there.

No desires are left, Mā, on the pyre

for the fire burns in my heart,

and I have covered everything with its ash

to prepare for Your coming.[14]

A model in which the 26-Myr mass extinction cycle of Raup and Sepkoski (1984) is associated with the orbital period of a solar companion star is investigated. The required semi-major axis is about 88,000 A.U., or 1.4 light years. Its highly eccentric orbit (i.e. greater than about 0.9) periodically brings the companion into the dense inner region of the comet cloud where it perturbs the orbits of large numbers of comets, initiating an intense comet shower in the solar system which results in several terrestrial impacts over a period of 100,000 to a million years. The companion probably has a mass in the black dwarf range of 0.0002 to 0.07 solar masses, depending on its eccentricity and the density distribution of comets in the inner cloud, and is potentially observable in the infrared.[15]

In the article 'Are Periodic Mass Extinctions Driven by a Distant Solar Companion?', published in the journal *Nature* in 1984, authors D.P. Whitmire and

---

14.   R.F. McDermott, *Singing to the Goddess: Poems to Kālī and Umā from Bengal* (Oxford: Oxford University Press, 2001), 74–75.

15.   D.P. Whitmire and A.A. Jackson, 'Are Periodic Mass Extinctions Driven by a Distant Solar Companion?', *Nature* 308 (1984), 713–715.

A.A. Jackson speculate on the existence of an undetected star in our solar system, constituting, together with our sun, a binary star system.

In a paper published in the same issue of Nature, M. Davis, P. Hut and A. Muller baptise the unseen star:

> If and when the companion is found, we suggest it be named Nemesis, after the Greek goddess who relentlessly persecutes the excessively rich, proud and powerful. We worry that if the companion is not found, this paper will be our nemesis.[16]

Interestingly, the theory of the existence of Nemesis emerged as a possible explanation for the cyclical repetition of mass extinction events on Earth registered in the fossil record. The recurring passage of the hypothetical dark star across the Oort cloud, a region located at the deep boundary of our solar system and populated by billions of comets, was deemed responsible for the distortion of the orbits of the icy worlds inhabiting the cloud, which would then be cast across our solar system and impact the earth, causing planetary devastation and bringing life to the brink of annihilation.[17] If Nemesis was indeed out there, then, according to the calculations proposed by Davis et al., it would now be at its maximum distance from the sun, and the next wave of catastrophic collisions should arrive about 15 million years from now.

Despite the fact that no firm trace of Nemesis has been found, and possibly never will be, and despite the theory of the 26-Myr mass extinction

---

16. M. Davis, P. Hut, and R. A. Muller, 'Extinction of Species by Periodic Comet Showers', *Nature* 308 (1984), 717.

17. Nick Land on cyclic mass-extinction events: 'In order to actually up the game, nothing quite substitutes for a super-compressed catastrophe (or mass extinction) which cranks evolution to the meta-level of superior "evolvability". By gnawing-off and burning entire branches of life, crises plowing deep into the X-risk zone stimulate plasticity in the biosphere's phyletic foundations. [...] Gnon isn't Malthus. It's the thing toasting Malthus' liver—in the fat-fed smoldering ashes of the biological kingdom it just burnt down.' N. Land, 'The Harshness', in *Reignition: Nick Land's Writings (2011–)*, <https://github.com/cyborg-nomade/reignition>, Tome 4, 189.

cycle being strongly contested, the legacy of Nemesis survives in the imagination of countless conspiracy theorists and in the sensational titles of publications on the web. The idea of a dark, deadly twin to our life-giving sun, proposed by astronomers for an exquisitely scientific reason and without the pretension of suggesting any kind of cosmological truth, offers us a glimpse into the abyss of a universal horror: that the sun, in its burning, offers us a vital energy that is not without *retribution*, and that the same burning that we experience as nurturing and vibrant is, in itself, the sacrificial pyre to its own deranged greatness: 'a certain madness is implied, [...] because it is no longer production that appears in light, but refuse or combustion'.[18] Nemesis was never found because, as the speculations of several paranoid theorists point out, it is hiding behind the sun, which engulfs it in its brilliance, making us all blind to the truth of our coming extinction; the dark companion of the sun *is indeed the sun itself*. From this perspective, the name of the goddess Nemesis, daughter of the night goddess Nyx, appears particularly fitting in its association with the Greek word νέμειν, meaning *to give what is due*. Extinction is the price we pay for our existence, the fuel consumed and forever lost, the surplus of energy we cannot grasp; it is the *necessity* of expenditure, that is, the *spontaneity* of our existence, since 'the verbal root of spontaneity, PIE *spend- (to make an offering, perform a rite, to engage oneself by a ritual act), contains this sense of sacrifice and self-offering, just as we speak of the spontaneous as something "surrendered to", as to a whim. The spontaneity of authentic transformation is also thus a species of death, of surrendering to the expiration of what is untenable.'[19]

Civilisation, as the bright twin of our binary Sun, 'has the form of an unsustainable law',[20] and appears as the desperate negation of spontaneity as it aggregates itself in architectures of horrendous symmetry; nonetheless,

---

18.   G. Bataille, 'Rotten Sun', in *Visions of Excess: Selected Writings 1927–1939*, tr. A Stoekl (Minneapolis: University of Minnesota Press, 1985), 57.

19.   N. Masciandaro, *On the Darkness of the Will* (Milan: Mimesis International, 2018), 34.

20.   Land, *The Thirst for Annihilation*, xix.

if we stare long enough into its feverish light, it reveals itself in its *nigredo*, as a cancerous proliferation, no less revolting than a corpse being nibbled by countless contorting worms. The shimmering temple of God, the perfect balance of His Kabbalah, the great 'humanizing project',[21] is but a sub-product of the godless precipitation of matter into darkness, 'a precarious stabilization and complication of solar decay'.[22] The history of civilisation is always told backwards, as seen through the lens of an impossible time machine; there is no true thermodynamic paradox in the existence of life, because it is not a process of aggregation, but rather an acceleration of disaggregation, a mindless engine consuming itself to death. The martyrdom of Christ on the cross is the necessary sacrifice for the preservation of the patriarchal order of the One God Universe,[23] revealing the inevitably dissipative nature of the Kingdom of God and expiating the thermodynamic sin of organic existence, so that, as the flesh of the creator is slaughtered, the darkened sun 'hiddenly gives witness to a zone of occult identity between the immanent summit of perfection and the kenotic abyss of God's self-dereliction'.[24] Cast out at the edge of our known universe, like a ritual scapegoat venturing into the desert, the Black Sun responds with an *invasion* of fiery comets from the sky, because there is no real outside to store its excess—it is life itself that is being sacrificed.

NIBIRU OR THE GREAT CITY OF BABYLON

The great planet:

At his appearance: Dark red.

The heaven he divides in half

as it stands as Nibiru.[25]

21.   Ibid.

22.   Ibid., xviii.

23.   See Ccru, 'Lemurian Time War', in Ccru, *Writings 1997–2003* (Falmouth and Shanghai: Urbanomic/Time Spiral, 2017), 33–52.

24.   Masciandaro, *On the Darkness of the Will*, 98.

25.   Z. Sitchin, *The Twelfth Planet* (New York: Harper, 1976), 242.

What is the terrible ruby star

that burns down the crimson night?

What is the beauty that flames so bright

athwart the awful dawn?

She has taken flesh, she is come to judge

the thrones ye rule upon.

Quail ye kings for an end is come

in the birth of BABALON.[26]

In his infamous 1976 book *The Twelfth Planet*, conspiracy theorist Zecharia Sitchin proposed an argument in favour of the existence of an unseen planet in our solar system, based on his interpretation of ancient Babylonian cosmology and astrology. This planet, the astronomical incarnation of the god Marduk, patron deity of the City of Babylon, was responsible for the creation of the earth when, smashing against the lost planet Tiamat, it tore her apart; one part of her would constitute our planet, and the other the asteroid belt and the comets of the solar system. In this very literal and simplistic transposition of the Babylonian creation myth as told in the ancient Babylonian text *Enûma Eliš*, the collision of Marduk with the planet Tiamat was the moment of the insemination of our dead, uncreated world:

There was no premeditated 'seeding'; instead, there was a celestial collision. A life-bearing planet, the Twelfth Planet and its satellites, collided with Tiamat and split it in two, 'creating' Earth of its half. During that collision the life-bearing soil and air of the Twelfth Planet 'seeded' Earth, giving it the biological and complex early forms of life for whose early appearance there is no other explanation.[27]

26. J. Parsons, 'The Book of Babalon', *Hermetic Library*, <https://hermetic.com/parsons/the-book-of-babalon>.

27. Sitchin, *The Twelfth Planet*, 256.

Marduk, our original metropolis, is according to Sitchin inhabited by the race of the Anunnaki, whose name was historically used to refer to the Gods and Goddesses of the pantheons of ancient Mesopotamian religions, but who, rather than spiritual beings, are a species of superintelligent and all-powerful aliens. Seeing that life on Earth was but a defective and debased version of the life that had evolved on Marduk, the Anunnaki intervened in the development of the primates populating Earth with biological engineering, creating Homo Sapiens in their own image, and dominating the ancient Babylonian civilisation as gods. Ignoring his clear religious connotation as a solar deity, Sitchin insists that Marduk is some kind of rogue, sunless planet that reached the solar system from outer space, not creating, but rather colonising our Earth; it is an invading force acting from the outside in, rather than an expanding force extending from its centre. Rather than creators, the Anunnaki, also referred to as Nefilim, the ancient biblical race of giants, are described as settlers: Sitchin insists that 'the story of the first settlement of Earth by intelligent beings is a breathtaking saga no less inspiring than the discovery of America'.[28] The city of Babylon—the 'Gateway of the Gods'[29]—was the first outpost of this planetary expansion, a hyper-technological spaceport connecting Earth to her alien invaders. Owing to the cyclic nature of Marduk's encounters with the earth, it was named *Nibiru*, 'planet of crossing'.[30]

Sitchin's pseudo-historical narrative was a brilliantly fascinating work of science fiction, destined to influence our image of extraterrestrial intelligent life and ancient human civilisations for decades to follow, but his impact extended far beyond the limits of mere fiction, entering the domain of astrology and prophecy. Firstly, it is significant to point out that, as is the case for Apophis and Nemesis, the supposed existence of an undetected faraway planet in our solar system is rooted in an ongoing scientific debate

28. Ibid., 283.
29. Ibid., 150.
30. Ibid., 240.

about unexplained aberrations in the orbits of other celestial bodies in the Kuiper Belt, which, according to recent mathematical modelling,[31] could be accounted for by the presence of a large unobserved planet hiding beyond Pluto, nicknamed *'Planet X'* or *'Planet Nine'*. Secondly, while Sitchin's prophecy remains somewhat incomplete, hinting at a vaguely defined *End Of Days* associated with the return of Nibiru, his work was completed in the 90s by Nancy Lieder, who was supposedly contacted by aliens warning her about an incoming cataclysm owing to the passage of Nibiru into the inner solar system, which would cause the earth to be destroyed; the inevitable catastrophe was, and still is, being covered up by governments and institutions, in order to avoid a global wave of panic and nihilism that would crush the social, political, and economic order of the world. Quoting from the archive of Nancy Lieder's website *ZetaTalk*:

Article: <6ftpfq$sd5@dfw-ixnews5.ix.netcom.com>
Subject: Planet X/12th Planet Cover-Up Mechanism
Date: 1 Apr 1998 16:20:10 GMT

[...] The panic that would ensue from a general announcement of the forthcoming cataclysms would in and of itself be deemed a disaster to avoid. Beyond the concerns of the banking industry, which would collapse due to lack of confidence in the continuing worth of many assets, and beyond the concerns of industry which requires the faithful attendance of its employees in order to function, there is concern about possible looting, suicides, mass migration of peoples, and never-ending demands that the government do something.[32]

---

31. See K. Batygin and M. E. Brown, 'Evidence for a Distant Giant Planet in the Solar System', *The Astronomical Journal* 151 (2016), 22.
32. N. Lieder, 'Re: Planet X/12th Planet Cover-Up Mechanism', *ZetaTalk*, 1998, <http://www.zetatalk.com/usenet/use00561.htm>.

A great deal more could be said about the theory of the Nibiru cataclysm and its impact on contemporary culture.[33] Two aspects of this visionary epic of extinction are particularly relevant to us for the elaboration of a *catastrophic astrology*: the reversal of the original timeline of the Mesopotamian creation myth and the mysteriously recurring association between the City of Babylon and the Apocalypse. The final impact with Nibiru that will put an end to humanity as we know it mirrors exactly the creation of the earth from the remains of the planet Tiamat; in Sitchin's own words, somehow 'the roles of, and references to, Tiamat and Earth appear to be interchangeable. Earth is Tiamat reincarnated'.[34] In other words, the Nibiru cataclysm is not simply the death of our world, but rather a *birth in reverse*: instead of being shaped out of the flesh of some sacrificed Original Mother, arising from formless darkness into light, life is sucked into a disintegrated future, reversing the patriarchal narrative of progress. From the perspective of human civilisation, Nibiru is thus a time-travelling monstrosity that comes *from* the future, *for* the future, realising the self-fulfilling prophecy of annihilation summoned by the same humanity that it created. Nibiru is not merely a planet, but the spaceship of an invading alien civilization, whose technological advancement allows it to understand that the only possible, energetically efficient outlook for the advancement of their species is disintegration.[35]

---

33. '– The earth is evil. We don't need to grieve for it.

    – What?

    – Nobody will miss it.

    – But where would Leo grow up?

    – All I know is, life on Earth is evil.

    – There may be life somewhere else.

    – But there isn't.'

    Melancholia, dir. Lars Von Trier, 2011.

34. Sitchin, *The Twelfth Planet*, 231.

35. 'The only way to get more tight-feedback under current conditions is by splitting, in every sense. That is the overwhelming practical imperative: Flee, break up, withdraw, and evade. Pursue every path of autonomization, fissional federalism, political disintegration, secession, exodus, and concealment. Route around the Cathedral's educational, media, and financial apparatus in each and every way possible. Prep, go Galt, go crypto-digital, expatriate, retreat into the hills, go underground, seastead, build black markets, whatever works, but get the hell out.' N. Land, 'Quit', in *Reignition*, Tome 2, 767.

Nick Land on the energetic economy of gravity:

> Lift-off, then, is merely a precursor to the first serious plateau of anti-gravity technology, which is oriented towards the more profoundly productive task of pulling things apart, in order to convert comparatively inert mass-spheres into volatile clouds of cultural substance. Assuming a fusion-phase energy infrastructure, this initial stage of off-world development culminates in the dismantling of the sun, terminating the absurdly wasteful main-sequence nuclear process, salvaging its fuel reserves, and thus making the awakened solar-system's contribution to the techno-industrial darkening of the galaxy.[36]

A sufficiently advanced civilisation will have to surrender to the inescapable law of thermodynamic *nemesis*—the fact that no more can be put together than is being torn apart; from the inertial reference system of an accumulating economy, whose timeline runs from dismemberment to aggregation, any disaggregating force is an invader collapsing backwards from the future. It is thus unsurprising that, as stated by Sitchin, 'Marduk was coming into the solar system not in the system's orbital direction (counterclockwise) but from the opposite direction':[37] Nibiru, entering our world from the deep outside, is a planet forever in retrograde, because our sun-propelled gravitational time-loop prevents us from grasping the universe's entropic drive toward destruction. Tiamat is no longer a primitive beast slaughtered on the altar of human civilisation, an original virgin to conquer and destroy. She is 'the Vast Abrupt, and the crossing',[38] She is 'the Great Propeller',[39] silently permeating our universe, undetected until She crashes into our reality. She is the future, and the future is female.

---

36. N. Land, 'Lure of the Void', in *Reignition*, Tome 2, 749.
37. Sitchin, *The Twelfth Planet*, 219.
38. N. Land, 'The Cult of Gnon', in *Reignition*, Tome 4, 166.
39. Ibid.

The idea that futurity is inherently feminine, and that femininity is the grave that Mesopotamian solar patriarchy excavated for itself unknowingly, is contained in the *Book of Revelation* in the figure of the whore of Babylon. Babylon shares with Nibiru a blurred definition of her identity: altogether she is a woman, a Goddess, a city and a civilisation; both of their names, meaning respectively *the gateway* and *the crossing*, do not indicate a particular place or time, but rather a relation between places and times. Both are associated with redness, as they are red with the blood of childbirth and the blood of slaughter; both stand and both fall at the End of Days. On a more superficial level of interpretation, Babylon incarnates a morally dissolute civilisation that thrives on wasteful consumption and celebrates the pleasures of the flesh; as city of the Tower, she is associated with unconstrained technological advancement beyond the boundaries of anything natural or human. Impure and artificial, decadent and oriental, implanted with shimmering prosthetic jewels, she is the Western dream of the city of the Future.[40] Babylon is described in contrast with an opposing version of femininity, expressed by the figure of the Celestial Mother bearing the child of God; but somewhere in the desert they fuse together, becoming one and the same. The feminine *Prima Materia*, dismembered to give birth to the kingdom of God, is the apocalyptic Beast that 'once was, now is not, and yet will come up out of the Abyss',[41] undead, crawling backwards from the future through the gates of Babylon to extinguish herself in a glorious fire together with everything that She created.

---

40. 'The Western civilization in which Modernity ignited was ultimately combusted by it. From an Occidental Traditionalist perspective, Modernity is a complex and prolonged suicide. An Ultra-Modernist, who affirms the creative destruction of anything in modernization's path, assumes an alternative criterion, inherent to Modernity itself. It asks: What had to happen to the West for it to become modern? What was the essential event? The answer (and our basic postulate): Zero arrived. [...] In Europe, zero was an alien, and from the perspective of parochial tradition, an infection. Cultural resistance was explicit, on theological grounds, among others. Implicit in the Ontological Argument for the existence of God was the definition of non-being as an ultimate imperfection, and 'cipher'—whose name was Legion—evoked it. The cryptic Eastern "algorism" was an unwelcome stranger.' N. Land, 'Zero-Centric History', in *Reignition*, Tome 4, 195.
41. Revelation 17:8, NIV.

Gaze into the sky, for the Future has come.

Mark our words: She is the Mother, the Devourer and the Fires that Consume the Universe.

Burn, love, and understand.

Today is the twilight of the God of Man.

LT

SPECTRAL MATERIALISM

Our instruments had intercepted minute random fragments of a prodigious
and everlasting monologue unfolding in the depths of this colossal brain,
which was inevitably beyond our understanding.

Stanislaw Lem[1]

HYDROGEN

In school they loaded me with tons of notions which I diligently digested,
but which did not warm the blood in my veins. I would watch the buds swell
in spring, the mica glint in the granite, my own hands, and I would say to
myself: 'I will understand this, too, I will understand everything, but not
the way they want me to. I will find a shortcut, I will make a lock-pick, I will
push open the doors.'

It was enervating, nauseating, to listen to lectures on the problem
of being and knowing, when everything around us was a mystery pressing
to be revealed: the old wood of the benches, the sun's sphere beyond the
windowpanes and the roofs, the vain flight of the pappus down in the June
air. Would all the philosophers and all the armies of the world be able to
construct this little fly? No, nor even understand it: this was a shame and
an abomination, another road must be found.

Primo Levi[2]

Chemists are all afflicted by a strange, morbid *melancholy. A black humour*
that exhales from our twisted stills, and which is perhaps only a strange

---

1. S. Lem, *Solaris*, tr. J. Kilmartin, S. Cox (London: Faber, 1970), 22.
2. P. Levi, *The Periodic Table*, tr. R. Rosenthal (New York: Schocken, 1984), 26.

contagion caused by intimate daily contact with the intoxicating vapours of our solvents. It is said that even the brightest mind in human history, that of Isaac Newton, was momentarily overshadowed by the poisonous miasma of his alchemical mercury when, in search of the Gold of the Philosophers, he allowed himself to be plunged into the creeping darkness of chemical trans-formation. Moreover, the experience of experimental chemistry occupies a traditionally ambiguous position in the grand scheme of the sciences. Where the physics experiment is typically framed in order to provide a confirmation or refutation of a theoretical hypothesis formulated in advance, chemical synthesis has an intrinsically productive and transformative nature, having as its primary objective the generation of a new substance, and only as a collateral purpose—assuming it is possible at all—the construction of a predictive and generalised model of its field of knowledge.

In fact, it is curious how much the vision of science as the luminous triumph of reason over matter seems to be completely shattered when it encounters the test of life in the laboratory. It is not uncommon, within the walls of chemical laboratories, for fatalistic, even *magical*, thinking to spread about the forces controlling the outcome of certain operations of synthesis or techniques of analysis. In a confused grey area between superstition and irony, I have seen votive candles appear next to excessively capricious instruments, and apotropaic talismans based on animal remains forgotten in the dustiest corners of lab counters. The spectre of *irreproducibility* haunts everyone when, countless times and for no apparent reason, the material escapes the operator's control. On the other hand, it is not uncommon for a chemist's skill in his field of expertise to be described using categories that are difficult to define, such as *sensitivity* and *intuition*, indicating a mysterious and incommunicable *elective affinity* between certain human minds and certain inanimate substances.

When, for the first time, the solutions to Erwin Schrödinger's equation for the hydrogen atom were calculated with pen and paper, chemistry could for a brief moment be considered a solved problem. On the other hand, while physics had succeeded for centuries in predicting with startling accuracy the behaviour of the macroscopic world by means of its equations of motion, directing with impeccable elegance the celestial symphony of the stars, chemistry had to make do with prophetic and obscure *periodic numerologies*, remaining of necessity a radically experimental science. Indeed, the strictly microscopic nature of the molecular world for centuries made it undetectable by conventional means of human investigation, leading to the formulation of hidden nondeterministic systems of affinities and correlations to describe these unthinkable motions.

It is important to bear in mind that the chemical problem is not trivially limited to a question of scalability in classical physics. It is no coincidence that almost every general chemistry course begins by drawing a line between *physical transformations*, which do not change the molecular nature of a body, and *chemical transformations*, in which the atomic organisation of matter is modified. This distinction, which appears to us to be quite natural and obvious, contains a subtext that is often overlooked: that, somehow, there must be a discontinuity between our understanding of the macroscopic world and the microscopic understanding of the molecular world, and that the laws identified by the physics of macroscopic bodies cease to be valid on a smaller scale. If atoms and electrons were no more than miniature versions of ordinary bodies, every transformation would be *physical* (in the sense described above) and chemistry would have no reason to exist.

This qualitative difference between the molecular and macroscopic worlds was set out extremely clearly by Schrödinger, who pointed out that the deterministic laws of the physics of macroscopic bodies are merely the statistical result of innumerable microscopic phenomena, about whose mechanisms we have, in principle, no experimental guarantee; indeed, we cannot even assume that the very concept of *mechanism* is applicable on an atomic and subatomic scale. It was only with the advent of quantum theory that physics finally gained some theoretical weapons with which to question chemistry, that heretical and rebellious discipline that for centuries had been disinherited from the ranks of respectable sciences. The analytical solution to the problem of the hydrogen atom can therefore be seen as the missing piece that made it possible to build the long sought-after continuity between the physics of macroscopic bodies and the chemistry of molecular matter. However, it is important to emphasise two aspects that trouble any such unified portrait of contemporary science: the first, more technically, concerns the impossibility of extending the same analytical approach to more complex chemical systems; the second, more generally, concerns the place of quantum theory in relation to classical physics.

In principle, one might think that, once the mysterious rules of the quantum game are revealed, any chemical problem, whatever its complexity, can be solved by applying the same principles; in reality, any system more complex than the hydrogen atom—that is, any molecular system—is an analytically unsolvable problem. For this reason, quantum chemistry has had to rely on numerical and computational methods, intrinsically approximate and often supplemented with experimental information, to describe with satisfactory accuracy the state and evolution of a molecular system from a theoretical point of view. Even these methods, however, are to date unable to replace the synthetic experimental approach, except to a very limited extent. In this sense, chemistry remains, by its very nature, a radically indeterministic science—*there is no* single, coherent set of laws that can analytically and accurately predict the evolution of a chemical reaction under its actual experimental conditions.

As regards the computational aspect, it is important to bear in mind that the intensive computational methods used by quantum chemistry could, in the not-too-distant future, be rendered obsolete by artificial intelligence. In a recent study published in the journal *Nature*, an AI was charged with devising efficient synthetic strategies for the preparation of small organic molecules. Devoid of any notion of physics, the machine was able to produce results comparable to those of its human counterparts using only the experimental procedures contained in previous articles in the literature.

We do not know whether the mind of this contemporary silicon alchemist harbours the ultimate laws of physics, or whether it is rather inhabited by magical, occult connections.

Naturally, the most immediate approach to the description of a chemical reaction is to think of it as the result of a series of collisions between rigid spheres, like a tiny game of billiards. This is a view that fits into the perspective of the more traditional atomism, in which one imagines that matter is made up of microscopic individual units whose behaviour is analogous to that of ordinary macroscopic bodies. In these terms, then, all chemistry would be easily describable by means of classical physics, and every chemical reaction could be studied by means of relatively simple *in silico* simulations, similar to those of a video game. The different outcome of each collision would essentially depend on the distribution of the initial conditions, and the difficulties in making exact predictions would depend exclusively on our *ignorance of the initial state* of the system, owing to its excessive complexity.

Although this approach is, in some contexts, a useful modelling tool, it is totally unsuitable for describing and predicting the actual chemical behaviour of molecular systems for a number of reasons, first and foremost its inability to account for *chemical bonding*. In fact, the difficulty of modelling chemical reactions is far more radical than a simple problem of incomplete information. The chemical reaction is a strictly quantum phenomenon, which can in no way be described by the classical model. Chemical bonding is, classically, a completely inconceivable phenomenon, because in the classical theory there is no way to justify the fact that a certain atom—classically understood as a rigid microscopic sphere—binds to others according to specific and recurrent proportions. In order to formulate any theory of chemical bonding, one must necessarily admit that the microscopic world is dominated by a *strange statistics*—that of the Pauli exclusion principle—and that microscopic matter manifests an inherent *discontinuity*, expressed in the discrete nature of the molecular excitations and vibrations that constitute the foundation of the chemical event.

This is a fundamental point because, in the practice of chemical synthesis, the quantum properties of matter become manifest and unavoidable on the scale of direct experience. In this sense, to think of quantum mechanics as something that manifests itself exclusively on a microscopic scale, accessible only through sophisticated modern technology, is inaccurate and misleading. *Everything chemical is a quantum phenomenon*, including the metabolic reactions that keep us alive. Not in the commonly understood sense that there is some *wave component* in all bodies, even macroscopic ones, which can however be translated in practice by approximating their behaviour to the classical one, but in the sense that chemistry, by its nature, *cannot be approximated* to any reasonably functioning classical model. No wonder Isaac Newton was himself an alchemist, when even his elegant theory of bodies in motion paled before the spectral behaviour of this weird quantum matter. We can therefore begin to see how the chemical laboratory constitutes a kind of liminal space, in which contact is established between two apparently irreconcilable regimes of matter: the macroscopic-statistical and the microscopic-quantum. It is legitimate to ask oneself how far it is possible to access quantum matter, and under what conditions this encounter can be translated into a form of scientific knowledge proper. This general problem has been at the centre of a long scientific and (necessarily) philosophical debate, initially opened by the same scientists who had been protagonists in the formulation of modern physics.

Given the enormity of the issue we are dealing with, and the huge number of authors who have dealt with it, I cannot aspire to give a complete picture of it here. I shall confine myself to addressing the problem of quantum indeterminacy, presenting it first from the point of view of the physicists who contributed the most to its formulation, with particular emphasis on the scientific and epistemological debate between Werner Heisenberg and Erwin Schrödinger. These two authors can be thought of as representing two different and irreconcilable approaches to the quantum problem: Heisenberg's approach, which postulates indeterminacy as the ultimate limit of scientific knowledge of bodies, beyond which the problem of the existence and nature of quantum matter is essentially meaningless, and Schrödinger's approach, which accepts the contingency as a real attribute of the particle, in the face of which the old view of matter must be entirely reformulated, abandoning the corpuscular model and embracing the wave model.

The history of science is often seen as a succession of discoveries, each surpassing the previous ones and tracing a straight line identical with the progress of human knowledge, but neglecting how often conflicting visions of the same phenomena, all formally correct, can coexist. The most egregious case is the formulation of the new quantum physics through the approach of matrix mechanics, proposed by Heisenberg, and that of Schrödinger's wave mechanics; the two formulations, which later turned out to be mathematically equivalent, and which had managed to lead in an analogous way to the solution of the problem of the hydrogen atom, implied two radically different visions of matter. This old scientific debate, now filed between the lines of the introductory paragraphs of physics textbooks, is well known and largely resolved. However, hidden between the snares of mathematical formalism and the romanticised biographies of its authors, there is still an open wound.

The theoretical apparatus that accompanies quantum mechanics implicitly posits a profound separation between matter at the moment of measurement, which we can broadly understand as matter that *manifests itself*—regardless of whether it is visible to a human observer, an instrument, or any classical body—and *matter itself*, which we can understand as being in a state chronologically prior to measurement, or, more generally, as matter that does not interact with any classical observer. Such a separation, by no means unprecedented in the history of Western thought, was however a completely new problem in the strictly scientific sphere. Whereas previously the scientist could speculate on whether or not there was *something out there* and what its properties were, without worrying too much about it and remaining well within the limits of the world of measurable matter, with the rise of modern physics that *thing out there* suddenly invaded the field of science, imposing itself in an overbearing way at the centre of a debate that was previously purely physico-mathematical rather than philosophical.

The most representative moment of this debate was undoubtedly Heisenberg's formulation of the uncertainty principle in 1927:

> Every observation of scattered light coming from the electron presupposes a photoelectric effect (in the eye, on the photographic plate, in the photocell) and can therefore also be so interpreted that a light quantum hits the electron, is reflected or scattered, and then, once again bent by the lens of the microscope, produces the photoeffect. At the instant when position is determined—therefore, at the moment when the photon is scattered by the electron—the electron undergoes a discontinuous change in momentum. This change is the greater the smaller the wavelength of the light employed— that is, the more exact the determination of the position. At the instant at which the position of the electron is known, its momentum therefore can be known up to magnitudes which correspond to that discontinuous change. Thus, the more precisely the position is determined, the less precisely the momentum is known, and conversely.[3]

Heisenberg's explanation, which today remains the most well known and commonly accepted, is that the experimenter's act of observing the particle brings about a *perturbation* of its trajectory which cannot be arbitrarily reduced until it becomes completely negligible. And it is precisely because of the ineliminable interference of the observer that the particle, previously undisturbed in its original state, cannot be known completely.

---

3.   W. Heisenberg, *Quantum Theory and Measurement*, ed. J. A. Wheeler, W. H. Zurek (Princeton, NJ: Princeton University Press, 1983), 64.

This interpretation is essentially based on the idea that the quantum particle is a corpuscle with a trajectory along which it moves unperturbed until it is observed by the experimenter, whose observation 'hits' the particle with what we could define as 'cognitive radiation'. Although this explanation may appear to be an intuitive and scientifically objective justification of the problem of indeterminacy, it carries strong assumptions about the nature of the particle, assumptions that the principle of indeterminacy itself renders necessarily invalid. In fact, this view raises two fundamental problems. The first is related to the fact that it attributes intrinsically classical characteristics to the quantum object, i.e. it assumes that the particle is at all times endowed with a trajectory. This is in stark contrast with the wavelike behaviour manifested by quantum objects, for example in the well-known double-slit experiment, where an understanding of particles as corpuscles is essentially incompatible with the possibility of their producing interference phenomena. The second, more general problem is that in this account, indeterminacy is reduced to a question of incomplete knowledge, without the traditionally accepted view of classical physics being radically challenged. A similar criticism was made by Schrödinger in his 1950 essay entitled 'What is an Elementary Particle?', where he wrote:

> I fully agree that the uncertainty relation has nothing to do with incomplete knowledge. It does not reduce the amount of information attainable about a particle as compared with views held previously. The conclusion is that these views were wrong and we must give them up. We must not believe that the completer description they demanded about what is really going on in the physical world is conceivable, but in practice unobtainable. This would mean clinging to the old view.[4]

---

4.   E. Schrödinger, 'What is an Elementary Particle?', *Annual Report of the Board of Regents of The Smithsonian Institution* (1950), 183–196: 187.

The 'old view' to which Schrödinger refers here is not classical mechanics as a whole, but rather one of its fundamental assumptions, namely that every body studied can be treated as an *individual* with specific properties that locate it in time and space. In his essay 'Are there Quantum Jumps?', Schrödinger fiercely criticises the corpuscular view of matter, i.e. the 'nightmare that physical events consist in continual sequences of little fits and jerks, the handing over of energy corpuscles from one particle (or group of particles) to another'.[5] In this sense, Schrödinger's thinking anticipates the proposal put forward by James Ladyman, David Spurrett, Don Ross, and John Collier in their 2007 essay *Every Thing Must Go*, in which they challenge the attachment of metaphysics to the corpuscular model, despite the abundant evidence that speaks in favour of its overcoming:

> The metaphysics of domestication tends to consist of attempts to render pieces of contemporary science—and, at least as often, simplified, mythical interpretations of contemporary science—into terms that can be made sense of by reference to the containment metaphor. That is, it seeks to account for the world as 'made of ' myriad 'little things' in roughly the way that (some) walls are made of bricks. Unlike bricks in walls, however, the little things are often in motion. Their causal powers are usually understood as manifest in the effects they have on each other when they collide. Thus the causal structure of the world is decomposed by domesticating metaphysics into reverberating networks of what we will call 'microbangings'—the types of ultimate causal relations that prevail amongst the basic types of little things, whatever exactly those turn out to be.[6]

5.   E. Schrödinger, 'Are there Quantum Jumps?: Part II', *British Journal For the Philosophy of Science* No. 3 (1952), 233–242: 241 [translation modified].
6.   J. Ladyman, D. Spurrett, D. Ross, and J.C. Collier, *Every Thing Must Go* (Oxford: Oxford University Press, 2007), 4.

The concept of the *domestication* of scientific theories by the dominant cosmological view is particularly interesting for our purposes, because it allows us to place Heisenberg's interpretation of the uncertainty principle within a broader context. It is not merely a simplification that fails to account for the complexity of the physical phenomenon of indeterminacy, but rather a deliberate attempt to place the new quantum theory within a *collisional* view of physical phenomena and our knowledge of them.

The fact that this view has been so successful, essentially reducing the problem of quantum indeterminacy to a microscopic game of marbles, may, as suggested by Ladyman, be interpreted as a desire to remain anchored in the reassuring image of a world made up of individuals, rejecting the fluid and relational nature of quantum matter. In fact, both Ladyman and Schrödinger focus on a refutation of the traditional concept of *individuality* applied to quantum particles, emphasising that this must be dismantled or at least radically reworked, in order for it to be applicable to the experimental evidence and mathematical models of the new physics. For both authors, the calling into question of particle individuality derives naturally from the statistics of quantum objects, which implies the indistinguishability of particles in *entangled* states. In Schrödinger's words:

If we wish to retain atomism we are forced by observed facts to deny the ultimate constituents of matter the character of identifiable individuals. Until recently, atomists of all ages, for all I know, had transferred that characteristic from visible and palpable pieces of matter to the atoms, which they could not see or touch or observe singly. Now we do observe single particles [...]. Yet we must deny the particle the dignity of being an absolutely identifiable individual.[7]

The pervasive description of Heisenberg's uncertainty principle as the result of a collision is therefore a symptom of the domestication of quantum theory

---

7.   Schrodinger, 'What is an Elementary Particle?', 191.

to our familiar corpuscular worldview, and at the same time a domestication of quantum matter to human knowledge.

In many ways, the contemporary subatomic myth implies a very precise cosmological vision, one in which the active position of the experimenter studying the material is clearly separated from the passive position of the particle being investigated, in a process whose violence is well exemplified, in Heisenberg's story, by the catastrophic impact between the particle and the beam of light that strikes it. From this point of view, the originary nature of the particle before its interaction with humankind is a simple theoretical assumption which, in fact, is given no relevance: it is a hypothetical substratum whose only purpose is to be transformed into active knowledge through the intervention of the observer. This is evidenced by the fact that Heisenberg himself is hesitant to attribute any form of reality to quantum matter per se: 'there is no "substance" that follows specific laws, but only complexes of connections which we can experience and that when we describe them we also occasionally use words like substance or matter'.[8] In a certain sense, then, the natural result of such an approach is the conclusion that the particle does *not exist* until it is known—which is not only absolutely paradoxical and counterintuitive, but also contains the disturbing subtext that the human is a kind of demiurge, ceaselessly producing matter through knowledge.

Heisenberg's unidirectional approach to the knowledge of particles is rightly challenged by Karen Barad in her essay *Meeting the Universe Halfway*, where she uses the concept of *diffraction* to propose a vision of knowledge in which the clear separation between the knowing subject and the known object is broken, and knowledge emerges as a *phenomenon of interference* between the two. To support her proposal, Barad refers to the principle of complementarity proposed by Bohr in 1927 to reconcile the corpuscular and wavelike views of quantum matter. The fundamental assumption of

---

8.   W. Heisenberg, *Reality and its Order*, tr. M.B. Rumscheidt, N. Lukens, I. Heisenberg, ed. K. Kleinknecht (Cham: Springer, 2019), 36.

this principle is the idea that the measuring apparatus must be considered an integral part of the physical phenomenon, and therefore cannot be separated from the object being studied; not only are the corpuscular and wave motions mutually complementary, but they also manifest themselves in different and mutually exclusive instrumental set-ups:

Since individually determinate entities do not exist, measurements do not entail an interaction between separate entities; rather, determinate entities emerge from their intra-action. I introduce the term 'intra-action' in recognition of their ontological inseparability, in contrast to the usual 'interaction', which relies on a metaphysics of individualism [...]. A phenomenon is a specific intra-action of an 'object' and the 'measuring agencies'; the object and the measuring agencies emerge from, rather than precede, the intra-action that produces them. Crucially, then, we should understand phenomena not as objects-in-themselves, or as perceived objects (in the Kantian or phenomenological sense), but as specific intra-actions.[9]

Setting out from a contestation of individualism as a constitutive principle of matter, Barad elaborates the idea that there is a mutual influence between the object studied and the apparatus that analyses it, and that there can be forms of knowledge other than the unidirectional one proposed in Heisenberg's model. What Barad seems to overlook with regard to Bohr's interpretation, though, is that the measuring apparatus and the object of study cannot really be placed on the same plane. For Bohr, in fact, the fundamental condition of possibility for measurement is that the apparatus used must be considered *classical,* and must therefore be of a substantially different nature to the quantum object. In this sense, Bohr's measuring apparatus acts more as a sort of translator, serving to reconcile the quantum behaviour of matter with classical language, without being directly involved in any interference phenomenon. In other words, Bohr's complementarity presupposes

9. K. Barad, *Meeting the Universe Halfway* (Durham, NC: Duke University Press, 2007), 128.

the establishment of an underlying asymmetry which is constitutive of the experiment and cannot be considered as a simple product of intra-action.

In fact, the necessary condition for any interference phenomenon to occur is that two or more waves should interact with each other, i.e. interference is a fact that concerns the interaction of quantum bodies with other quantum bodies. It is easy to understand how such a system lies far from the mental experiments formulated by Heisenberg or Bohr, whose fundamental assumption is that we are observing a single particle isolated from all others; in this sense, the individuality of the particle is an axiom opportunely programmed into the measuring apparatus, rather than an actual property of the quantum particle. Here we can once again refer to Schrödinger, who emphasises that the possibility of treating quantum particles as individuals is strictly dependent on their *density*: it is possible to study quantum objects in such a way that they exhibit a kind of individuality, provided that the *density of states* available to them is sufficiently low. In other words, it is necessary that the amount of interaction between the studied quantum object and other quantum objects is sufficiently small for the corpuscular model to be considered valid. When the density increases, the behaviour of particles can only be understood according to the wave approach, which excludes any treatment of particles as individuals. In Schrödinger's words:

One has the impression that the more the individuality of the particles is suppressed by the increase in their density, the more the corpuscular model becomes inadequate to describe them, and must be replaced by the wave model. For example, in the electronic rings of an atom or molecule the density is extremely high, since almost all the states within a certain region are occupied by electrons. The same applies to the so-called free electrons within a metal.[10]

---

10.   Schrodinger, 'What is an Elementary Particle?', 194 [translation modified].

It is interesting to note that Schrödinger mentions here three particular cases in which the wavelike behaviour of matter emerges in an inescapable way: atoms, molecules and crystalline solids. In all of these contexts, which essentially encapsulate the field of investigation of chemistry, one is not dealing with an isolated particle interacting with a classical apparatus, but with a legion of interpenetrating quantum bodies, whose boundaries are unclear to the point of vanishing altogether. Experimental chemistry, then, is concerned not with defining trajectories for solitary, non-interacting particles, but rather with witnessing the fluid, multifaceted potential of quantum matter in perpetual resonance with itself.

The celestial harmony of classical physics is perfectly accommodated to the human ear, so much so that, more or less voluntarily ignoring the progress of contemporary physics, we continue to marvel at the incredible consonance between microcosm and macrocosm, deceived by the extraordinary naturalness of the Newtonian accord. The subatomic visions of quantum matter are the inaudible beat of a dance that does not concern us: a liquid symphony in constant dissonance, which matter murmurs to itself in solitude.

NITROGEN

Now the five months of anxious waiting had passed: from among us eighty freshmen had been selected the twenty least lazy and foolish—fourteen boys and six girls—and the Preparation laboratory opened its doors to us. None of us had a precise idea of what was at stake: I think that it was his invention, a modern and technical version of the initiation rituals of savages, in which each of his subjects was abruptly torn away from book and school bench and transplanted amid eye-smarting fumes, hand-scorching acids, and practical events that do not jibe with the theories.

Primo Levi[11]

---

11.   Levi, *The Periodic Table*, 34.

The experience of the chemical laboratory is a ritual of deep communion and incommunicable solitude. Every laboratory I have set foot in was unique, but each shared with all the others a peculiar and indefinable atmosphere, a bit like churches. Maybe it's the smell of the solvents, the uninterrupted ticking of the magnetic stirrers, the flickering glow of the burning instruments, the hum of the extractor hoods, the ghostly hiss of the water running through the pipes. I remember how, upon entering a synthesis laboratory for the first time, confronted with the reagents on display on the counter, I was over-whelmed by a feeling of dangerous intimacy, as if that dead matter, which I had to tame and interrogate with my red-hot irons, could in turn penetrate through the confines of my skin and contaminate me irreversibly. The work of synthesis has a certain almost initiatory quality: there are experimental experiences that are remembered as milestones in one's training as a chem-ist, and which—even though they have now almost fallen into disuse—are regularly repeated in teaching workshops, because you *have to have been there, at least once in your life.*

Perhaps it is because of this curious tendency of special chemistry toward esotericism, or perhaps because of my unusual nocturnal readings, that, during one of my innumerable curricular laboratories, I was visited by a strange dream.

My colleagues and I, dressed in our white coats, were gathered in an underground laboratory of our department, where we were preparing to take part in a strange ritual. One by one, we approached a large steaming dewar from which there emanated an icy blue luminescence. The luminous liquid was then extracted by means of a long needle and injected under our skin, leaving an arcane mark on our left arms. When it was my turn, the man in charge of this mysterious procedure examined my forearms, tattooed with the alchemical symbols of sulphur and mercury—a reminder of my naive and enthusiastic freshman days, when my vague notions of science blended with a confused fascination with the occult. 'You forgot Nitrogen', he said in a tone of remorse, before going on to cauterize my flesh with liquefied gas.

The experience of encountering liquid nitrogen is undoubtedly one of the most intense and impressive milestones for newcomers to chemical synthesis. Although easily rationalised, the properties of this substance appear paradoxical and disturbing, so distant are they from any phenomenon we are accustomed to witnessing: it is a strangely dry liquid which burns the skin like a flame only to vanish spontaneously in a frenzied freezing boil. For water-based life forms like us, its state functions are necessarily alien, evoking the extraterrestrial landscapes of remote moons, covered by oceans of incomprehensible fluids.

The word *azoth*, coined in 1787 shortly after the element's discovery by the Scottish chemist Daniel Rutherford, and which to this day remains the Italian word for nitrogen—*azoto*—refers to the inert nature of the gas, which, unlike oxygen, cannot be used by living beings to drive the organic molecules they eat to produce energy. For this reason, it took its name from the Greek ἀ-ζωή, meaning 'lifeless'. Curiously, numerous mediaeval and Renaissance alchemical texts, long before nitrogen was identified as a chemical compound, contain recurring references to a miraculous substance called *Azoth*. As is well known, many terms currently in use in the chemical sciences—including the names of many elements and substances, as well as numerous preliminary techniques and pieces of experimental equipment—derive more or less directly from the alchemical tradition; it is therefore plausible that, in choosing the name for the newly discovered substance, the chemists of the time were influenced by alchemy, which was still widely practiced.

The word *Azoth*, according to a kind of Kabbalistic etymology presented by Basil Valentino in his treatise of the same name in 1613, was interpreted as a kind of magic formula in which the occult meaning of the Great Work was realised:

And as with everything else, from the greatest to the smallest, the beginning and the end come from God, the A and the O, the omnipresent. The Philosophers have graced me with the name Azoth, with the Latin letters A and Z, the Greek a and I, the Hebrew א and ת, Aleph and Tau, which added together give 'AZOTH'.[12]

The word *Azoth* therefore contains a kind of intrinsic circularity, and it is precisely because of this circularity that its realisation is the crowning achievement of the alchemical work. Several authors insist on the identification of Azoth with the *Elixir* or *universal medicine*, which contains the key to the transmutation of metals into gold and eternal life. The circularity of Azoth is the same as that of Ouroboros the serpent, another alchemical symbol in which the mystery of the Great Work is concealed.

In spite of its many vital and positive associations, Azoth remains surrounded by a certain ineradicable ambiguity, which can be likened to the creeping restlessness that surrounds the symbol of Ouroboros. If, on the one hand, Azoth is the expression of a condition of total equilibrium, as registered in the phonetic-Kabbalistic interpretation of its name, this equilibrium has a deadly and chaotic aspect to it, which converges on the definition of nitrogen as the ἀ-ζωή. In fact, in alchemy and in the Hermetic tradition as a whole, the union of opposing polarities can be achieved via two processes—a centripetal action which *coagulates* opposites in a productive synergy, or a centrifugal one which *dissolves* them in a state of sterile primordial chaos—in which equilibrium is achieved through maximum thermodynamic multiplicity.

To tell the truth, from the first moment I read the word, I could never help associating *azoto* with something obscure and vaguely demonic. The aforementioned treatise on chemistry attributed to Basil Valentino actually has a rather obscure origin, according to the alchemist Fulcanelli dating back to

---

12.   B. Valentino, *Azoth* (Rome: Edizioni Mediterranee, 1988), 105.

tenth-century Arabia and particularly to the work of Muhammad ibn Umail al-Tamimi.

Although this attribution is controversial to say the least, there is little doubt that the word *Azoth*, like many others in the alchemical and chemical vocabulary, has its roots in the Arab world. The word's association with the Near East reinforces the effectiveness of the curious assonance between alchemical Azoth and Lovecraftian Azathoth, the absolute monstrosity that seems to play a central role in the inhuman cosmology of the *Necronomicon*, the grimoire of black magic of the mad Arab Abdul Alhazred.[13] Indeed, returning to Basil Valentino's definition, the main characteristic defining the alchemical Azoth is its undivided nature, which, however, cannot be attributed to any kind of individuality in the strict sense of the word: 'I am one, and many are in me.' Azoth, or *First Matter*, is a kind of *undetermined substratum* from which the alchemical work must necessarily proceed and in which it must necessarily end, but which—unlike Heisenberg's particle—does not appear as a mere theoretical presupposition that is functional for human determination; it is precisely from its undetermined nature that Azoth draws its miraculous alchemical characteristics. The numinous and indeterminate nature of Azoth connects it back to a mythological *primordial chaos*, the very *chaos* from which it is derived.

According to Lovecraft's cosmology, at the centre of 'Ultimate Chaos' there 'sprawls the blind idiot god Azathoth, Lord of All Things, encircled by his flopping horde of mindless and amorphous dancers, and lulled by the thin, monotonous piping of a demoniac flute held in nameless paws.'[14]

Several of Lovecraft's tales contain numerous references to paradoxical and disturbing chemical and physico-chemical phenomena which act as silent

---

13.   The similarity was pointed out by Ben Woodard in his essay *Slime Dynamics. Generation, Mutation, and the Creep of Life* (Winchester: Zero Books, 2012).

14.   H.P. Lovecraft, 'The Haunter of the Dark', *The H.P. Lovecraft Omnibus 3: The Haunter of the Dark and Other Tales* (London: HarperCollins, 2000), 294.

messengers of the unnameable entities that inhabit the sidereal spaces beyond human comprehension. It is therefore plausible that Lovecraft himself was influenced by the then very recent scientific discoveries about the quantum nature of matter, relativity and atomic physics.

The most representative case is undoubtedly the 1927 story 'The Colour Out of Space', in which a mysterious meteorite strikes and irreversibly contaminates the New England town of Arkham. A central element of the story is the enigmatic properties of the substance from space, which loses its mass in the form of heat, radiating a disturbing luminescence of indefinable colour. For Lovecraft this photochemical monstrosity represents the apotheosis of an indescribable horror, something infinitely distant from ordinary human experience, yet at the same time radically and terrifyingly material:

[...] and over all the rest reigned that riot of luminous amorphousness, that alien and undimensioned rainbow of cryptic poison from the well—seething, feeling, lapping, reaching, scintillating, straining, and malignly bubbling in its cosmic and unrecognizable chromaticism.[15]

This aspect is highlighted by Graham Harman in his essay *Weird Realism: Lovecraft and Philosophy*, in which he underlines the essential complicity of the scientific eye in constructing the horror of Lovecraft's work:

The usual opposition is between enlightened modernism and anti-modern obscurantism. Either the scientist dismisses the gullible fetishes of witch doctors and theosophists, or these mystics dismiss science as having access to nothing but a shallow version of a more terrible cosmic truth. Despite Lovecraft's alleged materialism (and he is certainly a materialist in part), his attitude to the problem is quite different. For Lovecraft, cult rituals and

---

15.   H.P. Lovecraft, 'The Colour Out of Space', *The H.P. Lovecraft Omnibus 3*, 267.

the scrawlings of Medieval Arab wizards stand in a perfect continuum of knowledge with the most advanced modern science.[16]

Lovecraft's choice to convey cosmic horror through the indescribable chromatic properties of a mysterious substance out of space is particularly effective. On the other hand, of all the properties of matter, *colour* has always fascinated alchemists more than any other, so much so that the entire Alchemical Work was divided up according to the different colours of the substances obtained.

In fact, the spectral properties of chemical substances are those least open to intuitive explanation without recourse to radically qualitative, or even spiritual, theories, which by their very nature cannot be included in the most rudimentary atomistic models. Unlike the immaterial ghosts of the most classic horror stories, which are of a strictly spiritual nature and can infiltrate the minds of their victims by causing a form of interference of a purely intellectual nature, Lovecraftian spectral substance manifests itself in the form of a physical contamination, in which the real horror is not so much the alien origin of the monster as the discovery of its disturbing intimacy with the human.

Indeed, contagion operates on the basis of a morbid principle of similarity, in which the contaminating substance must have sufficient affinity with the contaminated body to allow a reciprocal interaction, according to the well-known chemical-alchemical principle *similia similibus solvuntur*. The sick luminescence of the Arkham meteorite moves with equal ease through organic and inorganic matter, from well water to animal organisms, all the way to the human mind which, plunged into unnameable madness, is equally susceptible to its frightening influence. In this respect, the colour out of space acts as a simple revealer or prophet of the ultimate anxiety: the idea that *we ourselves*, in some perverse and incomprehensible way, *are spectres*, and

---

16. G. Harman, *Weird Realism: Lovecraft and Philosophy* (Winchester: Zero Books, 2012), 116.

that the *blackness* that consumes us is a resonance that proceeds inexorably from the very core of the matter from which we are made.[17]

In chemistry, the spectrum of a substance is generally defined in terms of the variation of a certain property of that substance as the frequency of the radiation that it interacts with changes. Most often, when we talk about the spectrum, we are referring to the optical characteristics of molecules: in this case, the property studied is generally the light absorption, which determines colour, or emission, in phenomena such as fluorescence or phosphorescence. It was the observation of the spectral characteristics of matter, and particularly hydrogen, that paved the way for the formulation of the quantum-mechanical model of the atom that we know today.

Originally, spectra were obtained by breaking down the light transmitted by the substance under study according to wavelength using a prism, and exposing a photographic plate to it. The image obtained in this way showed thin dark zones, placed in the spectrum with surprising regularity, and corresponding to the wavelength of the radiation absorbed by the substance, which became known as *absorption lines*.

Spectroscopy, curiously enough, originated in astronomy; the first spectra observed were, to all intents and purposes, *colours out of space*. The first observation of spectral lines dates back to the early nineteenth century, when the English chemist William Wollatson observed that the spectrum of sunlight was not perfectly continuous, but was separated by small interruptions; these spectral lines were catalogued a few years later by the German physicist Joseph von Fraunhofer, after whom they are named today. Long before modern spectroscopy, the first scientist ever to develop a bizarre theory of space waves was Kepler, who argued, in accordance with his harmonic vision of the universe, that the stars could act upon human beings with their light rays through an elaborate system of geometric assonances.

---

17.   See R. Negarestani, 'The Corpse Bride: Thinking with Nigredo', *Collapse IV: Concept Horror,* ed. R. Mackay, D. Veal (Falmouth: Urbanomic, 2008), 129.

This vision had its roots in the not strictly scientific conviction that there was an occult symmetry between microcosm and macrocosm, such that the human soul and the surrounding universe were somehow united by the same susceptibility to specific spherical harmonies. From this perspective, the Lovecraftian meteor is a totally eccentric and disharmonious spatial object, whose resonance with living matter is a bleak litany of death.

In light of quantum mechanical discoveries about the wavelike nature of matter, the potential interactions of atoms and molecules with light have been widely studied and understood. The key to spectroscopy is the concept of quantum *jumping*, i.e. the idea that quantum objects can only be found in certain states, characterised by discrete energy levels. In reality, as Schrödinger pointed out, the idea of the quantum *leap* does not account for the complexity of the dynamics of quantum interactions, and testifies not so much to the discontinuity of atomic and molecular phenomena as to the inadequacy of our understanding of them.

In analogy with Kepler's speculations, our contact with the boundless vastness of space, as well as with the visceral depths of molecular matter, is inevitably mediated by the vibration of a mysterious accord. At this point, we can perhaps allow ourselves to surrender to the poignant poetry of this extraterrestrial chemical-physical dialogue; a communication painfully encrypted in absence, constructed out of furrows of interstellar silence carved into the dim light of our knowledge. Spectra are but the remote trace of a relationship of resonance—the one-dimensional shadow of an infinitely more complex, and infinitely distant, interaction.

MERCURY

Did chemistry theorems exist? No: therefore you had to go further, not be satisfied with the quia, go back to the origins, to mathematics and physics. The origins of chemistry were ignoble, or at least equivocal: the dens of the alchemists, their abominable hodgepodge of ideas and language, their

confessed interest in gold, their Levantine swindles typical of charlatans or

magicians; instead, at the origin of physics lay the strenuous clarity of the

West—Archimedes and Euclid. I would become a physicist, ruat coelum:

perhaps without a degree, since Hitler and Mussolini forbade it.

Primo Levi[18]

The history of alchemy is a long story of ambiguities and misunderstandings. The most obvious and widely debated question about this ancient discipline is whether it should be considered simply as a primitive form of science, or whether it should be understood as a magical-religious initiatory path. Although there are very good arguments for both positions, ultimately none of them seems to me to be conclusive. The urgent need to classify the alchemical experience as either one or the other emerges, perhaps, from the fear that in it there is a dangerous contamination between two worlds that we tend to treat as separate and irreconcilable. While the intrusion of any mystical aspect into scientific work is undoubtedly seen as a danger to its objectivity, on the other hand, surprisingly, the idea that experimental experience can become a legitimate channel of access to the spiritual dimension is often considered equally unacceptable, and has often been interpreted as a desecration of deeper Hermetic truths.

Several authors, including Carl Gustav Jung in his *Psychology and Alchemy*, have argued that the alchemical experience is based on a kind of synergy between the psychological aspect, which is internal to the human being, and the strictly scientific-material aspect of experimental work. Taking up this idea, the physicist Wolfgang Pauli—one of the most influential scientists involved in the formulation of quantum mechanics—coined the concept of *Hintergrundsphysik* to indicate the indissoluble correlation between science and psychoanalytic archetypes, hoping that modern physics,

---

18.   Levi, *The Periodic Table*, 55–56.

via Bohr's concept of complementarity, could heal the Copernican schism between physis and psyché, reuniting them in a new unity:

The general problem of the relation between psyche and physis, between the inner and the outer, can, however, hardly be said to have been solved by the concept of 'psychophysical parallelism' which was advanced in the last century. Yet modern science may have brought us closer to a more satisfying conception of this relationship by setting up, within the field of physics, the concept of *complementarity*. It would be most satisfactory of all if physis and psyche could be seen as complementary aspects of the same reality.[19]

For Pauli, for the contemporary scientist, the real philosopher's stone would be, as it was for the ancient alchemist, the reunification of spirit and body and the descent of the *soul into the world*, made possible by the most advanced discoveries in theoretical physics and psychology. Indeed, from the idea that a kind of miraculous synergistic relationship of mutual determination can be established between the quantum object and the apparatus that studies it, a broader mythology can easily be deduced, in which the human mind and the material world are united in a harmonious union, similar in many ways to that pursued by the Hermetic and alchemical traditions.

The complementarity postulated by Bohr, however, while constituting a pragmatically effective answer to the problem of the indeterminacy of the quantum particle, is an essentially limited instrument which presupposes, in its very operation, the maintenance of a clear distinction between the quantum properties of the particle under study and the classical properties of the measuring apparatus. In other words, Bohr's complementarity does not admit any possibility of authentic conciliation between quantum matter itself and the knowledge of the experimenter. The particle, in its state prior

19.   W. Pauli, 'The Influence of Archetypal Ideas on the Scientific Theories of Kepler', in *Writings on Physics and Philosophy*, tr. Priscilla Silz, ed. C. P. Enz, K. von Meyenn (Berlin and Heidelberg: Springer, 1994), 260.

to interaction with the human, remains a *physis* in an inaccessible beyond, whose very existence is incompatible with that of the *psyché* that studies it. The completion of the alchemical-quantum work is, rather, a poisonous *reverse philosopher's stone*, consisting of the revelation of the incommensurable distance between human reason and matter.

In this text I have tried to suggest the ways in which scientific investigation constitutes a privileged channel of contact with dimensions of reality that are radically alien to human experience, and how this contact is achieved in a particularly disturbing way in the encounter of the experimental chemist with quantum matter. In fact, the advent of the quantum model has opened up a bifurcation between two possible approaches to the problem of matter in science. On the one hand, the unknowability of the quantum particle in its pre-measurement state may provide grounds for a radicalised thinking, unheard of in the strictly scientific sphere before modern physics, which denies the ontological autonomy of matter; since it is not possible to know the particle in its original state, it would be meaningless to attribute to the particle itself any form of existence independent of its manifestation. Taking this conception to its extreme, it is the human experimenter themselves who creates matter with their own gaze at the moment it manifests itself. Taking a more cautious stance, one could argue that matter exists in different ways depending on its manifestation—whether the experimenter chooses to use one measuring device or another. This thought, which we can define as correlationist, in reference to Quentin Meillassoux,[20] assumes that matter and the mind that studies it are necessarily correlated, so that matter is always necessarily decentred with respect to the human gaze.

Alternatively, quantum mechanics can open the way to a new form of thinking about matter, which we could call *spectral materialism*, in which indeterminacy leads to the renunciation of traditional atomism, replacing

20. Q. Meillassoux, *After Finitude: An Essay on the Necessity of Contingency*, tr. R. Brassier (London and New York: Continuum, 2008).

it with a reinterpretation of matter as *self-resonance*. This vision frees matter from its dependence on the gaze of the experimenter, allowing us to intuit, through the mathematical-geometric image of the *spectrum*, the trans-individual dimension of quantum interaction. The spectrum is not, as correlationist thinking would have it, a deficient form of human knowledge, but emerges as the trace of an unobservable relationship of matter with itself. In this respect, then, returning to Meillassoux's reading, spectral matter is inherently *fossilised*, because the spectrum, as the mathematical shadow of the quantum object, constitutes a privileged connection, indeed the only possible connection, between human experience and a *matter without us*.

The letters written by Isaac Newton between 1669 and 1696 show signs of a dramatic physical and psychological attrition, culminating in an almost complete mental collapse in 1693. Reading his correspondence, at times one comes across obscure and disjointed phrases, unusual spelling mistakes and unjustified outbursts of anger, accompanied by tales of bizarre physical afflictions and strange alterations in his handwriting.

It is now widely accepted that this sudden deterioration of the scientist's psychophysical condition was an unmistakable symptom of mercury poisoning.[21] The dating of the incriminating writings corresponds almost exactly to the period during which Newton is thought to have begun taking an interest in alchemy, working tirelessly day and night in his laboratory with large quantities of mercury; he himself reports in his writings that he inhaled and tasted salts and amalgams in his feverish search for the mystery of the transmutation of metals into gold.

It is plausible that episodes of intoxication like those suffered by Newton were very frequent among the alchemists and scientists of the time, at least those who were wealthy enough to purchase expensive mercury compounds for their research. In the light of such evidence, it is difficult to subscribe

---

21.   L.W. Johnson and M.L. Wolbarsht, 'Mercury Poisoning: A Probable Cause of Isaac Newton's Physical and Mental Ills', *Notes Rec. R. Soc. Lond* 34 (1979), 1–9.

to the view of alchemy as a strictly philosophical and disembodied path in which experimental work played only a symbolic role, or acted as a mere cover for deeper mysteries. On the contrary, not only was the research into the transmutation of metals perfectly authentic, but it is reasonable to think that many of the more theoretical aspects of Hermetic philosophy took shape from the experimental activity, and not vice versa. The poisonous exhalations of mercury, the central element in alchemical transmutation, afflict the minds of those who are exposed to them with a slow but inexorable melancholy, which can evolve, as it did for Newton, into depressive episodes and a gradual dissociation from the surrounding reality. The *nigredo*, the material and spiritual putrefaction that the alchemist had to pass through in order to reach the completion of their work, could then be understood as a more or less deliberate form of intoxication.

This interpretation may seem naive, but is only apparently so. The aim is not to reduce the magical-religious dimension of the alchemical experience to a simple hallucination caused by careless contact with dangerous chemical compounds, but rather to bring *chemical matter*, back to the centre of the alchemical narrative in place of the *human*. The movement of alchemical work is not so much one of irradiation from the human mind into matter, as a certain reactionary revisionism of the Hermetic tradition would have it, but rather one of *contamination* of the mind by matter; in other words, in the alchemical process it is not human knowledge that sheds light on matter, but matter that infiltrates with its shadowy tentacles the mind of the subject that studies it.

If, in the alchemical laboratory, this infiltration is realised through a literal intoxication, in which inorganic matter insinuates itself into organic matter, revealing its *living death* and undoing it in an inexorable putrefaction, the contemporary chemist is confronted with a different, but analogous, form of *nigredo*. The quantum particle may maintain a semblance of individuality, as in the experiment imagined by Heisenberg, only at the moment in which it is supposed to be treated as an isolated body which collides against a measuring apparatus and *collapses* into an essentially classical state. On the other hand, in chemical systems, matter reveals its own necessarily undulatory nature, which manifests itself to the experimenter via its spectral properties. Spectra, in the broad sense, are transversal geometrical structures emerging from the interaction of quantum bodies with other quantum bodies; from this point of view, chemistry, being essentially concerned with the study of the reciprocal interactions between atoms and molecules, is by definition a spectral science. Assuming that it is not possible to draw a definite boundary between one quantum object and another, spectra are what remains of an incessant monologue of matter with itself: in this sense, the study of the chemical object takes place at the price of a disintegration of the subject that studies it, which must lose its individuality, dissolving in the oceanic nature of quantum matter.

In 1900, Paul Drude proposed a model for metallic bonding which was supposed to account for the electrical and thermal conductivity properties of solids. The model, which was entirely classical, assumed that metals consisted of a lattice of atomic nuclei, between which electrons could move freely, forming what is commonly referred to as a *sea of electrons*.

This formulation, which was later set aside in favour of more accurate quantum-mechanical models, was unsuitable for describing the electronic properties of solids, but it contained an interesting insight: the bizarre and counterintuitive idea that hidden behind the solid appearance of metals is a microscopic *liquidity*. In fact, crystalline solids, including metals, can only be studied by admitting the complete delocalisation of their electrons, which—with a little poetic licence—may be imagined as resonant waves on a single, unconfined ocean. Moreover, the fascination of scientists with the idea of a miraculous liquid metal with infinite multiform powers, capable of creating or dissolving any other metal, long predates modern physics, and has its roots in ancient Hermetic philosophies.

I have always imagined the ocean of Solaris as a shimmering sea of mercury. In his 1961 novel, Stanislaw Lem recounts the journey of a scientist to the space base of a planet inhabited by a single, titanic organism that covers it like an enormous ocean. The enigmatic alien creature appears at times to be sentient, if not actually intelligent, capable of interacting with the surrounding environment and even of altering the orbit of the planet it inhabits, in order to ensure its survival. However, it seems to resist any form of communication with human explorers, responding in a totally unpredictable way to any attempt at contact, and preferring instead to engage in what Lem calls a constant *ontological self-metamorphosis*, from which emerge 'fragments of an intelligent structure, perhaps endowed with genius, haphazardly mingled with outlandish phenomena, apparently the product of an unhinged mind'.[22] The ocean creature finally breaks the silence with its human visitors when, following a massive X-ray bombardment, it begins to conjure up mysterious anthropomorphic apparitions, drawing upon the memory of the inhabitants of the base. These creatures are distorted and monstrous reflections of human beings, endowed with consciousness but unable to remember anything about their past lives, seemingly immortal and condemned to come back to life every time the protagonists try to destroy them.

The ocean of Solaris is the perfect example of *spectral matter*: an essentially inaccessible object[23] that resists human investigation, a *hyperchaos*[24] that acts as a perfectly formless substrate from which disjointed fragments of geometric structures with obscure symmetries sometimes emerge. Its relationship with the human cannot be translated into an exasperated solipsism: the ocean is a *radical other* which, as witnessed by the numerous experiments of the protagonists, cannot simply be reabsorbed into the human mind, reducing its monstrous manifestations to a form of hallucination

22.   Lem, *Solaris*, 24.

23.   See B. Konior, 'Unlearning Habitual Cosmologies: Reading Stanisław Lem at the Event Horizon', in *Dispatches from The Institute of Incoherent Geography* 1:4 (Flügschriften, 2019), 39–46.

24.   See Meillassoux, *After Finitude*.

or madness. The ocean is undoubtedly *out there*, but its relationship with scientists is not one of *complementarity*, i.e. of mutual determination, but rather one of destructive interference, of mutual indetermination. The more the ocean and the human mind get together, the more they confuse one another, producing something deformed and frighteningly blasphemous.

In the last, poignant chapter of Lem's work, the protagonist questions the possibility of the existence of an imperfect, 'sick' God, who 'created eternity, which was to have measured his power, and which measures his unending defeat'.[25] The ocean of Solaris, the indeterminate amorphous chaos that sleeps in the abyss beyond the light of the instruments of science, is, like Azathoth and the alchemists' quicksilver, 'the first phase of the despairing God',[26] a *blind idiot* god perpetually engulfed in a delirium of eternal solitude. The recurring image of the *demented god* conveys the disquiet of the revelation that the ultimate dimension of matter is essentially alien: no anthropomorphic demiurge, good or evil, could ever have produced the quantum horror, because its very existence is radically incompatible with that of any reason.

The world with which we are familiar is, in reality, haunted by phantasms, by the remains of structures of interference that emerge from the constant, solitary vibration of a liquid substrate that unites us in an indissoluble embrace, whose *fearful action* can cross any distance. Like the ancient alchemical warning,[27] the spectral vision of quantum matter commands us to descend into the bowels of the matter that composes us, where, in the incomprehensible vibration of the molecular substance, the exasperating beat of a monstrous drum resounds incessantly.

And through this revolting graveyard of the universe the muffled, maddening beating of drums, and thin, monotonous whine of blasphemous flutes from

25.   Lem, *Solaris*, 197.

26.   Ibid., 198.

27.   *Visita Interiora Terrae, Rectificando Invenies Occultum Lapidem.*

inconceivable, unlighted chambers beyond Time; the detestable pounding and piping whereunto dance slowly, awkwardly, and absurdly the gigantic, tenebrous ultimate gods....[28]

LT

---

28.   H.P. Lovecraft, 'Nyarlathotep', in *The Doom that Came to Sarnath* (New York: Ballantine, 1971), 57–70.

II

NOTES ON GOTHIC INSURRECTION

GOTHIC INSURRECTION

We are sinking into a new Middle Ages. Traditionalism, fundamentalism, and the regressive policies of the new Right are corroding modernity from within, holding back its driving force, and bending technological means to military, propagandistic, and repressive ends. Extreme climate phenomena, epidemics, armies from the East pressing at the borders of the West, greedy commercial corporations, financial crises (increasingly reminiscent of waves of famine), apocalyptic paranoia spawned by millenarian cults—these are the divine plagues raging on a tormented planet. One would almost be tempted to say that the past has never been so close to the future, to the point where we cannot help but doubt whether the modern age was nothing more than one long dream: the Promised Land, peaceful and skilfully governed by cybernetics, is turning into a cybergothic nightmare marred by conflict, bigotry, and superstition. Indeed, across the globe, reactionary movements are calling for the end of modernity and a return to various prior configurations.

THE SPECTRAL DIMENSION

In *Specters of Marx*,[1] Jacques Derrida, the founder of deconstruction, introduces a useful concept for understanding such retro-progressive trends: the notion of 'hauntology', i.e. the analysis of the phenomena of the return of ghosts of the past (so-called *revenants*). Even before Derrida, Walter Benjamin had already addressed the reactivation of past events—as in the case of the recovery of the cultural and political heritage of ancient Rome

---

1.   J. Derrida, *Specters of Marx: The State of the Debt, the Work of Mourning and the New International*, tr. P. Kamuf (London and New York: Routledge Classics, 2006).

by Robespierre and the French revolutionaries. For Walter Benjamin, this kind of access in the present to the corridors of the past represents 'a tiger's leap'[2] that cuts through the linear flow of history, i.e. a creative reworking of the relics of a lost age. Without this constant activity of theatrical disguise, which goes from travesty to farce and from farce to tragedy, history itself would be nothing more than a succession of indistinguishable instants. Setting out from this assumption, Derrida points out how this short-circuit forces us to admit the impossibility of solidifying the ground of history once and for all, declaring the series of past events 'dead and buried'. In fact, in various ways, historical time seems to manifest catastrophic tendencies, capable of reversing the present into the past, altering the course of events.

However, unlike Benjamin, Derrida deals with a different kind of historical event: those that were foreseen or hoped for, but never came about. One of the most famous examples is found in the opening words of the *Manifesto of the Communist Party*: if, as Marx writes, 'a spectre is haunting Europe', it is because the timeline that this spectre brings with it, as if dragging its chains behind it, was never realised, and has sunk into the abyssal ruins of history. Hauntology, therefore, also deals with a particular kind of historical non-event: those 'lost futures' that can perhaps be reactivated in the present.

The revolution is the catastrophe embodied by this spectre, the unexpected event that could strike the world like lightning, altering the normal course of events. Both in the case of Benjamin's future-past and that of Derrida's events that never happened, the calendrical progression that moves inexorably from the past toward the future is broken by an interaction that is apparently impossible, both historically and physically: an element that has now disappeared or which never happened, an absent or materially irretrievable event, appears in that very section of the chain that launches itself from the present toward the future. And yet, as Derrida himself points out, it would be a serious mistake to believe that this is some sort of cyclical

---

2.   W. Benjamin, 'On the Concept of History', in *Selected Writings Volume 4, 1938–1940*, ed. H. Eiland, M.W. Jennings (Cambridge, MA: Harvard University Press, 2003), 395.

phenomenon (the eternal return of the identical): the ghost does not coincide with the person whose name it bears, it does not share the same flesh, nor the same bones, nor the same intentions; it is an atmospheric,[3] insubstantial, and yet terribly material double, capable of shaking, screaming and murmuring from the shadows, the historical and biographical foundations upon which individuals and communities rest.

In turn, our transition from the cybernetic to the cybergothic era denotes a paradoxical union between the apex of modernity, represented by digital technologies and hyper-connectivity, and the Middle Ages, a period charac- terised by great political fragmentation, a terrifying proliferation of natural, economic, and political disasters, and the dizzying transcendence of Gothic architecture. We find ourselves caught between a reactionary nostalgia for a time we never experienced (and which perhaps never existed) and the disturbing phantasmal return of an era that is alien to our historical continuum. The only escape route is upwards, as the gloomy cathedrals of the thirteenth century remind us.... Flapping out in the twilight of civilisation, like bats.

Art is undoubtedly one of the main channels via which the spectres of the past find ingress into the dimension of the present. An example of historical discontinuity in the sense described by Benjamin can be found in the art of the French Revolution. In the paintings of Jacques-Louis David, the death of Jean-Paul Marat—whose throat was slit in his bathtub by Charlotte Corday in an attempt to put an end to the revolutionary violence—echoes those of Socrates and Seneca, thinkers killed—or rather 'suicided'—by conservative political forces and fierce opponents of aristocratic excesses. David's *Death of Marat,* which portrays the Jacobin as a martyr of the revolution, soon became one of the symbols of the world that Marat himself had helped to build.

An example of the second type of discontinuity, analysed by Derrida, is provided by Mark Fisher. In a 2007 interview (which would later be included

---

3.   See E. Thacker, *In the Dust of this Planet* (Winchester: Zero Books, 2011).

in the anthology *Ghosts of My Life*), Fisher applies Derrida's hauntology to the music of William Bevan, the real name of the electronic producer Burial, at the time the leading light in the dubstep scene. At stake here is the legacy of rave culture (or what Simon Reynolds called the 'hardcore continuum'): While much of dubstep is determined by an intensification of previous styles and by the use of flat, claustrophobic and oppressive musical devices, Burial's electronics, on the contrary, unfold in atmospheric spaces traversed by sonic remnants and distant echoes of sampled voices, heavily contaminated by soul and hip-hop. It's not that Bevan's compositions re-elaborate on any artistic or cultural heritage: on the contrary, 'Burial's is a re-dreaming of the past, a condensation of relics of abandoned genres into an oneiric montage. His sound is a work of mourning rather than of melancholia, because he still longs for the lost object, still refuses to abandon the hope that it will return.'[4]

Bevan grew up far from the rave scene, yet Burial's music manages to evoke its broken dreams and hopes. More than ten years after Fisher's interview, one does not have to look far to find a long list of similar examples in contemporary music: hypnagogic pop, vaporwave, post-punk revival, ambient, lo-fi, thrash metal, bubblegum pop, etc. Burial is only one of countless examples of the nostalgic reactivation of a past that was never lived and a future that never came to be, a fact that leads us directly to the heart of the problem: if nostalgia and a longing for an imaginary past are the affective bases of the reactionary, then how can the ruins of a lamented 'monumental' history[5] be reconciled with the reactivation of lost futures? How to welcome the coming cybergothic era without setting foot in the wreckage of fascism?

---

4. M. Fisher, 'Downcast Angel: Interview with Burial', *The Wire* 286 (December 2007), 27–31: 28.

5. F. Nietzsche, 'On the Uses and Disadvantages of History for Life', *Untimely Meditations*, tr. R.J. Hollingdale, ed. D. Breazeale (Cambridge: Cambridge University Press, 1997), 57–124, in particular 67–69. 'Monumental' history would correspond to mythical history, understood as insurmountable and superhuman, capable of inspiring posterity and instilling a feeling of reverence in those who look back at it.

The answer may come from the music scene, and from a particular genre where one would least expect it: black metal. A genre that is in itself nostalgic, animated by yearning for a lost yet recoverable purity—a purity of sound, and a purity of attitude with regard to the audience, the press, and large-scale distribution. Although poetically and stylistically centred on the themes of death, disappearance, and the annihilation of everything that exists, black metal is one of the most reactionary, conservative musical genres, and the one most associated with mediaeval imagery. Unsurprisingly, in the hands of the extreme Right, it seems to morph very easily into a form of ethnic, nationalist, and traditionalist advocacy. However, some aspects of early black metal may allow us to better understand this reactionary and anti-modern desire, allowing us to introduce a particular form of 'double vampiric-spectral spiral', a characteristic that I will try to illustrate here through the musical work of two classic bands: Bathory and Darkthrone.

The nostalgia of European black metal seemingly harks back to a mythical, rather than historical or religious, past, thus allowing us to oppose the reactionary nature of the new Right with a kind of temporal distortion different from that advocated in recent times by the 'alt'-Right. For this reason, it will first of all be necessary to address the concept of *neoreaction*—i.e., as we shall see, the closest relative, both theoretically and linguistically, to the historical category *cybergothic*.

TIME SPIRAL

Neoreaction, or NRx, or even Dark Enlightenment, is a movement inspired by the writings of Nick Land, the father of accelerationism, and Mencius Moldbug aka Curtis Yarvin, a computer scientist and political theorist.[6] The neoreactionary proposal consists in a kind of open-ended programme for the dissolution of modernity, devised within a political framework that has room

---

6.   For the full text of Nick Land's *Dark Enlightenment,* see N. Land, 'Dark Enlightenment', in *Reignition*, Tome 2, 9–145. The entirety of Yarvin's work is available in the archive at *Unqualified Reservations,* <http://www.unqualified-reservations.org/>.

for neo-monarchists, fascists, ethnonationalists, social Darwinists, transhu-
manists, techno-commercial accelerationists, neo-cameralists, anarcho-cap-
italists and even some anarcho-copapists. Unlike the classic reactionary
and traditionalist movements, neoreaction, while representing a revival of
the Enlightenment project, does not reject the scientific achievements of
modernity, but proposes to make use of all available scientific and technical
means to achieve its goals—namely, the fragmentation of nation-states into
a myriad of city-states and micronations, the destruction of universalism,
and the end of representative democracy.

A further element that distinguishes NRx from common reactionaryism
(and even from the new Right) is that, although it too considers democracy
and a universalism of rights to be the principal causes of a process of
economic and cultural decadence, its exponents do not propose as their
ultimate goal the restoration of an ancient Edenic splendour. On the contrary, neoreaction advocates a reworking of political realism based on the
concepts of dissipation and metastability: nothing lasts forever, violence and
oppression are the laws that govern the universe, which is why it is necessary to govern ruthlessly, designing small but manageable and robust social
structures. According to NRx, democratic-progressivist-universalist thinking
has ignored the brutal reality of the facts in its attempts to enclose the cruel
spontaneity of nature and human beings within an imaginary world revolving
around equality, solidarity, and the assumption that nature, and particularly
human nature, is inherently benevolent. On the basis of these assumptions,
the West attempts to allow the cohabitation of different economic interests,
ideologies, religions, genealogies and ways of life, thereby condemning its
political and cultural institutions (i.e. schools and universities) to mediocrity
and subjugation by 'minority lobbies', bowing their heads before the rule
that everyone is special and worthy of respect. Egalitarian ideas are so
deeply rooted in Western society and history that they make it necessary
for neoreaction itself to analyse and examine its own theoretical production
in detail. Land writes:

The very last thing neoreaction has to usefully declare is I have a dream. Dream-mongering is the enemy. The only future worth striving for is splintered into myriads, loosely webbed together by free-exit connections, and conducting innumerable experiments in government, the vast majority of which will fail. We do not, and cannot, know what we want, anymore than we can know what the machines of the next century will be like, because real potentials need to be discovered, not imagined.[7]

Curiously, NRx has dubbed the ensemble of forces it opposes (mainstream media, academia, etc.) the 'Cathedral', alluding to their hypothetical religious origins, which, it contends, have become secularised over the centuries—a tradition that can be traced back to the Renaissance, the cradle of universalist humanism and the era of hypothetical liberation from the dark yoke of the Middle Ages. In order to overthrow the 'unitarian' hegemony of the Cathedral, the most famous theoretical elaboration of neoreaction proposes a strategy of *exit* from current State formations via the constitution of autonomous guilds and regions, united by economic, ethnic, or religious ties, leading to the foundation of corporate metropolises governed by CEO-monarchies, administrative councils, and police forces.

By reactivating old concepts, values, and methods of investigation and adapting them to the contemporary world—thereby managing to unite different or conflicting interests and positions around the same objective— neoreaction effectively collapses the past into a multi-dystopian future (from a democratic or anti-authoritarian perspective). As Land himself points out:

To translate 'neoreaction' into 'the new reaction' is in no way objectionable. It is new, and open to novelty [...] it not only promotes drastic regression, but highly-advanced drastic regression. Like retrofuturism, paleomodernism, and cybergothic, the word 'neoreaction' compactly describes a time-twisted

---

7.   N. Land, 'Neoreactionary Realism', in *Reignition*, Tome 3, 126.

vector that spirals forwards into the past, and backwards into the future. [...]
[N]eoreaction is a time-crisis, manifested through paradox.[8]

With the help of Land's philosophical genius, neoreaction, well aware of the fact that (in the words of Deleuze and Guattari) no one ever died of contradictions, has successfully managed to think ontological, political and existential plurality, and moreover to do so without degenerating into regret and nostalgia for an uncontaminated world—in the process helping to tip the Enlightenment project into the dark cauldron of boiling oil of the new Middle Ages. A victory that has been paid for dearly: by asserting that order can only emerge from chaos and violence, NRx fully exposes its flank to even more chaotic and violent forces, to ancient horrors that are only apparently dead.

In order to confront neoreaction, we will have to penetrate deeply into its own camp, finding different uses for the weapons it has developed. Perhaps, by making both the reactionary spirit and the thirst for black metal annihilation our own, we will be able to hit this many-headed adversary from behind and decapitate it, as if with a well-aimed slash of the sword. Easier said than done, though. The icy sound of black metal screeches, croaks shrilly and tries to attack us with its claws: it does not like to be analysed, summarised or glossed. Ultimately, it doesn't like anything at all.... As soon as a verdict is pronounced, black metal rejects it: fleeing into the past when questioned about the future, hurling itself into the most distant future (the apocalypse) when questioned about the past.

Flying through the ages like an immortal crow, black metal abandons the present in its quest for ever more refined and ever more immoral cruelties: when it gets bored of the Middle Ages, it will take on ancient Greece or Mesoamerican civilisations, return to haunt the Norse myths it holds so dear, or contemplate the end of the world. Neoreaction should fear this black creature,

---

8.   N. Land, 'The Idea of Neoreaction' and 'Neoreaction (for Dummies)' in *Reignition*, Tome 3, 92, 25.

for although it possesses its own chrono-paradoxical capacities, it wishes neither to constitute nor to liberate anything. As a purely negative spirit, it is compelled to deny, again and again, every theory, every practice, every instance and every earthly collectivity, always pushing itself further. The *blackster* rarely manages to master both faculties of the black beast, merely remaining blind like old Odin, staring either into the anti-cosmic void or the fantasised splendours of bygone eras. However, to become chrono-warriors, we must strive to acquire both magical eyes.

THE CALL OF THE BEAST

Although heavy metal and rock have always dealt with Satan, pagan myths, and witchcraft, the primordial black metal of bands such as Venom, Mercyful Fate, Bathory, and Hellhammer/Celtic Frost has turned these tenuous ties into a kind of symbiotic fusion. After a few albums centred on Satanism, necromancy, and assorted provocations, it was the Norwegian band Bathory, founded by the legendary Tomas 'Quorthon' Forsberg, that gave birth to what would become one of the most famous sub-genres of black metal: so-called 'viking metal', characterised by an extensive use of traditional instruments and pagan themes. The mutation becomes even more striking if one compares Bathory's first viking album, *Hammerheart* (1990), with the music and lyrics of previous bands with similar themes, such as Manilla Road, Heavy Load, Manowar, Cirith Ungol, Omen, Virgin Steele, Brocas Helm, War-lord, and Blind Guardian. Prior to *Hammerheart*, metal generally referenced the *heroic fantasy* of authors such as Robert E. Howard, J.R.R. Tolkien's *high fantasy*, and the RPG universes of Dungeons & Dragons, aiming—as in the case of Venom's playful and desecrating Satanism—at a visual and musical spectacularisation of the themes it dealt with.

This nerdy approach took on two different forms during the 1980s and 1990s: on the underground side, it gradually merged—thanks to the enormous influence of Manilla Road and Cirith Ungol—into the sub-genre known as doom metal (in this case we are talking about 'epic doom metal'); on the other, it became mainstream, giving rise to the eternally adolescent sound of power metal and the hypermachismo excesses of bands such as Manowar.

After experimenting with slowdowns, Viking themes and acoustic breaks on *Blood Fire Death* (1988), Bathory's *Hammerheart,* however, did not so much define a third position, as a line of escape from the epic/power metal dialectic: still too fast for epic doom, yet too aggressive and techno-minimal for the emerging power metal. Bathory, with their strange mixture of heavy metal and punk rock, thus laid the historical, musical and ethnomusicological foundations of the emerging Scandinavian black metal, while at the same time taking care to reject this fourth possible categorisation, giving rise instead to a new type of folk music.

In a 1996 interview with Sigurd 'Satyr' Wongraven (member of the seminal Satyricon) for the fanzine *Nordic Vision,* Quorthon recounts his meeting with Randall J. Stephens, author of the book *The Devil's Music* (which focused on the vexed relationship between rock music, religion, and nationalism):

> I believe I had just released 'Blood Fire Death' and he asked why I was doing this Viking thing and if I didn't believe that this would lead to Nationalism and such. Then I said 'it is a fact, it is a historic fact'. For us it is a historic fact and a way to get an identity and those who don't know their history cannot manage the future. He commented on symbolism and then I pointed at his arms where he had a red star and a black arrow [...]. Then he said that it was not interesting about what people stand for, but that is an ideology that too. The communism in Russia was not communism, it was fascism. [...] [W]e shall justify our Nordic culture and our Nordic history so that it doesn't die out. If all people think in the way the government wants us to think then everything we fight for and like will disappear very fast.[9]

Although Quorthon later distanced himself from any form of traditionalism, one cannot help but give some weight to such statements. Nor can one

---

9.   *Nordic Vision* 5 (Winter 1996) <https://bathory.clan.su/publ/3-1-0-19>.

ignore the emotional charge of certain textual fragments from Bathory's work, as in the case of the following passage from 'Baptised in Fire and Ice'—a track that opens with fierce tribal percussion and seems to declare war on everything and everyone:

> Proudly my Father took me in
> his arms and walked outside
> where for the first time
> light struck me, newborn child
> and even though told when older
> I can almost recall the scene
> when he held me high up towards
> the most beautiful sky ever seen [...]
>
> I grew and learned respectfully
> the Earth, Wind, Water and the sky
> the powers that decided the weather
> and rule both the dark and light
> I heard the voices of the spirits
> of the forest call my name
> I saw the Hammer way up high
> cause lightning in the rain.[10]

The Bathory of the folk period is permeated by evocative soundbeds that leave no room to breathe; Quorthon's voice is an echo from distant times, while traditional instruments, acoustic ballads and samples of natural sounds seem to almost burst into the metal fabric of the songs, layered to create a sonic continuum across the tracks. In the midst of this ghostly habitat, folk, metal, and punk meet in the clearing of an era more distant than Burial's post-war London, namely the Scandinavia of pre-Christian peoples.

---

10.   Bathory, 'Baptised in Fire and Ice', *Hammerheart* (Noise Records, 1990).

Interestingly, in Bathory's albums post-1987 there is no trace of either anti-Christian positions or neo-pagan celebration: the stories of everyday life, the detailed descriptions of personal feelings and natural landscapes seem to emerge spontaneously from the dreamlike atmosphere, like fragments of one great collective dream.

Quorthon is the shamanic channel through which the spirits of ancestors and places express themselves. The hauntological characteristics of Bathory's Viking metal thus confirm that it belongs to the second type of chronological discontinuity, that dominated by nostalgia for a past that has never been lived and a future that has never been realised. The era evoked by tracks such as 'Foreverdark Woods' is the one in which mediaeval Christianity drowned pagan culture in blood (between the eighth and twelfth centuries), annihilating and stigmatising that barbaric world of which, over the centuries, the Viking people have become an emblem. As Quorthon himself suggests, knowing the past means knowing how to deal with the future, preventing economic interests and historicism (the typically Western and modern idea that time and human progress coincide) from burying biographies, myths, practices, and world views forever.

The first spiral of European black metal, the hauntological one, has as its protagonist a mythical character whose contours remain somewhat vague: the barbarian. The term derives etymologically from the Greek word βάρβαρος, which denotes the babbling stranger, i.e. the foreigner who cannot speak Greek and who only speaks a language characterised by the repetition of similar syllables. In ancient Greece, the exclusion of the foreigner from the sphere of linguistic intelligibility is accompanied by his marginalisation from the political and social life of the city (Aristotle himself, originally from the Macedonian city of Stagira, never acquired any property rights, being forced to rent the building in which he founded his school).

As is well known, habits of this kind soon turn into commonly accepted facts: being deprived of speech and unable to participate in politics—an activity essentially based on discourse—the barbarian is more like an animal than a human, being disenfranchised and outside of history. A judgement that would only become more severe over the course of time, as testified to by Thomas Aquinas's *Summa Contra Gentiles* (1269–1273): in this case, the barbarian is exemplified by the figure of the 'gentile', an umbrella term which, from one era to another, has designated the lunatic, the heretic, the Muslim, and the atheist. The very theoretical premise of the *Summa* bears with it a certain symbolic violence: for Thomas the fundamental truths of the Christian faith are in themselves evident to the natural intellect—that is, to the intellectual capacities with which human beings are universally endowed. It follows implicitly that those who persist in denying or refuting these truths must necessarily be, if not sinners in bad faith, then idiots, madmen, or creatures unfortunately deprived of a capacity for natural illumination—once again, beasts.

In the West, the historical boundary between human and nonhuman shifts following this series of concepts: speech, political participation, and reason. Being on the wrong side of the boundary means being a barbarian or semi-barbarian. The term *barbarian*, therefore, designates those individuals and groups who, in every age, become the principal target of the collective violence of those on the 'right' side of it, i.e. the civilised (those who have learned to live in the city). However, for the civilised person, the barbarian also represents the magmatic, inscrutable multitudes on the other side of the line: wild myriads, born of chaos, who flock to the border to cross it and invade the civilised world. In the nightmares of humans, the barbarian par excellence is therefore the *berserker*, the warrior-shaman who, clad only in animal skins, fell into a sort of trance-like state or spiritual possession, fighting in an undisciplined manner, outside the ranks, sometimes even with bare hands, without pain or fatigue. As the Icelandic historian and poet Snorri reports in his *Saga of the Ynglingar*:

They went without shields, and were mad as dogs or wolves, and bit on their shields, and were as strong as bears or bulls; men they slew, and neither fire nor steel would deal with them; and this is what is called the fury of the berserker.[11]

The link between the *berserker* and ferocious beasts such as bears or wolves, however, is not limited to metaphor; according to legends, these barbarian warriors were actually able to assume the form of their totem animal, blurring the boundary between beast and human in a *weird* (bizarre or mysterious) way—a problem, that of the exact distinction between 'becoming-bear' and 'becoming-a-bear', which cannot but torment the civilised boundary-setter. In the words of Land in 'Spirit and Teeth', to be a *berserker,* i.e. to be a wolf or a were-bear or any other human-beast, is

> to be inferior by the most basic criteria of civilization. Not only is the discipline of political responsibility alien to them, so is the entire history of work in which that discipline is embedded. [...]. Compared to the piety, morality, and industriousness of its superiors it exhibits only laziness, disobedience, and an abnormally unsuccessful repression of all those traits of the unconscious which Freud describes as 'resistant to education'.[12]

These are all aspects also highlighted by the French poet Arthur Rimbaud, who wrote in *A Season in Hell*: 'From my ancestors the Gauls I have pale blue eyes, a narrow brain, and awkwardness in competition. [...]. I am well aware that I have always been of an inferior race'[13]

Recalcitrant to education, discourse, and rational calculation, the barbarian is alien to Western logocentrism, or rather to that centrality of word and argument which, since ancient Greece, has dominated our cognitive and relational paradigms. It, however, has different ways of knowing the

---

11. Quoted in M. Eliade, *Rites and Symbols of Initiation: The Mysteries of Birth and Rebirth,* tr. W.R. Trask (New York: Harper & Row, 1965), 81.

12. N. Land, 'Spirit and Teeth', in *Fanged Noumena*, 182–83.

13. A. Rimbaud, 'Bad Blood', in *Complete Works* (New York: Harper Collins, 1967), 220.

world and relating to it: *I heard the voices of the spirits of the forest call my name*, says Quorthon, or some Norse spectre that speaks through him. The barbarian does not draw permanent boundaries, preferring to pass from one dimension to another as necessary: *Man and beast was one, and the gods of the sky walked the face of the earth.*[14] The forest spoke with a non-human voice, the gods had not been relegated to an unreachable sky, humans had not been separated from nonhumans; nature was one thing and, at the same time, many things continually engaged in knowing, relating to, and interpreting one another. This is a mystical paradigm, not a religious one, organised in terms of coordinates rather than as a series of commandments: the mountains, for example, could be petrified giants, alluding to an epic battle between the forces of primordial chaos and the gods of nature; in this case, the extraction and working of iron from the belly of the mountain would allow one to draw upon the strength of these ancient giants, but also upon the divine, or technological, wisdom of forging.

Bathory's pagan nostalgia has little to do with nationalism or reaction-aryism; it is more to do with regret for a broken world, for the violation of nature, for the subjugation of Europe to the law and culture of the dominant 'race'. The spectral world that Bathory's music channels into our time (the 'Middle Ages' it embodies) is non-Christian, non-rationalist, non-humanist and non-universalist. However, unlike the neo-amanuenses of corporate neoreaction bent over their source code, for the non-civilised nomadic barbarian the economy is a matter of plunder or domestic management, not mass production. The Roman historian Ammianus Marcellinus asserts of the Huns that

> No one in their country ever plows a field or touches a plow-handle. They are all without fixed abode, without heart or law, or settled mode of life, and keep roaming from place to place, like fugitives, accompanied by the wagons

---

14. Bathory, 'Blood and Iron', *Twilight of the Gods* (Black Mark Production, 1991).

in which they live [...]. In truces they are faithless and unreliable, strongly inclined to sway to the motion of every breeze of new hope that presents itself, and sacrificing every feeling to the mad impulse of the moment.[15]

For the barbarian, war, the means of pillage, does not represent a general mobilioation of ranks, bodies and disciplined formations (i.e. a vast police operation), nor a conquering impetus animated by the desire to found a state or an empire, but a disorderly assault, mostly followed by an escape or a ransom demand.

Together with ancient ways of interpreting the world and an attempt at reunification with nature, the barbarians bring the fury of war and conflict into the cybergothic era. Deleuze and Guattari write in *A Thousand Plateaus*:

> The battlefield [...] is a complex aggregate: the becoming-animal of [warriors], packs of animals, elephants and rats, winds and tempests, bacteria sowing contagion. A single *Furor*. War contained zoological sequences, before it became bacteriological. It is in war, famine, and epidemic that werewolves and vampires proliferate.[16]

And that's exactly where we're going to hunt: vampires.

RETURN OF THE VAMPIRE

Founded in 1987 as a death metal band, Darkthrone have embraced Norwegian black metal since their album *A Blaze in the Northern Sky* (1991). With their seminal 1994 album *Transilvanian Hunger*—dedicated, as the cover states, to 'all the evil in man'—they transformed the genre into something radically new. The production almost seems to border on noise, and the

---

15.   A. Marcellinus, *Roman History*, tr. J. C. Rolfe (Cambridge, MA: Loeb, 3 vols, 1986), vol. 3., XXXI, 2, 10–11, 385.

16.   G. Deleuze and F. Guattari, *A Thousand Plateaus*, tr. B. Massumi (Minneapolis: Minnesota University Press, 1991), 243.

extremely repetitive melodies combine to weave a sickly, spectral web. The blast beat, the drumming style that has characterised black metal since the second wave, forms the backdrop to all the tracks, helping to produce an extremely alienating atmosphere. The result is a minimalist masterpiece, as *Transilvanian Hunger* contains in a few tens of minutes the very essence of the *eerie*: endless repetition with minimal variations, silences that stun the listener as they break through the noise, and no trace of artistic elaboration or intelligent thought. Pure automatism, anonymous, unconscious, impersonal; a work that could have been composed by the wind moving through the mountain rocks or by a machine, and which, in some ways, recalls the mystical drone of Keiji Haino's *So, Black is Myself* or Sunn O)))'s *Flight of the Behemoth*.

Transilvanian Hunger totally abandons itself to the drive to extremity characteristic of heavy metal, totally saturating the field of the possible: at this level of static and sonic expansion, there is no way to go further. As Hunter Ravenna Hunt-Hendrix of the American band Liturgy writes, '[*Transylvanian Hunger* is] total, maximal intensity. A complete flood of sound. An absolute plenitude [...] a dead and static place, a polar land where there is no oscillation between day and night [...] purity, totally absolute, selfsame and eternal'.[17] In the title track of the album, the disincarnate screams of Ted 'Nocturno Culto' Skjellum's articulate disjointed phrases and words, which almost seem to arise from the mind of a predator absorbed in the hunt:

Transylvanian hunger, cold soul [...]

The mountains are cold, soul, soul

Careful, pale, forever at night [...]

Embrace me eternally in your daylight slumber

To be draped by the shadow of your morbid palace

Oh, hate living

---

17. H. Hunt-Hendrix, 'Transcendental Black Metal', *Hideous Gnosis: Black Metal Theory Symposium*, ed. N. Masciandaro (CreateSpace, 2010), 53–65: 56–57.

The only heat is warm blood

So pure, so cold [...]

Hail to the true, intense vampires [...]

Beautiful evil self to be the morbid count

A part of a pact that is delightfully immortal.[18]

With their references to Transylvania and the 'morbid count', Darkthrone celebrate their alliance with one of the most famous forces of evil, the vampire: 'Careful, pale, forever at night [...] / A part of a pact that is delightfully immortal'. *Transilvanian Hunger* sonically materialises eternity, managing to represent its temporal dimension—an almost impossible feat for figurative art. But as is the case with the vampire, condemned to live forever without ever being able to see the light of day again, the price to pay is ice and total lifelessness.

To understand this kind of negative condition, mediaeval scholastic philosophy developed a bizarre ontology of absence, according to which cold is the absence of warmth, death the absence of life, and evil the absence of good.[19] A series of absences that, paradoxically, make us perceive our own presence (that 'non-being' that we perceive when something is missing, in melancholy and nostalgia). On the basis of this theoretical intuition, we can see that the time manifested in works of art such as *Transilvanian Hunger* is inhuman or even inorganic: the time of 'non-death'—of the mysterious presence of absence, a world populated by impersonal forces and entities that, although not alive, cannot be called dead, i.e. without agency (golems, vampires, spectres, corpses or inanimate objects, mists, deities, atmospheric phenomena, minerals, microorganisms, viruses, sentient machines, etc.).

As is also evident from its various references to vampires, trolls, demons and castles, *Transilvanian Hunger* is a wholly Gothic work, focusing on the themes of darkness, the unknowable, and supernatural horror. In addition

---

18.   Darkthrone, 'Transilvanian Hunger', *Transilvanian Hunger* (Peaceville Records, 1994).

19.   See T. Aquinas, *On Evil*, tr. R. Regan, ed. B. Davies (Oxford: Oxford University Press, 2003).

to a type of mediaeval architecture, the term 'Gothic' also denotes a literary genre originating in the eighteenth century and including authors such as Walpole, Radcliffe, Polidori, Maturin, and Lewis, as well as exponents of the so-called 'Gothic Revival' (or 'neo-Gothic') such as Mary Shelley and Bram Stoker. In the stories of these authors, evil—in the form of supernatural creatures— bursts into the everyday lives of innocent individuals, tormenting the protagonists or bringing to the surface gruesome buried truths: such is the eternal Gothic struggle between darkness and light, between truth and lies, brilliantly represented in films such as *Nosferatu* (dir. F.W. Mirnau, 1922).

In the Gothic novel, the Middle Ages, ever-present both architecturally and as a historical background, represents the superstition and cruelty of premodern times. It is precisely the appearance in the present of creatures and forces believed to be the product of the perverse imagination of the Middle Ages that gives rise to the doubt, or rather the certainty, that the modern age has chosen to remove horrors beyond imagination from its cognitive horizon. Gothic time, therefore, is not isomorphic to the Middle Ages; rather, it is an eternal and motionless time, suspended below the veil of the present, ready to seize those human beings naive enough to go snooping around in the dark recesses where evil hides (dungeons, castles, cemeteries, crypts and ruined churches).

No novel in this genre has left such a mark on the collective imagination as Bram Stoker's *Dracula* (1897). This horror novel, set in the 1890s, tells the story of young lawyer Jonathan Harker, who is sent to Transylvania to arrange the purchase of some real estate in England on behalf of the elderly aristocrat Dracula. As is well known, Harker soon discovers that Dracula is an ancient vampire who, wishing to prolong his eternal life and satiate his thirst for blood, has decided to move into the beating heart of modern Europe. Having managed to escape from the count's castle, Jonathan returns to England to confront the vampire and save the soul and life of his bride. If in the Gothic novel the forces of light are usually represented by Christian morality, within the neo-Gothic setting of *Dracula* we witness the birth of a new alliance between religion, the bourgeoisie, science, and capital. For the vampire, in fact, will find himself hindered by a strange axis which, rather than symbolising the meagre yet unshakable forces of humanity, seems a perfect representation of the values of modern European society.

In *Dracula,* the team of 'good guys'—armed with crosses, cloves of garlic, holy water, and consecrated hosts—is made up of a superstitious old scientist, Dr Abraham Van Helsing, the rich Texan Quincey Morris, noted psychiatrist Dr Seward, nobleman Lord Arthur Godalming, and finally the two protagonists, Jonathan and Mina Harker—the immaculate knight and the damsel in distress. The forces of evil, on the contrary, appear smaller and more improvised: the team of 'villains', although led by a young and vigorous Dracula, is made up of just one of Seward's most serious patients, the schizo-paranoid zoophage Renfield, the count's vampiric 'brides', and a group of gypsy-nomads who escort Dracula and facilitate his movements. The dual relationship between the two groups is based not only on religious and moral concepts (good versus evil), but also on economic, historical, and social distinctions: the insane versus the sane, eroticism versus true love, the poor versus the rich, the aristocracy versus the bourgeoisie, the past versus modernity. This marked contraposition of roles means that the reader spontaneously identifies with the tragic figure of the vampire, who thus becomes one of the most important *dark* figures of modernity, enabling his gradual transformation into the antihero made famous in Anne Rice's novels.

These clear distinctions, however, also help highlight the immoralism and anti-modernism that characterise the Dracula character. In this regard, it is interesting to note how Stoker's Dracula possesses characteristics that immediately recall a barbaric heritage: wild animals are his natural allies and he himself can transform himself into a wolf or a bat; moreover, on several occasions Dracula invokes the Norse deities Thor and Odin in the name of his Hun and Viking ancestors. A connotation consciously sought by the author who, not content with reviving the bloodthirsty Vlad III 'Tepes' ('the Impaler') Dracula, at the same rewrote his genealogy, tracing a symbolic line of descent between the ferocious barbarians subjugated by the Christians and the demonic predator protagonist of the novel

Although the real Vlad III was already considered by his contemporaries to be a 'savage' and inhuman tyrant—to the to the point of being portrayed feasting in the shadow of a pile of corpses—it is precisely Stoker's portrait that returns the Count, or rather the Prince of Wallachia, to the race to which he rightfully belongs, the barbarian race. During the second half of the 1400s, Vlad the Impaler was the guardian of the eastern borders of the Empire: he defended Wallachia from the continuous invasions of the Turks—by whom he had been held hostage as a child—making several sallies into their territory to mercilessly exterminate his enemies. During this period, he became infamous throughout Europe for his brutal cruelty, as expressed in acts that were not without a certain creative element: he impaled without distinction rich and poor, religious and infidels (taking care only to have the nobles impaled on poles covered with silver and placed a little higher than the others); he asked the Sultan's emissaries, who had come to collect overdue tributes, to remove their turbans in his presence and, receiving a flat refusal, had the turbans nailed to the heads of the diplomats; in 1459 he invited to dinner two merchants who had displayed contempt toward him, let them eat, then had one of them disembowelled and his entrails, still full of food, served to the other, then had the survivor's throat slit, had him cooked, and fed him to his dogs; in 1460 he had ten thousand people impaled and covered with honey so that they would die tormented by insects.

The insane parable of Vlad III came to an end in mysterious circumstances around 1476, following a betrayal by his younger brother Radu and the Wallachian nobles who had allied themselves with the Sultan Muhammad II in order to consecrate a peace that would allow trade routes to be reopened and the nobility's ancient privileges to be restored. To Vlad's hyperbaric trajectory of war and extermination, the nobility and the merchant class opposed a peace of convenience or, better, a low-intensity war, following a pattern that would soon spread throughout Renaissance Europe. The vampiric resurrection of

Vlad in *Dracula*—foreshadowed in several popular legends shortly after his death—can be read in light of the macabre seventeenth-century treatise *On the Chewing of the Dead,* according to which the undead corpse digs, scratches, and snarls from within its tomb in an attempt to free itself, so that it can once again walk the earth sowing death and destruction. Clearly, we are faced here with a chronological discontinuity of the first kind, as outlined by Benjamin, in which the past bursts into the present in an altered form. The second temporal spiral of black metal is vampiric, and concerns the return of the undead, an event that sharply truncates linear time, producing unpredictable, chaotic effects that are elusive from any rational point of view.

In addition to amplifying the barbaric characteristics already evident in the historical Dracula, Stoker has another brilliant intuition: the vampire can transform himself into fog (a metamorphosis he uses to break into his victims' rooms, make himself invulnerable or flee far away). This is the most bizarre transformation and the most radically related to Dracula's non-living nature; an atmospheric transformation that brings to mind the icy atmosphere of *Transilvanian Hunger.* Gothic time, the inorganic time of the vampire, is contained in Dracula's body and is, so to speak, its obscure essence, the double negation of the individual unity: he is and is not Vlad III and, at the same time, he is and is not Dracula. For this reason, *Dracula* could be defined as the 'definitive' gothic novel, a work of pure emotion (also owing to its narrative structure, made up of diary entries and scattered letters, memories and vague impressions). In this sense, Dracula's thirst for blood is a pure urge for atmospheric dissolution—a desire that originates in the anonymous, impersonal, and inorganic world from which the vampire springs: the afterlife.

It is, therefore, a threat from an alternative timeline or even from another dimension. Dracula's Middle Ages is neither a lost future nor a possible future, but an alien catastrophe suspended in time: the pure possibility that the human world could be annihilated by forces beyond the comprehension of human beings. In the eyes of his contemporaries, the historical Vlad himself embodied the negation of mediaeval values and Christian morality and, in the judgement of posterity, was the antithesis of Renaissance humanism and universalism—characteristics which, in some ways, anticipate the anti-human and apocalyptic aspects of the literary Dracula.

Although neoreaction also speaks of an inhuman, indifferent, and catastrophic time, it deludes itself into believing that it can control or mitigate time's cataclysmic effects through the coordinated employment of social microstructures, governmental techniques based on scientific knowledge, and massive recourse to the means of police violence. As evidence of the illusory nature of this belief, Marx, in the first book of *Capital*, compares the capitalist accumulation machine to a vampire (thus inaugurating the cybergothic era)[20] in an analogy that also helps us to understand the ending of Stoker's novel. In the last pages, Dracula is cornered and stabbed in the heart, whereupon he turns to dust—but not before, for a brief moment, an expression of peace crosses his face. The narrator interprets this expression in a moral sense, attributing it to relief at being freed from his tormented existence, consisting of crime and eternal damnation. However, the Marxian analysis, and what we have said so far here, would seem to indicate that a different interpretation is more appropriate: the vampire has returned to his place of origin, the atmospheric-inorganic world, only to be reincarnated in the complex cybernetic system of machines and monetary flows that shapes Capital, waiting to once again unleash his annihilating fury. The Anthropocene, the age of ecological catastrophe, is the era through which the cybergothic age winds like a snake.

GOTHIC APOCALYPSE

The journey from the pre-Christian era to the end of the Middle Ages has finally come to an end; we have returned to the precise moment when we were aiming to strike a blow against all forms of reactionaryism and retroprogressivism.

---

20. K. Marx, *Capital: A Critique of Political Economy*, tr. S. Moore, E. Aveling (New York: Random House, 1906), Part III, Chapter 10, 257.

Jumping schizophrenically from one epoch to another, we have seen how both modernity and neoreaction, whatever they may say, are founded on the same error of judgement: both have been too optimistic, both have underestimated the possibility that there might be 'something' bigger and scarier than themselves. That something is the Gothic Insurrection: the first product of the entry into the cybergothic age.

We have seen how, unlike the double neoreactionary spiral described by Land (which advances toward the past and retreats toward the future), the double vampiric-hauntological spiral thrusts the past forward and makes the future retreat, crushing the present. Where the first marches toward the restoration of an ancient order, the second is marked by the brutal removal of an era from the time *continuum*: the barbarian hordes ride toward the future, while the apocalypse advances from the end of time. More like a meat grinder than a time machine, the black metal double spiral is a chrono-abolitionist device:[21] if neoreaction looks at modernity as a deviation that directly leads to a 're-emergence' of the Middle Ages, the Gothic Insurrection recognises the Christian, mercantile, colonial and logocentric Middle Ages as the root from which the modern capitalist West arose.

The emerging cybergothic era does not therefore correspond to a simple return to the historical Middle Ages or to an actual barbarian tribe (which would really mean getting away with very little), but to a perverse vampiric resurrection of the Middle Ages, effected through the reactivation of a mythical past. This tendency can be broken down into three fundamental metabolic processes: the rewriting of barbarian genealogies, a lycanthropic proliferation, and an atmospheric metamorphosis. A triad that, in turn, can be further subdivided into three twin dyads, in which the first element represents the incubation phase (the present situation), the second the result

---

21. See A. Ireland, 'The Poememenon: Form as Occult Technology', *Urbanomic Documents* (2017), <https://www.urbanomic.com/document/poememenon>. Ireland writes: 'The future, marked up by the immanent unfolding of the spiral, has already been determined diagrammatically, while remaining, from the inside, a harbinger of the unknown'.

of a global process: fragmentation and autonomy; mixing and hybridisation; indetermination and impersonality. Drawn by the spiral's double clockwise-anti-clockwise vortex, we are broken down, decomposed, and put back together again in new, bizarre configurations—how astonishing to discover oneself a human-animal-plant-language-archive-machine-bacterial-colony!

The Gothic Insurrection takes the demonic saying 'I am Legion' literally, propagating and accelerating in every direction this vector of the spatiotemporal, psychic, bodily and conceptual molecularisation of the modern world. This event seems to have already been recorded by one of the most notorious and infamous Western political theorists. In *Leviathan*, in the chapter 'Of Spirituall Darknesse', Thomas Hobbes analyses through the Holy Scriptures the arrival of the 'Kingdome of Darknesse':

> Besides these sovereign powers, *Divine*, and *Humane* [...] there is mention in Scripture of another power, namely that of *the rulers of the Darknesse of this world*, *the Kingdome of Satan*, and *the Principality of Beelzebub over Daemons*, that is to say, over Phantasmes [...]. [T]he Kingdome of Darknesse, as it is set forth in these, and other places of the Scripture, is nothing else but a *Confederacy of Deceivers* [...].[22]

In other words, a multitude of prophets, poets, visionary oracles, sorcerers, witches and shamans who, in opposition to the one Truth of God and the State, profess enigmatic, often contradictory or even incompatible doctrines, contaminating the body politic and causing its fragmentation (in the form of civil war).[23]

In his book *In the Dust of this Planet*, Eugene Thacker (following in the footsteps of Carl Schmitt) shows how the paradigm that sustains and

---

22.   T. Hobbes, *Leviathan*, ed. C. Macpherson (London: Penguin, 1980), 627.

23.   See V. Garton, 'Leviathan Rots' *Urbanomic Documents* (2017), <https://www.urbanomic.com/document/leviathan-rots>.

nurtures political orders, establishing Truth each time, is analogy, i.e. the assumption that there is or should be some degree of similarity between the cosmic order and the political order. This is the Image of the World, an imaginary representation of reality through which human beings attempt to circumscribe the forces of chaos, in order to establish order; in essence, as Thacker himself asserts, the cosmo-political order assured by Truth would have the same practical status as a protective circle in a magic ritual. For Thacker, however, the analogy comes up against some obvious limitations:

> The analogical model assumes a few key factors: first, that 'out there' there is an accessible, revealed and ordered world that can serve as a model or guide in the development of a political system 'in here' [...]. Second, this analogical relation is assumed to be a one-way street, that is, that the discernible order of the world flows directly into the constitution of politics, whereas, of course, there are a large number of ways in which this direction is reversed [...]. Finally, Schmitt's analogical paradigm is decidedly anthropocentric, since it takes it for granted that politics—like theology—has first and foremost to do with the human (and, in this sense, the Hobbesian analogy of the body politic is the most explicit example of this anthropomorphic property of the political).[24]

It is precisely the supernatural horror propagated by the heralds of the Kingdom of Darkness that spreads doubt as to whether the world order is false, and it is for this reason that for Hobbes, as for every defender of the established order, it is necessary that they be unmasked as 'deceivers' and corrupters of the Truth. The cosmo-political model, however, reveals its fragility from the moment when the proliferation of false prophets is compounded by the unexpected destruction caused by natural catastrophes: in addition to the 'Children of Darknesse', Hobbes counts divine will, i.e. chance and indeterminacy, among the main threats to the safety of the state unit. It

---

24. Thacker, *In the Dust of This Planet*, 96.

is precisely because politics does not solely have to do with humans that the ecological catastrophe of the Anthropocene appears as the most concrete manifestation of an enigmatic and malevolent will or, even worse, of the icy indifference of an empty heavens; the cosmos will remain silent while the earth collapses under our feet, along with all the certainties and beliefs to which we have so far clung.

As will be evident by now, the Kingdom of Darkness (Babylon?) is not a place but a time: the time of danger and dissolution. It is the time of the Gothic Insurrection, in which the multitude of the dead, situated beyond time, is unleashed upon the world, tearing it to pieces, channelled and propagated by the voices of possessed oracles. It is the time when the world, or rather the Image of the World, shatters—without any hope of return—and the most 'deviant' world views proliferate indefinitely. Unity dissolves into an ocean of singularities, the universal into the particular. To paraphrase Marx: 'From each according to his insurrection, to each according to his desire'.

Satisfied with its work, the black metal crow, perched on the edge of time, sees what we can only anticipate: it watches the planet plunge into chaos, burnt alive by the new barbarians.

But who are the new barbarians?

CK

EXTINCTION

The enemy is no longer ecstasy, but redemption.

Stephen Metcalf[1]

Among the most heartbreaking and unbearable works of art of recent years, the music video 'Cry Alone', the first single from Gustav Elijah Åhr/Lil Peep's posthumous album *Come Over When You're Sober pt. 2*, has earned a place in my heart, remaining, as far as I'm concerned, undefeated in morbidity to this day. The reason for my personal preference is easy to state: behind the mall goth aesthetics, the ugliness of the video, the nauseating repetitiveness of the song and the grunge revival in trap sauce that no one asked for, there is a narrative as simple and effective as it is unconscious and involuntary, as poignant and monstrous as it is kitsch and in bad taste. 'Cry Alone' is comparable to a particularly obscene and detestable yet clumsily trashy Halloween decoration. A human skull used as a Jack O'Lantern.

The video for the song is an ungainly pastiche of images that depict Peep walking through his old high school as if he were a ghost, Peep sitting in a hotel room, and fragments of his school yearbook. The images are extremely lo-fi, in keeping with the grunge sample that underpins the whole song. The *nigredo* that makes this digital artefact essentially *cursed* is, as in any self-respecting ritual, repeated cyclically before each refrain, and is activated by a simple magic formula: 'Tell the rich kids to look at me now'. The ritual formula achieves its effect by secreting a kind of impalpable black substance and subverting the trap topos to which Peep was most likely referring: for

---

1.   S. Metcalf, 'Introduction: "Even When the Heart Bleeds"', in F. Nietzsche, *Hammer of the Gods: Apocalyptic Texts for the Criminally Insane*, tr. ed. S. Metcalf (Sun Vision Press, 2012), 12.

if these phantom rich kids who haunt the trapper's memories were to take the trouble to go and see where Gustav has ended up, rather than finding him a success story climbing the music charts, they would find photos of his corpse, spread online on the day of his death, 15 November 2017.

This sentence, then, takes on a revolting character that turns it into a funeral lament repeated—at the time of writing—more than 24 million times on YouTube, going from being a moment of social revenge to being a most classic and didactic example of tragic irony. We, the omniscient spectators, already know that our hero is going to die, but we are forced to helplessly watch his words resonate within an ultra-Calvinistic universe, a cosmos where everything is monstrously linear and predetermined. Lil Peep, unaware of what is about to happen, unknowingly records a macabre 'reach out and touch faith' for the total depression generation, a groan that invites us to access his martyrdom. Like the voice of the flutes in Greek tragedies, the catatonic repetition of 'Tell the rich kids to look at me now' combines *singing* and *wailing* to form an inhuman chimera. As described by Eugene Thacker in *Infinite Resignation*: 'The mourning voice [the flute] of Greek tragedy constantly threatens to dissolve song into wailing, music into moaning, and voice into a primordial, disarticulate anti-music.'[2]

Why dig up and celebrate this particular image, one of the many fragmentary testimonies that make up the digital martyrology that Peep left us after his death? This atheological saint and this godless martyrdom harbour an extremely detailed metaphorical description of the temporality in which we are immersed, which mediates and informs our psychic, collective, and individual lives. In other words, it is a trash parable that narrates, again unintentionally, the way we perceive time on both subjective and social levels. Before explaining what I mean by this, however, I must necessarily take a step back and turn to my main interlocutor: CK, author of 'Gothic Insurrection'.

CK's text also begins with a metaphorical description of the temporality in which we live—a present haunted by a remote past that does not want to

---

2.   E. Thacker, *Infinite Resignation* (London: Repeater, 2018), 16.

remain in its grave. According to CK, following VM's analysis,[3] the present is currently in the grips of a temporal paradox that has essentially resurrected the Middle Ages. Rather than looking toward the future which, as Mark Fisher argues in *Ghosts of My Life*,[4] is slowly being erased, our present rots with the corpses of a past that is returning to the present, plunging us into a hellish version of Nietzsche's much-vaunted Eternal Return. The temporality that characterises us, both as individual prisons of flesh and as a society, is a closed circle in which the future is replaced by an endless repetition of the ghosts of our past.

In order to support this reflection, CK calls into question one of the most influential schools of thought in the contemporary philosophical debate on chronopolitics: Mark Fisher's aforementioned reinterpretation of Jacques Derrida's *hauntology*. This theory is, at first glance, completely acceptable. After all, every sphere of our social life seems to be suffocated by a total retromania, by the revivals of the revival of the revival. We live in an open-air Overlook Hotel, we ride a snake that keeps eating its own tail, and we inhabit a world in which the present only ever regurgitates before us faded copies of a time we feel we have already lived. The future is dead.

As natural and self-evident as this theory may seem, I believe that the situation is far worse and far more suffocating than CK suggests. I believe, in fact, that at the basis of this circular temporality that characterises our New Middle Ages there lies an apocalyptic, neo-Millennialist and tragic linearity, marked by the firm conviction that our destiny is already totally and irretrievably written. The endless repetition of the past is merely the symptom of a deeper temporality, marked by a future which, far from being cancelled, is all too present, but already decided in advance. This future, which makes every attempt at action futile and doomed to failure—and

3. V. Mattioli, 'Il medioevo digitale', *Il Tascabile* (2018), <http://www.iltascabile.com/linguaggi/il-medioevo-digitale>.

4. M. Fisher, *Ghosts of My Life: Writings on Depression, Hauntology and Lost Futures* (Winchester: Zero, 2014).

which in turn generates the time of hauntology—can be summed up in a single term: *extinction*.

Indeed, our present is obsessed with the idea that we are about to be annihilated, that the world as we know it will be obliterated, that our time is a straight line to total destruction—which is why we cling to a past marked by the absence of this awareness. From learned discourses on existential risk,[5] and in their wake the whole bandwagon of educated secularised ecomillennialism that Alexander Galloway has called 'warm pride',[6] via the litany of class malaise[7] to the general inarticulate feeling that there is essentially nothing left to do (defined by Fisher as 'capitalist realism')[8] what we might term the *Zeitgeist* (a decidedly stale word), as Ray Brassier rightly observed in his masterpiece *Nihil Unbound*,[9] is devoted in its profound essence to the countenance of our disappearance from the face of the earth. *Our temporality, then, is not hauntological, but tragic, in the harshest sense of the term.* Like Christ in Gethsemane, we already intimately know our future passion and accept this determinism as if it were a historical necessity, clinging to the fetish of times past. As Emil Cioran says, modern humanity has 'opted for tragedy'.

This brings us back to our martyr, Lil Peep. If our chronopolitical hypothesis works, then Peep becomes the embodiment of this intimate sense of predestination which is widespread throughout the social body. Peep is the manifestation of our destiny: an inglorious, unredeemable end, anticipated by a parade of premonitions of what lies ahead, confirming the *necessity* of this extinction. *I swear I mean well, I'm still going to hell.*

---

5.   For example, N. Bostrom, 'Existential Risk Prevention as Global Priority', *Global Policy* 4:1 (2013).

6.   A.R. Galloway, 'Warm Pride', *Culture and Communication* (2014), <http://cultureandcommunication.org/galloway/warm-pride>.

7.   R.A. Ventura, *Teoria della classe disagiata* (Rome: Minimum Fax, 2018).

8.   M. Fisher, *Capitalist Realism: Is There No Alternative?* (Winchester: Zero, 2009).

9.   R. Brassier, *Nihil Unbound: Enlightenment and Extinction* (Basingstoke: Palgrave, 2007).

Clearly, this revision of hauntological chronopolitics needs to be put to the test by other case studies. In other words, it's not enough for Lil Peep to demonstrate how widespread the tragic temporal structure is within the social body for us to affirm that the vision of the world according to which we are destined to vanish into oblivion—what we will call *passive extinctionism*—has become our mother tongue.

Fortunately, material that can be used as an example of our passive extinctionism is, in my view, plentiful: from Roko's Basilisk making its way into pop culture to the far-fetched success of neo-Millenarian conspiracy theories, which in a very short period have become one of the most consumed products on the most 'family-friendly' platform on the web, YouTube.[10] For this reason, I will restrict the sample of cultural material under analysis and, in imitation of Eugene Thacker's *In the Dust of this Planet*,[11] will focus on horror, convinced that horror, taken to the right degree of abstraction, can release a conceptual power that no other genre can hope to rival. In particular, I will consider *Halloween* (dir. Green, 2018) and *Hereditary* (dir. Aster, also 2018), two shining examples of tragic temporality.

BLOOD RITES

Forty years after the Haddonfield massacres in Illinois, Laurie Strode—the girl who survived the first *Halloween*, released in 1978—is still in hell. Michael Myers, her tormentor, has been locked up in prison for decades, perpetually engrossed in his luciferous hexichasm, but she continues to prepare for his return. She lives in a house littered with weapons and traps, with rooms transformed into mazes of manacles, armoured doors and a basement/crypt concealed by a complicated automatic mechanism.

---

10. Shane Dawson, currently one of the most popular figures on the platform, is a prime example of this 'family-friendly apocalypticism'. Dawson is now a maker of documentaries which celebrate the gothic and barbaric splendour of the new platform capitalism, but he owes his success largely to his viral videos covering, in incredibly millenarian fashion, the various conspiracy theories born of the hive mind in which we are all immersed.

11. E. Thacker, *In the Dust of This Planet* (London: Zero, 2011).

This meticulous preparation for the resurrection of her very own prince of darkness has, however, taken its toll: Laurie has become estranged from her niece, ostracised by the rest of the family, and lives far from everyone, afflicted by a long list of addictions, phobias, and psychophysical disorders. In other words, this is a woman with no future and no present, devoured by absolute evil as embodied in the silent masked visage of Michael Myers, and by her past.

Even limiting ourselves to this brief summary, it seems clear that the latest chapter in the horror saga created by John Carpenter explicitly works against my revision of hauntological temporality, and gives credence to that proposed by CK. Leaving aside the fact that the new *Halloween* is an objectively hauntological product to the core—being the umpteenth sequel in a saga that survives thanks to our attachment to characters and narrative formats from over forty years ago—the story it tells seems clearly to be obsessed with a past that paralyses the present and banishes what remains of the future. Laurie, the protagonist of the story and the character we are supposed to identify with, is a walking corpse with no existential horizons or possible futures, anxiously awaiting the return of her past. Laurie Strode is the very incarnation of the hauntological subject, trapped in the putrescence of the past.

But the ending of the film destroys this interpretation. Predictably, Michael Myers has escaped from his imprisonment and has done everything possible to reach Laurie. After a long struggle, Laurie manages to lock him in the basement, leaving Michael with no way out. She then burns down the house, throwing her own past into the fire. *Burn me down till I'm nothing but memories, I get it girl....*

However, the film ends with a decidedly predictable 'twist': the camera swiftly frames all the rooms in the house one by one, clearly showing that Michael Myers is not in there—he is still on the loose. For those who know the saga we are referring to, it is an ending that is not surprising at all. In fact, the 1978 film already ended in exactly the same way: Michael Myers falls out of a window, 'the good guys' (outside and inside the film) are convinced that he is dead and that the nightmare is over, but he actually escaped. *Halloween* repeats *Halloween*, nothing has changed.

The really disturbing thing about this ending—and, above all, about the profound sense of déjà vu that it provokes in the viewer—is that it clearly shows how, underneath the hauntological theme that dominates the story, there is another, hidden temporal paradox: behind the hauntology lies the horrifying idea that the script, not only of the film but of the whole saga, was already written all along, that it comes from a future already established from the very start. The film and the saga in general were destined to end like this, it is a sentence without appeal. Moreover, what testifies to this paradoxical temporality as the true horror of this film is that we viewers already knew all along how it was going to end. There is no surprise or astonishment, and the ghosts of the past are little more than epiphenomena of a temporal noumenon that smiles out at us at the end of the film, showing its fangs.

Halloween concludes by showing us its true face: the whole saga is underpinned by a predestination with no escape route, made of the same substance as the attitude I have called passive extinctionism. The problem, then, is not the slow erasure of the future, but the peremptory and merciless assertion of a future that is necessary and already written. In other words, the problem is not hauntology but tragedy, understood as a temporal structure in which the future is given as an unavoidable fact underlying the continuous return of the past. The story goes like this: silent death, embodied by Michael Myers, comes from the future and condemns us to extinction. Everything has already been written, so all we can do is lock ourselves in and prepare our bunker.

If this temporal anarchitecture in which time runs in reverse and the future imposes a rigid and deadly structure upon the present and the past weren't depressing enough, the situation becomes even more chilling when we examine the second example of tragic temporality, also released in 2018: *Hereditary.*

Hereditary is essentially the story of a ruthless and luciferous matriarchy. The film opens with the funeral of Ellen Graham, the matriarchal figure of the protagonist family, and all the events that take place in the film revolve around her occult will which, from beyond the grave, directs a sacrificial rite consisting of decapitations and Lovecraftian madness, inflicted upon her family with the aim of invoking Paimon, one of the central demons of *The Lesser Key of Solomon*.[12] *Hereditary* is, in a nutshell and without going into too much detail, the representation of a ritual that comes true thanks to the dark forces that vow every single action represented to a precise future result. Every detail of this film, from the title to the exotic symbolism that punctuates the scenes, is a concentration of absolute predestination, in which every gesture is destined to fulfil a future already ordered by forces that come from places where the human mind cannot venture.

Clearly, the tragic temporal structure in this case is blatant and explicit. In *Hereditary*, time flows backwards, and everything that happens is simply the result of the activation of a hidden predestination. What is interesting, however, is that neither the spectators nor the protagonists of the film *fully understand the predestination that informs the whole film*. The tragedy just happens and that's it—at the end of the film, no one knows precisely what it was that caused such pandemonium, we just know that it happened. *Hereditary* is pure fatality without cause: we understand the mechanism and the general logic of the story, but we never really understand *why*. Ellen never explains her intentions, Paimon never directly reveals himself, the reasons behind all of this remain a mystery.

This pure fact, this impenetrability of the motivations that guide the ritual staged by *Hereditary*, in my opinion exemplifies the final element that completes the implicit philosophy of passive extinctionism. This form of tragic temporality that holds us captive is also generated by the fact that the world we live in seems to have become cognitively ungraspable. The cosmos in

---

12. S.L. MacGregor Mathers and A. Crowley, *The Lesser Key of Solomon* (Bristol: Mockingbird Press, 2016).

which we are immersed (and we must indeed speak of a cosmos, given that the order of things seems immutable, as if it has always been perfectly given) seems clearly destined for self-destruction, but it is too complex and too absurd for mortal and intellectually limited beings like us to understand. Our temporality is marked by an unknowing that is involuntary and absolute, light years away from that proposed by the mystics and by Georges Bataille, the most disturbing and most fundamental philosopher of the twentieth century, an unknowing that destroys all possibility of intervention in the tragedy in which we are protagonists. As Eugene Thacker writes in the first pages of *In the Dust of this Planet*:

> The world is increasingly unthinkable—a world of planetary disasters, emerging pandemics, tectonic shifts, strange weather, oil-drenched seascapes, and the furtive, always-looming threat of extinction. In spite of our daily concerns, wants, and desires, it is increasingly difficult to comprehend the world in which we live and of which we are a part. To confront this idea is to confront an absolute limit to our ability to adequately understand the world at all—an idea that has been a central motif of the horror genre for some time.[13]

In short, *Hereditary* allows us not only to analyse, once again, the time of tragedy, but also to complete the conceptual structure that justifies and reproduces passive extinction, the philosophical and temporal horror that we have tried to expose.

Passive extinctionism is thus essentially composed of three fundamental characteristics: (1) time flows in reverse, going from a future that has always been present toward a past that becomes, a posteriori, the activation of this same future; (2) time has only one direction and only one possible point of departure: extinction; (3) this tragic temporality is sustained by a complete inability to grasp its motives, and the world generated by it.

---

13. Thacker, *In the Dust of This Planet*, 1.

BARBARISM

Fortunately, horror is not only destructive but also generative.

Not only has horror produced an extremely accurate description of our temporal prison, it has also outlined a possible way out of this pernicious situation. More precisely, one film has shown more than anyone else what it means to break free from the time of tragedy: *Mandy.*

Mandy, director Panos Cosmatos's latest psychedelic folly (also from 2018), is the tale of a couple, Mandy and Red, who unwittingly end up practising two deadly magical rites. The first ritual is markedly tragic and very reminiscent of the dark forces described by *Hereditary*: through the invocation of chthonic warriors, Mandy conjures up biker demons of a markedly Lynchian type, and a sort of gang/cult of 'freaks' who subsequently decide to capture her and Red and sacrifice them. In a nutshell, the pair unwittingly destine themselves for death.

The second ritual, however, breaks the spell and subverts the tragic temporality. It is a totally paradoxical rite: Mandy has been captured and is about to be raped and killed by the leader of this mysterious redneck cult, a certain Jeremiah Sand. Jeremiah undresses in front of her, ready to embody the mania of the lord of tragedy. Mandy, however, laughs in the face of her tormentor. Mandy shows joy in the face of death, the same joy so celebrated by Acéphale's sacred conspiracy,[14] and Jeremiah goes mad. Mandy will be killed, but her jubilant death will trigger an implacable vengeance at the hands of Red, completely subverting what seemed to be the film's destiny.

As Nicola Masciandaro has quite rightly observed,[15] this laughter, so mystical and alien, splits the film in two. The image distorts under the pressure of the sound of Mandy's unconditional joy, every authority and every idol disintegrates, and Mandy becomes the vector of an Outside that breaks the

14.   G. Bataille, *The Sacred Conspiracy: The Internal Papers of the Secret Society of Acephale and Lecturers to the College of Sociology* (London: Atlas Press, 2018).

15.   N. Masciandaro, 'Laughing In(side) the Face of Evil: Notes on *Mandy*', *The Whim* (2018), <http://thewhim.blogspot.com/2018/09/laughing-inside-face-of-evil-notes-on.html>.

prison bars of tragic temporality. Mandy embodies *a mystical sovereignty that dismisses all sovereignty* and generates the possibility of a totally unknown future, open to radical novelty. Mandy's martyrdom is a barbaric immolation, in which the world is obliterated by an excess-sensation-re-demption that frees the cosmos from the time-trap of tragedy. Mandy is a wild abandonment, in which the victim takes possession of her own tragedy, affirming, as the philosopher and occultist Hakim Bey did: 'Ours is no art of mutilation but of excess, superabundance, amazement.'[16]

Moreover, while not understanding what is happening, this jubilant martyrdom transforms ignorance into non-knowledge, a direct emanation of an *inhuman darkness*. Mandy is, to quote Max Stirner, an *Unmensch*,[17] a monster who no longer has any relation to the human, who takes possession of himself without waste, turning tragedy into Dionysian power and into chaos and excess. 'I pray we could come to this darkness so far above light! If only we lacked sight and knowledge so as to see, so as to know, unseeing and unknowing, that which lies beyond all vision and knowledge',[18] says Pseudo-Dionysius the Areopagite. Mandy is pure *active extinctionism*.

This brings us directly back to CK's thesis. In fact, CK too, by way of a very dense analysis of Bathory's poetics and a rigorous exposition of various monstrosities, comes to affirm that the non-subject that will shatter the asphyxiated temporal paradox in which we are trapped is the barbarian, the monster that comes from outside, the protagonist of a multitudinous Gothic insurrection against the world.

> The Gothic Insurrection takes the demonic saying 'I am Legion' literally, prop-
> agating and accelerating in every direction this vector of the spatiotemporal,

16. H. Bey, *T.A.Z.: The Temporary Autonomous Zone, Ontological Anarchy, Poetic Terrorism* (Brooklyn, NY: Autonomedia, 1985), 37.

17. M. Stirner, *The Ego and Its Own*, tr. S. Byington (Cambridge: Cambridge University Press, 1995).

18. Pseudo-Dionysus, 'The Mystical Theology', in *The Complete Works*, tr. C. Luibheid (New York and Mahwah, NJ: Paulist Press, 1987), 138.

psychic, bodily and conceptual molecularisation of the modern world. [...] To
paraphrase Marx: 'From each according to his insurrection, to each according
to his desire'.

    Satisfied with its work, the black metal crow, perched on the edge of
time, sees what we can only anticipate: it watches the planet plunge into
chaos, burnt alive by the new barbarians

However, CK concludes 'Gothic Insurrection' by asking, paraphrasing
Nietzsche, who these new barbarians will be. But does it make sense, having razed the entire world, to conclude by wondering how to *identify* these
multitudes who will displace the existing regime and launch themselves
against the hegemonic temporality, whatever it may be? Without wishing
to be excessively polemical, I believe that the question is inessential: Mandy
allows us to bypass it completely. What is evident in Mandy's laughter is that
identification and Proper Names are obsolete structures in this kind of total
insurrection, destined to dismantle the tragic temporal mobilisation in which
we are immersed. What really matters, what unites and qualifies destruction
liberated from barbarian mysticism, is *what the insurrection does*, not who
or what it is. While the identity of the new barbarians remains mysterious,
their actions are crystal clear.

    The new barbarians as embodied in Mandy, in fact, do only one thing:
transform tragedy and decadence into sources of power and subversion.
Where biofascism[19] and the Dogma of the Right Hand see chaos and perceive the need for order, insurrection sees the blossoming of a thousand
new worlds and the virulent tragedy of this world surpassing itself. In the
words of Edmund Berger, the decadence in which the new barbarians arise
'is not decadence understood first and foremost as a moral stagnation or
reactionary theory of civilizational decay, nor as any sort of absolute law;
instead, decadence is a kind of aberrant moment in which the development

19.   T. Guariento, 'Dalla Parte Del Caos, Per Distruggere Il Biofascismo', *Not* (2018), <http://not.
neroeditions.com/caos-vs-biofascism>.

of productive forces is tossed out of joint from the creative turbulence that typifies the long-range evolution of industrial systems'.[20] Like Donna Haraway's cyborgs, the new barbarians are the bastard children of modernity and, through a state of permanent destitution, help it toward its obsolescence.

This is no tragedy: it is the monstrous aura of the real movement that abolishes the present state of affairs. *When we die, bury us with all our ice on.*

EM

20.   E. Berger, 'Waveforms: Art and the Revolutionary Transformation in the Age of Blockchain', *ŠUM* 10:2 (2018), <http://sumrevija.si/en/eng-sum10-2-edmund-berger-waveforms-art-and-the-revolutionary-transformation-in-the-age-of-blockchain/>.

GOTHIC (A)THEOLOGY: SOME NOTES ON GOTHIC INSURRECTION AND ACTIVE EXTINCTIONISM

In what follows, I would like to attempt to outline some brief reflections on the two writings entitled 'Gothic Insurrection' and 'Extinction', of which EM and I are the authors and which, prior to this publication, have already found their way onto the web.[1]

Despite the obvious differences (some attributable to aesthetic prefer-ences, some to genuine theological disagreements), both writings attempt to rework and reimagine a common legacy: that of Unconditional Acceler-ationism (U/Acc), a countercultural current clearly distinct from both Left Accelerationism (L/Acc) and Right Accelerationism (R/Acc)—all of which are widely debated online, especially in the obscure digital crevasse known as #cavetwitter. The Gothic Insurrection—henceforth abbreviated as Goth/ Ins—is the theoretical entity that has emerged from this remodelling; it is a new paradigm, deeply rooted in the traditions of cosmic pessimism and Lovecraftian cosmicism, fuelled by a radical distrust of modernity and a calling into question of technological singularity. As far as I am concerned, I think that the main difference between U/Acc and Goth/Ins lies in the fact that, although Goth/Ins attempts to bring certain naturalist and neo-fas-cist perspectives to the boiling point, at the same time it borrows certain

1.   I would like to thank EM for having prompted this reflection, for the contents of which, however, I take full (ir)responsibility. I would also like to thank Edmund Berger, Vincent Garton, and S.C. Hickman for their valuable comments.

characteristics from neoreaction (NRx) that could be correctly defined as 'reactionary' or 'realist', as opposed to the optimism that still permeates all currents of accelerationism, even the catastrophic U/Acc.

FOR A CHAOTIC VISION OF TIME

A fundamental aspect of Goth/Iris is the attention it pays to the theme of temporal multiplicities, that swarm of virtualities that constitute the heart of temporal dynamics and which, far from being mere passive elements, are susceptible to a whole series of activations, perversions, and re-activations that culminate in the production of 'mutant' or 'undead' doppelgängers. The history of the world, as natural history, is nothing more than a stratification of events and processes that are never definitively 'dead and buried', but which continue to flow and exert an active force from a lower, or even sub-terranean, dimension than the present—events and processes that can also reappear in an altered form, upsetting our temporal perception. This characteristic pluriversality amounts to the preeminence of reality over imagination, i.e. the hierarchical superiority of natural processes over thought. This shift gives rise to a hypercomplex situation, of a natural-cultural kind, in which areas such as economics, or philosophy itself, are liable to return to a reflection on the various dimensions that make up the unity of reality (what are the limits of scientific thought, or those of artistic perception, for example?). This kind of philosophical analysis, therefore, would not only require a 'scientific vision', unattainable by phenomenological intentionality, but also a 'chaotic vision' based on the transience and unpredictability of both structures and natural laws.

By going beyond the classic distinction between past, present, and future—as well as the far more deeply rooted distinction between natural laws and possible worlds—the dual articulation of the virtual and the actual shatters every theoretical-practical concreteness, bringing it down to a level beyond our diagrammatic perspectives, our heuristics, and our planning, thus thwarting (directly from the transcendental plane) any kind of theoretical and ideological hegemony, totality or supremacy. From these simple axioms some important consequences may be drawn:

I. Principle of finite adaptability: no structure can 'live' forever or aspire to immortality, since such a goal would require that this structure should be able to implement de facto, from time to time and according to need, an infinity of virtual adaptations—a potentiality harboured only by nature itself.

II. Principle of absolute immanence: none of the parts is able to perceive or think of the whole to which it belongs, except at the cost of its own faculty of observation and contemplation; nature remains radically inscrutable, assuming characteristics that are supernatural to our eyes.

III. Principle of economy: No structure can arise, proliferate, or be generated where there are cheaper, or more immediately effective alternatives to the features and traits presented by environmental pressures; each part is subsumed within the whole, being powerless in relation to its dynamic developments.

IV. Principle of operational constraint: Even if cheaper and more efficient alternatives to the existing ones were to appear afterwards, the variations and developments of the structures would have been subject to *path dependency lock-ins* which, turning into operational constraints, would prevent the structure from retracing its steps.

Both point III and point IV relate to the very concept of *extinction*.

MUTANT DEGENERATION

I would now like to focus on EM's response to some of the questions and problems posed by Goth/Ins. 'Extinction' in particular seems to me to exemplify and summarise, with great precision, the critical aspects of the argument. EM writes:

> After all, every area of our social life seems to be suffocated by total retroma-
> nia, by revivals of revivals of revivals. We live in an open-air Overlook Hotel,
> we ride a snake that keeps eating its own tail, and we inhabit a world in which
> the present always regurgitates before it only faded copies of a time that we
> feel we have already lived through.
>
> The future is dead. [...] I believe that the situation is far worse and
> far more suffocating than CK suggests. I believe, in fact, that at the basis
> of this circular temporality that characterises our New Middle Ages there
> lies an apocalyptic, neo-Millennialist and tragic linearity, marked by the firm
> conviction that our destiny is already totally and irretrievably written. The
> endless repetition of the past is merely the symptom of a deeper temporality,
> marked by a future which, far from being cancelled, is all too present, but
> already decided in advance. This future, which makes every attempt at
> action futile and doomed to failure—and which in turn generates the time
> of hauntology—can be summed up in a single term: *extinction*.

I strongly agree with EM that chronological linearity, based on the paradigm of the 'fixed attractor' and thermodynamic annihilation, in turn produces numerous sub-oscillations linked to different sub-actors, thus superimposing upon the straight line the circularity of eternal return. I also agree that the extinction of our species, our people, the planet, and the universe itself is actually necessary—indeed, it would be terribly naive of me not to accept such an obvious and important point. I do not, however, agree that the impersonal process, or the multiplicity of impersonal processes, that lead out of the labyrinth and into death, is so prominent that what is, or what has

remained, in a state of virtuality is overshadowed: the past, 'the hauntological never-born' and all those obscure processes that unfold outside possible
access by our consciousness. We must not, therefore, confuse future-time,
mobilised by the attractor, with the attractor in-itself, i.e. with the final state
of each process. To paraphrase Isabelle Stengers, any attractor, however
powerful, would only pose a whole series of problems, to which bodies and
assemblages of bodies would have to respond by mobilising all the resources
at their disposal.

What I consider relevant, however, is the idea that 'passive extinctionism'
has become drastically insufficient. In fact, as EM himself states later on,
apocalyptic linearity would lead to new forms of 'active extinctionism', i.e. the
affirmative desire of some 'free spirits' (in Nietzsche's words) to actualize
a certain virtuality, with the full awareness that the culmination and source
of this life-filled virtuality is none other than death itself—understood as a
negating becoming, but also as the negation of annihilation itself. The double
spectral-vampiric spiral posited by Goth/Ins already entails—by virtue of
its vampiric side—a drive toward annihilation and a desire to return to the
inorganic (what we have termed the 'major attractor'). As in Nietzsche's
eternal return, however, it is power that returns, power as that which actively
eliminates passive and reactive forces, drawing them into a vortex of pure
destructive activity.[2] By admitting the passive/active dyad, we are forced
to assume, at the same time, this theoretical approach—which certainly
includes within itself the 'end of all things' but does not necessarily take it
as its metaphysical cornerstone. This end, apocalypse as absorption or reab-
sorption into nothingness, is not a problematic aspect, but rather the event
that marks the disappearance of all problems; it is therefore an 'irrelevant'
time that we know will come sooner or later, but whose temporal location
and modalities we remain unaware of. Nevertheless, this final blaze that will
consume the universe is an allegory of the ultra-nihilist creative destruction
offered by Goth/Ins—as well as a kind of founding myth for all nihilism.

2.   See G. Deleuze, *Nietzsche and Philosophy* (New York: Columbia University Press, 2006).

If the future is full of death, the past (in its threefold form: monumental, critical, and antiquarian) is the only alternative source of inspiration to the traditions and memories of a zombified world. Any predestined timeline is swept away by the reactivation, in mutant or undead form, of past or never-born elements, flanked by the disintegrating action of death and becoming: time, from this perspective, is in a process of ceaseless stratification and destratification. What is at stake here is the capacity of thought to create, i.e. to produce ex novo, as well as that of ordering along a straight line not only its chimerical lucubrations, but reality itself. As we can see from the analysis carried out by U/Acc, anti-praxis and anti-politics are not just one choice among others, but real alternatives—paradoxically practical and political—to the trivial wasting of time and energy. Whether we like it or not, there is no other choice but barbarism, the dissolution of the ways in which modernity was born and developed in the West. There is no other way out than the return of the past in an aberrant form, precisely because this past has already become actualised. Conversely, what is not at all certain is that modernity is capable of overcoming, destroying, or consuming itself without any 'external' intervention. This is exactly why, setting out from the idea of a hypothetical New Middle Ages, one would already be able to theoretically delineate this novel time as a mutant degeneration, and not as a return or revival of the Middle Ages themselves. It is precisely by virtue of barbarism, fragmentation, the reemergence of despotism, the ineffectiveness of politics, and social aberration that we can say that modernity has already died a crushing death and that anti-praxis is the only option left.

This brings me to the second point, and the final part of EM's text:

[...] CK concludes the text by asking, paraphrasing Nietzsche, who these new barbarians will be. But does it make sense, having razed the entire world, to conclude by wondering how to *identify* these multitudes who will displace the existing regime and launch themselves against the hegemonic temporality, whatever it may be? Without wishing to be excessively polemical, I believe that the question is inessential [...] [I]identification and Proper Names are obsolete structures in this kind of total insurrection, destined to dismantle the tragic temporal mobilisation in which we are immersed. What really matters, what unites and qualifies destruction liberated from barbarian mysticism, is *what the insurgency does*, not who or what it is. [...] The new barbarians [...], in fact, do only one thing: transform tragedy and decadence into sources of power and subversion.

In the face of these words, I would like to repudiate the unfortunate expression with which I concluded my paper. In my defence, however, I would like to point out that the use of the interrogative form should not be understood as a request for identification or subjectification (a 'freezing' interpellation capable of operating as an apparatus of capture). Instead, it could well function in the form of an oracular evocation. In essence it is a call to arms, but also an omen, an invitation to a barbaric proliferation and an anti-practical convergence—or, more precisely, to a convergence into absolute divergence. What is questioned by this call is the idea of the multitude in the singular.

The world has already burned yet, at the same time, has not yet burned enough: our principal opponents are still standing. Neoreaction, revivals of all sorts, optimistic statism, classical conservatism and police authoritarianism are getting louder and louder. Following EM, one could also suggest that the main enemy is our own need for identification, which is intensified by the terror of the invisible and undecidable. There is still much to be thrown into the flames, and there is still much to be said and done.

Having reached this point, however, I feel it would be useful to continue my reflections on EM's notes in order to examine a perspective on the gothic slightly different from the previous one, developed by two young authors, Vincent Garton and Miroslav Griško. A real anomaly, which has taken on the appearance of a bizarre 'post-accelerationism' of Christian provenance. I will try to summarise what I consider to be the most interesting elements of this current, attempting to identify the main points of contact and divergence with the theses set out in 'Gothic Insurrection'.

HORROR

Let us begin with two texts by Garton, an author better known than Griško and with whom many will be more familiar thanks to his important piece, 'Leviathan Rots'.[3] In the first essay that we will examine, 'Catholicism and the Gravity of Horror',[4] we find one of Garton's most brilliant insights: the highlighting of the profound affinities between the Outside of the accelerationist tradition—the inhuman, the alien or the catastrophe[5]—and the Divine as radical otherness, the absolute 'Other' of human and of creaturely space-time.[6] This is not, however, a purely eschatological or apocalyptic operation—centred on a temporal *apex* capable of bringing about a reversal of the Inside into the Outside—but a reactivation of historical projects that were prematurely interrupted. Garton invites the reader to a recovery of the origins of Catholicism, whose roots were corrupted by the advent of modernity, its evolution inscribed and subsumed within modern time, linear and irreversible. On the contrary, according to Garton, the mythical temporality that pervades Christianity is founded on a Time outside of time: a sovereign eternity, capable of delegitimising and displacing any element in the locally-bound transient series. Let us take a closer look at some of the passages in this text:

•

---

3.   Garton, 'Leviathan Rots'.

4.   V. Garton, 'Catholicism and the Gravity of Horror', *Jacobite* (2018), <http://jacobitemag.com/2018/07/05/catholicism-and-the-gravity-of-horror>.

5.   See N. Land, 'Machinic Desire', *Fanged Noumena*, 319–44, but also the following passage from 'Non-Standard Numeracies': 'For anything that can arrive when it wants, the best place to hide is non-existence.' Ibid., 534.

6.   See in particular the tradition of Rhenish speculative theology, specifically, Meister Eckhart's German Sermons: *The Complete Mystical Works of Meister Eckhart*, tr. ed. M. O'C. Walshe (Chestnut Ridge, NY: Crossroad, 2009).

An introduction to Catholicism can very well begin with horror. [...] To consider God is, primordially, to be struck by fear. The fear of God is the foundation of all wisdom [...].

The Christian cosmos is caught from the start in the torsion of an entanglement of historical time with infinity, in the operation of God's hand in material history. [...] [A]ll things are made subject to a judgment pronounced from a throne beyond time itself. To follow this unfolding of history is to be drawn [...] by an inescapable gravity of difference—the impulsive sense, familiar in the aesthetic of horror, of shadowy movements that overflow human comprehension [...] a radical freedom not of this world [...]. [...] [T]o be aware of an alien exterior to our perception is itself to sense God.

And again:

Under the compressive impulse of recent modernity, [...] the distinctively open future of the Enlightenment seems to be coming to a close. What is characteristic of this 'cyberpunk' age is the collapse of the boundaries not just between the future and the present—a 'future so close it connects'— but also the past: for progressives as much as conservatives, the future comes to be constituted by the recovery of historical projects prematurely foreclosed. The liberal understanding of Catholicism is ill-suited to this new context, in which 'progress' is no longer linear and consensus reality itself seems to be disintegrating. [...] [T]he postmodern metropolis with its Gothic darkness and its neon lights, its complex and unbearably persistent ethical disparities, points towards a potential rediscovery of the profundity of the human soul [...].

In the slightly later text 'The Limit of Modernity at the Horizon of Myth', Garton returns to the theme of recovering the past, clarifying and expanding the theoretical-political foundations of his project. In this case too, allow me to extrapolate a few passages:

The question is this: How does one conceive the future? For enlightened man, the future was to be constructed, a supposition embodied in an endless proliferation of utopian schemes. A quite different answer, however, was provided at the start of the twentieth century by Georges Sorel. The future, Sorel saw, is the product of *myth* [and] to 'construct the future' is therefore to elaborate a myth. The significance of myth is not, in this sense, in its truth or falsehood, but in its social effects [...].

Garton notes however that 'myth *cannot* be merely engineered'. In his words:

The fantasy of the speculative *philosophe* [...] was always *just* a fantasy, in its full pathological sense. [...] [F]ully enlightened man, in fact, even when he imagines he has mastered his mythic ground, sprawls beneath the symbols of a greater myth, which he can barely perceive: the 'illusion of progress'. [...] What is more, the illusion of progress is a myth that runs up far too easily against the limits of material production. [7]

Setting out from the speculative construction of an alternative Catholic Church to the existing one, Garton shows how mythological multiplicity is not totalised within this movement of historical re-institution. The 'disinte-gration' of time cannot, in fact, prevent other myths from tracing their own independent paths through the ruins of modernity. At the same time, we are reminded that modernity itself, exemplified by the Enlightenment, rests upon a mythical development: that of a self-intensifying historical progression, distributed along a univocal timeline. Modernity is unconsciously possessed by a myth, transformed into a blind spot, whose illusory and megalomaniac characteristics are explicitly defined by Garton as 'pathological', since they are part of the symbolic delirium of a paranoid temporality that aims to annihilate any alternative to itself.

---

7.   V. Garton, 'The Limit of Modernity at the Horizon of Myth', *Cyclonograph II*, 2018, <https://vincentgarton.com/2018/07/23/the-limit-of-modernity-at-the-horizon-of-myth/>.

The current process of the dissolution of this tendential vector can be deduced from the proliferation of numerous mythical images of the world, the fading of utopian thinking, and the recursive nature of the crises that capitalism periodically undergoes (and which produce a further increase in political, symbolic and social fragmentation).[8] As it fades, the future hoped for by Western modernity leaves room for new ways of recovering the past— or rather, *pasts* plural. And yet, although such recovery is possible—and indeed, quite within reach—to believe that myths can be merely fabricated or engineered would still amount to a profession of naivety. Reality always has the last word, and the only effective distinction between myths is their descriptive, prescriptive, and diagrammatic efficacy.

Garton's goth Catholicism fits perfectly into the recent horror revival (an exquisitely 'speculative' and 'folk' revival) while resonating with the powerful return of cosmic pessimism (see the works of two very different authors, Thomas Ligotti and Eugene Thacker). In this sense, the return of fundamentalism and irrationalism, which accompanies geopolitical and social fragmentation, is an important sign of a corresponding return of the sacred.

This 'rediscovery of the depths of the human soul'—that abyssal and inviolable interiority which places each and every one of us, individually, before Horror and the Absurd—sets the worldly and immanent action of the subject upon the basis of an ulterior, transcendent gesture, radically foreign to the performative subject. Drawn into the crucible of the sacred, fear and bewilderment are converted into glory, and the *Deus Absconditus*, who was thought to be hidden at the end of time—outside of time—turns out to have been all along hidden in plain sight, within the folds of creation itself.

> And he loves you more intensely than ever, because he remembers the obe-dience of you all, and how you received him with fear and trembling.
>
> St Paul, Corinthians 7:15

---

8.   On the topic of the repression of alternative designs to the Western-modern one, see also M. Tomba, *Insurgent Universality: An Alternative Legacy of Modernity* (Oxford: Oxford University Press, 2019).

HORROR *OR* TERROR

In 'Operation Eukaryotic Cell', Miroslav Griško takes the category of *horror* as his starting point, while drawing a clear line between it and a second concept, that of *terror*.[9] As Griško himself shows, this distinction can already be found in the critical work of Ann Radcliffe, who, in *On the Supernatural in Poetry* (1826), defines horror, on the one hand, as a feeling of annihilation and paralysis before an absolutely clear and distinct atrocity, and terror, on the other, as a dark veil of indeterminacy, positioned before a horror that is only foreshadowed. For Radcliffe, it is terror and not horror that has the greatest point of contact with the sublime,[10] since the anguished anticipation of terror 'expands the soul, and awakens the faculties to a high degree of life'[11] (on the contrary, the upheaval occasioned by horror can hardly be reconciled with aesthetic experience). Terror, moreover, is intimately related to the supernatural and to the enigmatic, ambiguous presence of obscure entities.

For Griško, this distinction is of theological status: horror, in fact, concerns the infinite metabolic cycle of the natural world (cosmic horror), while terror indicates a transcendent dimension, located beyond space-time (an 'otherwordly cosmic terror'). While Garton uses the tools of critical philosophy to identify the mythical roots of modern naturalism, Griško turns directly to theology and mystagogy: physics—based on the necessity of bodily death, the gratuitousness of history and individual existence, and the non-sense of thermodynamic apocalypse—must yield to the mysterious teleology of metaphysical eschatology. If the extermination of creation (Hobbes and Darwin's famous 'war of all against all') led to the appearance of intelligence, if, through natural selection, it can even be said to be the active cause of the

9.   M. Griško, 'Operation Eukaryotic Cell' (2018), <https://www.academia.edu/35500410/Operation_Eukaryotic_Cell_>.

10.   This is very similar to Edmund Burke's hypothesis in his *A Philosophical Enquiry into the Origin of Our Ideas of the Sublime and the Beautiful* and then Kant's in the *Critique of Judgment*.

11.   A. Radcliffe, 'On the Supernatural in Poetry', *The New Monthly Magazine* 7 (1826), 145–52.

appearance of intelligence, it is because God himself is infinite intelligence and supreme ruthlessness. The God of the Christian is the God of murder and war, hidden at the end of time, awaiting the annihilation of the world.

For Griško, the end of natural war corresponds to the gradual unveiling of a 'secret war' of which one may become conscious only through religious or sublime experience. Perhaps the aims of this war will sooner or later be revealed in a final, destructive jubilation; but while awaiting this supreme moment, the war can only get worse, becoming more and more insane and horrifying—until the arrival of the Exterminating Angel.

Let's take a look at a couple of passages from 'Operation Eukaryotic Cell':

Horror and terror name two forces of extinction, distinguished by the former's immediacy and the latter's remoteness [...] Horror describes outer war in its transparent brutalism, whereas terror names the hidden extinction at the heart of inner war. [...]

For Radcliffe, horror names a visceral, entirely corporeal violence, according to which 'cruel agents' enact a program of incessant slaughter. As a mechanism of perpetual liquidation, the predation dynamics of horror are consistent with knowable accretions of force that register themselves as translatable and relatable in the vivid description of physical injury: from the smashing of limbs to the slashing of throats. A discreteness of violence is found in the uniqueness of a local death; horror as such denotes the inexhaustibility of these local deaths in an interminable cycle of extinction. As a superior form of extinction, terror, in contrast, is a 'supernatural' threat occasioned by the 'obscurity' of something that is not yet realized. The predation dynamic of terror is conditioned by its remoteness; in terror the force of extinction is immanently inaccessible and therefore untranslatable. Above the immanent purposeless extinction of horror, terror in its remoteness implies 'the progress of (a) conspiracy', a holocaustic eradication that is enacted according to the intelligence of an objective which is not of this earth.

While Garton attempts to curb the eschatological aspects of the religious gothic—focusing on the disturbing manifestation of an infinite God silently penetrating a finite world—Griško, on the other hand, creates a dizzyingly transcendent, apocalyptic, and linear eschatology in which it is the world itself that unknowingly overflows into the infinity of God. In both cases, however, we find ourselves faced with a strong form of dualism: between immanence and transcendence, between the natural and the supernatural, between creature and divinity. In this sense, despite the obvious differences, Griško's orthodoxy is the key to understanding the fundamental assumptions of Garton's mythical theology. Deciding on which side of the fence to place oneself—on the side of immanence or on the side of transcendence— means, in fact, projecting oneself into an inner experience, carrying out an act of faith in the Absurd or, on the contrary, issuing an icy refusal of all transcendence.[12]

Both Garton and Griško make a (mystical-eschatological) wager on the Real: What is the ultimate foundation of creation, Nature or the God-of-Nature? A question which, in Nick Land's work, takes the form of a pure hypostatisation of indeterminacy: 'Gnon' (God-of-Nature-Or-Nature). Either the world has a purpose (and an end), or chance and meaninglessness reign. An impossible choice to make, a question whose answer will merely become spontaneously evident in time—'with' time. The Truth about the Real remains suspended at the boundaries of Time, in a lacerating instant.

Thou sayest that I am a king. To this end was I born, and for this cause came I into the world, that I should bear witness unto the truth. Every one that is of the truth heareth my voice.

Pilate saith unto him, What is truth?

Gospel according to John 18:37–38

---

12.   True faith, in this sense, always corresponds to a blind leap into the unknown—and immersion in a crazy shadow universe. See S. Kierkegaard, *Fear and Trembling*, tr. A. Hannay (London: Penguin Classics, 1985).

HORROR *AND* TERROR

The gothicism of 'Catholicism and the Gravity of Horror' and 'Operation Eukaryotic Cell' involves a subtle play of light and shade—something like the obscure Catholicism that permeates novels such as *The Monk* by M.G. Lewis, or Horace Walpole's *The Castle of Otranto*. The mysterious presence of the hand of God and the ethereal touch of the Devil—in turn concealed by a thick blanket of absence—alternate, intertwine and collide, raising toward the skies the forms of a dark speculative cathedral. In the Gothic novel, however, the Manichean clash between Good and Evil is only part of a far wider framework, which includes the icy power of the inorganic and death, the afterlife and its earthly thresholds populated by ghosts, vampires and the undead, desires (erotic and otherwise) that plunge protagonists into madness and depravity, and the enigmas of fate and predestination.

In *The Castle of Otranto*, for example, the deceased Alfonso becomes an increasingly (and literally) cumbersome presence—to the point where he comes to coincide with the castle itself, and explodes with rage. As for *The Monk*, its story is a mad race through the labyrinth of self-destruction, with the Devil in the role of occult director of a tale already written from the start (it is a work that may still be considered 'extreme'). The essence of the Gothic is a constant exploration of the secret life of the inorganic and the meanderings of the virtual—of that same 'presence of absence' that can be found among the mechanisms of memory, in melancholy, in the regularities of nature and, indeed, in myth.

From a certain point of view, however, Garton's work is still too 'naturalistic': How can one burn with faith and yet at the same time not bow down before the pure act that is not of this world? Having reached the heart of the Christian religion, it is still impossible to regard the Godhead—which goes beyond the anthropomorphic and human-centred vision of a creator-God—as a mere element of myth, or a sociological figure. Griško's apocalyptic God, on the other hand, has the distinction of being also the worst of demons: a fully alien, Lovecraftian entity, interchangeable with countless cosmic or hyper-technological nightmares (such as Hans Moravec's AI or de Hugo de Garis's Artilect, for instance). This Gothic deity would immediately appear ambiguous, perhaps even obsolete, in comparison to a hypothetical metropolitan *noir* deity: an invisible hand that traces out paths and weaves destinies, incarnating itself in dark alleys and revealing itself in fleeting moments of illumination, vertigo, and redemption. In all probability, only this gnostic proto-God, which imperceptibly combines a whole series of non-signifiant signs, could be effectively counted as belonging to the order of myth. Indeed, as Garton seems to sense, theology draws its strength from the weakness of a feeble contrast, not from the self-evident triumph of light over darkness. The triumph of glory and grace must always remain speculative.

However, unlike myth, religion can only grow larger by the minute, coming to occupy—like the avenging spectre in *The Castle of Otranto*—all of reality, producing excesses of abstraction and uncontrollable teleological prolifer-ations. In this vortex, every sign acquires a meaning, and every meaning converges, pointing in the same direction. Hunted down by paranoia, the Hidden God becomes more and more evident—and Griško's God, the 'Lord of Extermination' is but the last stage of a semiotic-religious delirium.

In spite of its undoubted theological fascination, the God of the Outside is one of the most obvious symptoms of the excessive linearity assumed by accelerationism (as well as a clear sign of a long-incubated monomania). In fact, we are faced with a relationship of perfect continuity with previous theoretical elaborations—rather than a kinship between L/Acc, R/Acc and U/Acc or a critical thread running through them. The obsessive-compulsive aspects, the monodirectionality and the extreme fluidity of the described processes (widely 'lubricated' from a philosophical point of view), are the product of the combining of a whole series of coarse concepts (bordering on pure fantasy) with theoretical frameworks within which the conflict is almost never empirically identified in its material singularity, but only in the form of empty universals, vague generalisations and abstractions of an idealist type. Aspects which, in some cases, relate only partially to certain currents and authors, but which, in other cases, seem to be deeply rooted in the entire theoretical complex.[13]

Accelerationism and its various derivations may have inherited from 'post-modern' philosophy a series of concepts and speculative territories characterised by great plasticity and fluidity, but it is always necessary to take into account the material constraints imposed by reality: the breadth of the operational margins does not allow for the creation of a new and more complex set of concepts.

The only field that can legitimately be defined as absolute, i.e. free of all constraints, is the real-material field, i.e. the space in which the world autoconstructs itself,[14] independently of any correlation (linguistic, mental, social or perceptive) and any access (conscious or unconscious).

From this perspective, the anti-naturalism put forward by a certain accelerationism and post-accelerationism has two contradictory yet sym-metrical faces. The first, widespread in the neo-rationalist and xenophilic spheres, is exemplified by the representationalist fallacy, which consists in claiming that nature is somehow 'unjust', and that human beings are capable of freely and voluntarily modifying their existential condition by acting on nature itself. But what is 'unjust' is in fact a specific definition of the concept of nature, which is purely modern and Western, i.e. historically and culturally situated—and not nature itself.

On the other hand, we can think nature as something plastic and mal-leable. An open totality, or an infinite set of spatiotemporal localities and micro-localities, performative processes, and concretions of memory. In this

13. This is the case with the rigid determinism attributed by many to 'hyperstition', or the ethnocentrism of most accelerationist currents. This future in which the techno-economy is nothing more than an indistinct, uniform mass, isn't it barely credible?
14. Here I follow in the footsteps of the research conducted by Ilya Prigogine. See for example D. Kondepudi and I. Prigogine, *Modern Thermodynamics: From Heat Engines to Dissipative Structures* (Hoboken, NJ: Wiley, 2014); I. Prigogine and G. Nicolis, *Self-Organization in Non-Equilibrium Systems* (Hoboken, NJ: Wiley, 1977).

sense, this conception of nature is in line with the idea that there is ample room for intervention, both technoscientific and evolutionary. Certainly, what humans cannot do, the self-initiated development of nature can, and vice versa; however, this space can in no way be said to be absolute and without objective material limits, since nothing partial and finite could claim to act directly on the infinite. The second anti-naturalist face is precisely the theological-paranoid one we have examined above, exemplified by an assertion of 'pure reason' according to which the sense of the world is external to the world itself; in this case, if nature is 'unjust' is because justice is not of this world.

It is evident that each of these two conceptions is marked by a certain degree of instrumental or ideological violence—a violence that cannot but be either speciesist or anthropocentric (bordering on the so-called 'strong anthropic principle'). Both, moreover, are based on a twofold metaphysical claim: on the one hand, 'something' could be capable of 'everything' (the finite is capable of implementing the infinite); on the other hand, things are not ontologically sufficient unto themselves (requiring an external entity, a superior rational principle, or an intrinsic end that certifies their existential or moral value). These two apparently contradictory positions demonstrate their paradoxical synthetic unity at the very moment when all objections based on a defence of organic finitude and partiality are branded as reactionary by militant anti-naturalists, and as nihilistic by theologians and metaphysicians. What cannot be endured in any way, after all, is the finitude, the marginality—and the vast burden of powerlessness—of the human being.

Moreover, the representational fallacy, the 'infinity fallacy' (which follows from it), and the eschatological paranoia seem to exemplify *ad absurdum* the secret idealism at the heart of accelerationism: the Singularity is inevitable, the universe itself has conspired to this end, and every single process since the beginning of time would have been nothing but an omen of the overcoming of matter by the omnipotence of a supreme AI. To remain steadfast in lucidity at this point is to keep in mind that not everything is already decided and not everything is inevitable, but also that, on the other hand, not everything is possible.

By locating the absolute—that which is totally free—in nature-matter, the Outside is positioned as immanent to every structure and as constitutively undecidable in its own virtuality. An atheological complex in which the horrors of death, conflict and degeneration are inextricably intertwined with the dark terrors of an impersonal, chaotic, disorganised, atmospheric and inscrutable field. That which is formless is opposed to that which has form and organisation. At the same time, this formless chaos is at the very basis of the production of form, it is transcendental with respect to it, because it constitutes the condition of its existence in time (something springs from nothingness). The Gothic, here, indicates precisely this coexistence of light and darkness, of manifestation and annihilation, of rise and fall. Forms do not preexist, they must be created or produced, starting from the absence of form—thanks to and in spite of its disintegrating action. The fluidity and plasticity of formless matter means that what is infinitely actual (the active production of forms, or *natura naturans*) can neither logically nor materially exhaust its own infinite virtuality (i.e. the different combinations and infinitesimal variations on the theme of actualised nature). The actual, therefore, is never definitively actualised, nor does it ever fully become itself, since the virtual is this very tension toward perpetual actualisation: becoming. The future, in this sense, is the chronotope in which the simultaneity of decadence and generation leads to the constitution of the past, while the present, as a threshold, presses for its own self-surpassing in the future. The play of becoming stands precisely on this threshold, where nothing is necessity, regularity or law—until its effective actualisation.

If there is any acceleration in Goth/Ins, it is precisely an acceleration of the virtual: accelerating the passing of knowledge, as Nietzsche invites us to do in *The Anti-Christ*.[15] In this sense, as a consequence of partiality and finitude, the unknown plays a fundamental role in the elaboration of a complex

---

15.   '[T]o guide the blade *here*—this is for *us* to do.' F. Nietzsche, 'The Anti-Christ', *The Anti-Christ, Ecce Homo, Twilight of the Idols and Other Writings*, tr. J. Norman, ed. A. Ridley, J. Norman (Cambridge: Cambridge University Press, 2005), 7 [§7].

capable of leaving behind the accelerationist hangover. Non-knowing and the unknown, in fact, anticipate the formation of knowledge at the same time that the latter believes it is moving toward them in order to conquer them. The unknown is never external to the world, but is situated in its very roots: How could knowledge be obtained without prior ignorance?

Everything we think we know at the moment is constantly thwarted by the virtual, and knowledge is nothing more than this continuous dynamic adaptation between the finite and the infinite. As in the gothic, the unknown bursts into the everyday, assailing all that is good, just and true—and, in essence, everything that is form and measure. By speeding up the thawing of structures, one proceeds toward the unknown, blurring the boundaries between the 'natural' and the 'unnatural', but also those between 'nature' and 'culture', or between 'possible' and 'impossible'. Gothic terror, in its purest form, does not correspond to the irruption of a series of transcendent entities into the plane of immanence, but to the disruption of the plane of immanence by itself, its laceration by the transcendental forces of chaos. Terror and anguish always dwell in the heart of death, and therein lies the root of all the horrors that befall us every day.

If, when reflecting on the power of the negative, we constantly look toward annihilation and death, it is because everything, sooner or later, fortunately, has its end—and it is this end that must be accelerated in every direction. The plurality of directions and possibilities is a wave that presses for the overcoming of any preconstructed future, and this is the real difference (the constitutive difference) between myth and religion. Myths and narratives are nothing but skeins of sense which segment and cross every plane of reality and every timeline: a whole series of paths that collide, intersect, alternate, and overlap, referring to possibilities that are entirely 'of this world'. A world that stands on its own shadow and on its own excess, rising, as if by magic, out of an ocean of darkness—in which the formless terror of nature lurks.

CK

LIFTING THE ABSOLUTE[1]

In this book you will find a 'subterranean man' at work, one who tunnels and mines and undermines. [...] Does it not seem as though some faith were leading him on, some consolation offering him compensation? As though he perhaps desires this prolonged obscurity, desires to be incomprehensible, concealed, enigmatic, because he knows what he will thereby also acquire: his own morning, his own redemption, his own daybreak?

Nietzsche[2]

Pankration (from *pan*, 'all', and *kratos*, 'strength') is an ancient fighting style somewhat akin to boxing, wrestling, or vale tudo, but totally lacking any time limits or demarcations such as rounds or weight categories. This brutal martial art first made its appearance among the Olympian disciplines in 648 BC and remained, at least until the fall of the Roman Empire, one of the most popular sports among the inhabitants of the Mediterranean. In pankration, to all intents and purposes an extreme sport, the only way to get out of a fight was to surrender, to lose consciousness, or to die—although,

---

1.   This text is taken from the collection of writings by the pseudonymous 'Bronze Age Collapse' entitled *The Search for Absolute Fitness: Plato as a Bodybuilder* (Agharta, 1991). Even though the identity of Bronze Age Collapse remains unknown, and despite the unreliability of the original text, *The Search for Absolute Fitness* is one of those writings that, circulating from hand to hand, has contributed significantly to the concept of the 'Gothic Insurrection'. The idea—developed by Bronze Age Collapse at the dawn of the 1990s in a crude and deliberately muscular way—that the present is to be overcome through joyous destruction and irresponsible immersion in a horrifically distant past, the neo-pagan atmosphere and autobiographical references that the author has disseminated in the essays that make up the work, are echoed in the writings of the Gruppo di Nun. We have therefore decided to offer readers a glimpse of this interesting piece of writing, in the hope that it will inspire others as it has inspired us.
2.   F. Nietzsche, *Daybreak: Thoughts on the Prejudices of Morality*, tr. R.J. Hollingdale (Cambridge: Cambridge University Press, 1997), 1.

according to historians, it would seem that there were also athletes who won even though they lost their lives.

Between 364 and 356 BC, pankration was dominated by the terrifying presence of Sostratus Sicionio, known as Acrochersite ('Mr Fingers') because of his obsession with finger-breaking and his vast catalogue of holds. Three times over, this ruthless fighter prevailed over the strongest men in the Mediterranean, beating all comers at the Olympics and also winning the Isthmian Games, the Nemean Games, and many other important titles. Around about the same time, during Sostratus's last years of glory, the young Aristocles of Athens—son of Ariston and Perictione; brother of Adimanto, Potone and Glaucon; descendant of Solon and, perhaps, of Apollo himself—participated in the Olympics, winning two titles in pankration. I like to think that it was Aristocles, the ancient philosopher who became as famous as Plato (from the Greek for 'big shoulders'), who gave Sostratus a taste of defeat, opposing the brutality of the Sicyonian with total bodily strength and harmony.

Imagine the mighty Aristocles grasping and crushing the hands of Sostratus, giving him a taste of his own medicine. After all, only a perfect alignment of muscular strength, instinct, intelligence, technical expertise, and experience—or at least the mere possibility that such an alignment could occur in the human body—could justify the existence of the discipline of pankration. Total strength, resulting from the conquest of the individual parts, from their subjection to the harmony of the whole: the founding myth of the philosophy of mind...and of wrestling.

As Yukio Mishima intuited in *Sun and Steel*, psychophysical harmony is first and foremost an Idea, in the full Platonic sense. It is a slow and arduous process of adapting one's body to a paradigm, a *techné* which in turn refers back to the model of classical education, through which one submits oneself to gradually more intense labours and more voluminous loads, to ever more refined exertions and to ever subtler dangers. Mishima cautiously maintained that 'beauty is always retreating from one's grasp'.[3] However, in the course of this process of adaptation, the body is not directed toward beauty, but *returned* to it.

Pay close attention, for I have dared to assert that harmony and beauty are things that preexist discord, ugliness, and dissimilarity—an extremely anti-modern, incredibly ancient (at least as ancient as the Way, Being, and non-duality), and yet universal assertion. That the human body is not by nature weak, passive, and sedentary, but powerful, active and dynamic— open to becoming and receptive to both confrontation and escape—is only the latest of the great truths to which modern science has assented. In bodybuilding, in wrestling, in running, in weight training and in survival, the body follows the same tendency toward the absolute before which the mind prostrates itself when it dwells on philosophical thoughts, the same tendency toward enhancement, recombination, speed and efficiency before which the whole universe bows.

It is for these reasons that the intellectual body, the wage-earning body—and, more generally, the battered body of the modern human being— discover in weightlifting one of the most basic facts of organismic experience: namely, that to exist means to insist, that life consists primarily of a series of efforts, of a perpetual effort, a *conatus*, a play of accumulations of tension and sudden discharges. The encounter with the cold steel of the dumbbells is the encounter with material concretion in its most inert and repulsive form; indeed, I would go so far as to say that there is a profound affinity between the body 'fallen' from its state of primordial dynamism and weightlifting equipment: both, in fact, seem to be of the same icy, crepuscular nature—just as, conversely, the dynamic body participates in the becoming of matter, recognising itself as part of its flaming flux. It is as if, by confronting and lifting matter, the human being lifts itself at the same time, becoming something like its own guardian angel or, better, *daimon*.

---

3.   Y. Mishima, *Sun and Steel* (New York: Kodansha America, 1970), 23.

It was Schopenhauer himself, in *The World as Will and Representation*, who proposed the body as the privileged vehicle of metaphysics: on the one hand, in fact, the body offers itself (in the words of Mishima) as 'depths of the surface', i.e. as the visible expression of individual interiority; on the other, as the seat of perceptions and of an 'instinctive' principle of causality—inherent in all living beings—it is the point of origin of all matter, i.e. of all activity in the universe, since perceptions and causality logically precede all objective activity.[4] From here one could go much further—as Nietzsche did—and assume that it is the activity of each individual body or corporeal collectivity, its closeness to the idea and its thirst for the absolute, that determines the cosmologies it inhabits. This should render entirely clear the meaning of the epithet *kalos kagathos* ('beautiful and good'), attributed in ancient times to those individuals who were psychophysically harmonious, resolute in battle, in action, and in speech, and endowed with an innate sense of rhythm and melody[5] (and how can we not think here of the feats of Herodotus's impertinent Hippocleanes, so distant from our stale Christian morality?). When the nature of a body is reactive, the universe around it becomes reactive, linear, and static; conversely, when the nature of a body is dynamic and enterprising, the cosmos turns into a cyclonic vortex—such is the origin of Nietzsche's Will to Power, a heroic and combative version of Schopenhauer's blind Will.

What a bizarre turn of events for philosophy, for the body to become the voice of the spirit and the source of all wisdom!

The industrial city and industrial society, with their noise, their annihilating rhythms and their junk food, are the products of a great upheaval. History did not end in them but retracted, curling into a kind of backwash. History

---

4.   See A. Schopenhauer, *The World as Will and Representation*, tr. E.F.J. Payne (New York: Dover, 2 vols., 1958), vol. 1, 5 [§2].
5.   See W. Jaeger, *Paideia: The Ideals of Greek Culture*, tr. G. Highet (New York and Oxford: Oxford University Press, 1939).

is not the history of human beings, nations, or tribes, but the living archive of the trials and tribulations that matter must endure in order to rise above itself. The pull-up bar, the most imposing and vertiginous object in every gymnasium, is the allegory of every vital impulse: by submitting ourselves to its inflexible judgement, we measure ourselves against the cosmos itself, raising ourselves above mortals.

If God were a lobster, and if the lobster were the yardstick for every human action and every rule of law, every true hero would prefer to be a star, a supernova or a black hole—to be able to glow from a great distance, or to devour the whole world with his soul.

If one were to set aside the dumbbells and barbells for a few minutes and pause to reflect on the philosophical status of the nerd leaving the gym every Friday night, one would at some point come across the modern myth of temporal linearity.

All too often in bodybuilding, the trainer does not perceive the whole process as a return to the body—to eidetic harmony or, better still, as a return to oneself—but as the journey to an 'other' destination, as a sort of pilgrimage or *una tantum* cleansing. A tendency marked by goals, deadlines and seasonal (mostly summer) events, and which is sure to cast any rookie determined to get to the beach as soon as possible into despair.

The pathetic efforts of modernity to refashion the moral, ontological, and aesthetic dignity of the body and spirit constantly come up against the impenetrable wall of corruption and impotence. A corruption and impotence generated by the introduction of the teleological and economic mechanisms introduced into the West by Christianity. Every sin and every 'wrongdoing' corresponds to a punishment and a new renunciation to settle the debt incurred; likewise, every process of purification is accompanied by a reward, according to the dictates of a pact and a promise made with a great creditor—in this case the future body, the centrefold body, beyond which there would be nothing but the oblivion of eternal rest. Without the demon of the eternal return, without the power of a Sisyphus or a Prometheus, assiduous bodybuilding is merely the worst form of nihilism, fully realised by the torment of steroids and the deadly, hyperreal atmosphere they bring with them. In the words of Mishima, the steel of the dumbbells is, more correctly, the means of 'restor[ing] the classical balance that the body had begun to lose, reinstating it in its natural form, the form that it should have had all along'.[6]

Somewhere between the hopeful heroism of natural bodybuilding and the hypertrophic nightmares of the Western gym there lies Greek sculpture, with a whole series of divine or semi-divine bodies distinguished by their apparently supernatural harmony and stature.

In the face of modern incredulity, it has often been said (especially in academic circles)[7] that classical sculpture 'idealised' the body. A hypothesis which, in the creature of spirit, cannot but provoke a scornful smile: how could Greek artists have idealised entire muscle groups in the smallest detail, without having had *concrete* models of flesh and blood at their disposal? Our level of corruption is such that we have become deaf to the call of god! Further evidence that messianic time is nothing more than a time of the constant postponement of every goal, and the stubborn postponement of eternal rest. It is not, therefore, a question of being part of a process of gradual and progressive improvement, but of an injunction to invert the very chronological course of history and biology: 'You must change your life!' The statuesque body of the god-athlete (living or merely depicted) acts upon the observer by means of its exemplarity, inspiring change and, at the same time, indicating the model to move toward. It is from this convergence of gazes that we can deduce how, in the Idea, being and being-exemplar may converge.

The inability of moderns to conceive of the antique body, then, resembles the inability of the child to imagine the true extent of its father's strength. Before Mediterranean antiquity, we are like children. Indeed, we are children in the face of all prehistory, the kingdom of the fearless hominids, and that

---

6. Mishima, *Sun and Steel*, 23.
7. And how could it be otherwise?

of the mighty creatures who preceded us. The reaction I ask you to embrace, therefore, is deeper and more titanic than that invoked by the frogmen.

What a palaeolithic—even geological—sadness to see a white collar where a cave bear could once have been seen!

When the Olympian gods defeated the Titans (the embodiment of the forces of wild nature), they banished their opponents to Tartarus, a dark place dominated by frost. In Tartarus—this sort of black hole, this gigantic hell—Kronos, time, the true father of the gods and the titans, became king once more, crushing under his heel every other being and every other principle. The strength of the Titans then waned, and they became docile and submissive creatures.

Like the Titans, we have been exiled into the bowels of the hollow earth, Agartha—into the darkness of our own bowels and our own pale desires. Such is the true meaning of the 'myth of the cave' and of Dante's journey. One day, our imprisonment will end, we shall return to the surface, and a new Golden Age will begin: the gods, spirits, and animals will speak once again, and their voices will resound, crystal clear; every man and woman will discover a god and a goddess within themselves, every fight will be accompanied by sweat and joyful laughter, every body will smell of flowers, honey, and oil, and the sun will shine on everyone equally. 'And thence we came forth to look again at the stars.'[8]

War is father of all things, king of all things.

Heraclitus[9]

---

8. D. Alighieri, *The Divine Comedy of Dante Alighieri: Inferno*, tr. ed. R. M. Durling (Oxford: Oxford University Press, 1996), Canto 34, I. 139, 541.
9. Heraclitus, *The Texts of Early Greek Philosophy: The Complete Fragments and Selected Testimonies of the Major Presocratics*, tr. ed. D.W. Graham (Cambridge: Cambridge University Press, 2010), 157.

Fools! Their reflections are not far-reaching, who expect what was not before to come to be, or that something will die out and perish utterly. For from what in no way is, it is impossible to come to be, and for what is to perish cannot be fulfilled or known, for it will always be there wherever one puts it at any time.

Empedocles[10]

The 'pseudonym' with which I pen these words does not conceal the subject of the athletic and philosophical endeavour; rather, it is the undertaking itself that drags the subject down into the dust, disrupts it, and strips it of all identity. *Palaistra* means, in fact, 'to struggle', or even better 'to throw down', 'to collapse'. And how could it be otherwise for Zeus?

Set upon set, lifting increasingly great masses of inert matter, the subject of weight-training brings their body closer to an impersonal, universal and anonymous form—the body of the god or goddess. This tension toward the unsolved, this desire to achieve an absolute *fitness* of body and spirit, is the motion that drives the universe, that structures its becoming and maintains its architecture.

When one thinks of the gods of antiquity, one imagines a whole pantheon of superior creatures, each of which embodies a principle, or the pure essence of a force; but the gods themselves were born of chaos, and had to scale the hierarchy of entities by their own strength until they reached the heights of Olympus. It is precisely because of this origin—common to everything that is—that they share with every other being the aspiration to embody a principle, a force, a certain atmosphere. The universe is 'a machine for the making of gods',[11] but the gods themselves (like the Homeric Ares) can bleed, subject as they are to the vortex of chaos, the supreme soul that generates and destroys

10.   Empedocles, *The Texts of Early Greek Philosophy: The Complete Fragments and Selected Testimonies of the Major Presocratics*, tr. ed. D.W. Graham (Cambridge: Cambridge University Press, 2010), 349.

11.   H. Bergson, *The Two Sources of Morality and Religion*, tr. R. Ashley Audra, C. Bereton (London: MacMillan, 1935), 275.

without mercy. The *anima mundi*—the fire that pervades even the most insignificant particle of this dimension—contains within it every possibility, every combination, every environment and every psychophysical adaptation. Living beings are merely contractions of its infinite activity, embodiments of its thought and manifestations of its power, because it alone harbours the supreme *fitness*: immortality as perpetual metamorphosis and as total effectiveness of action (which thus becomes 'gesture'). At the heart of reality, Phanes and Zagreo, Apollo and Dionysus, form and élan, face each other in a violent assault, tearing apart the cosmos and shattering space-time. 'The one and the many': not a philosophical problem, but the product of a *coincidentia oppositorum* and the diairetic proliferation to which this disjunctive synthesis gives rise. This is the real secret of the tension toward the absolute, as of any mimicry of natural rhythms on the part of human beings.

It was probably during the Great Oxidation Event—one of the darkest and most catastrophic moments in the history of the planet—that individual organisms, overwhelmed by environmental pressures, were forced to form the first cell federations in order to survive. In an attempt to return to harmony, the federation became the first form of organisation of living matter: the assembly of the many into a functional pseudo-unity. The microorganisms that animated a peaceful, indistinct mass discovered form, differentiation and specialisation, flexibility and perseverance. With distinction came toil and confrontation; with toil and confrontation came competition; with competition came victory, and mutualism and egoism became two sides of a single coin.

The sublime science of nutrition is the discipline upon which the delicate economy of the organismic federation is based. Blinded as we are by the mists of chaos, we perceive every attempt not to gobble up other living beings and the trash food that infests the hollow earth as a 'sacrifice'. The alchemy of flavours, macronutrients, and micronutrients, which our ancestors were repositories of, is now unknown to us; neither can we—except at the cost of unspeakable suffering—bid farewell to the panoply of sugar, salt, gluten, and added fats that infest packaged food.

Rejecting the food that our jailer feeds us is the first step toward a total revolt—the first step toward a full-blown 'great health', based on generosity and magnanimity toward oneself and others. Only an implacable resolution will be able to tear time from its hinges, cleansing our blood-stained hands and our soft underbellies. On the other hand, one might almost say that the planet is experiencing a felicitous alignment: in fact, it is only from the perspective of illness that one is able to recognise the features of a healthy body.

All the names of history, gathered to shake up and de-stress your slumbering spirits.

Writing while honouring and respecting the sacred competition is a burdensome task and a sacrifice. Every moment spent writing is a moment stolen from living thought, training, play, and carnal love: it could almost be said that writing is a symptom of the corruption that befell human beings ten thousand years ago. However, being a sort of 'original sin' and false consciousness, writing must be transvaluated and catastrophically overturned—grasped and lifted by hand, like the Atlas globe; we shall aim, therefore, at a majestic sincerity, at obtaining in speech the effectiveness of gesture: an operation allowed by the deadly and static nature of writing itself. We shall pay every attention and care not to become scribes, and will imprint the character of becoming on the being of the text. If Nietzsche advised us to think only while walking, we shall take care to make writing a marginal activity, devoting all our efforts to the search for and exposition of the truth, rooting our perspective in the impersonality of the absolute. Our aim will be to radiate each word as the sun radiates its rays.

According to the myth, Alexander the Great, upon his arrival in Greece, immediately received numerous visits, from intellectuals and philosophers, politicians and men of science; only Diogenes, the Cynic teacher who lived in a barrel in the public square, did not go to pay him homage. When Alexander finally met Diogenes 'the Dog', he found him lying in the middle of the street, sunbathing. Amazed and admiring the impudence of the philosopher, Alexander offered to grant him any wish he might have.

Staring him in the eyes, not budging an inch, Diogenes asked him to get out of the way, and return the sunlight to him.

This anecdote, already famous in ancient Greece, remains the essence of a sovereign and unyielding spirit, radiating a sunny warmth and infusing hilarity into every healthy and unashamed body. It is impossible not to dwell on the unusual properties of sunlight. Sunlight weeds thought out from its depths, forcing it to rise to the surface and quit every refuge, every classroom, every hermitage. No less important are its benefits to the body: through exposure to sunlight, the body instinctively becomes able to distinguish accurately between day and night, aiding sleep and stabilising mood (all too often conditioned in these dark times by enclosed spaces and irregular hours); likewise, through the metabolic action of the sun, the synthesis of vitamin D and calcium is made possible, substances in which much of the population, confined to homes and offices, is deficient.

Moreover, by offering themselves unconditionally to the greatest gift of heaven, the human being becomes part of a magmatic processuality that joins together plants, animals, and microorganisms in one and the same shared splendour. Just as it did billions of years ago, this cellular federation that is our body rejoices in the solar flux, invigorating itself and drawing power from it, relegating to the night-time hours rest, reproduction, and regeneration—in other words, all those subtle techniques of repetition and replication of the identical. In short, thanks to the warmth of the sun, the body becomes healthy, strong and beautiful, and the mind acquires the precious virtues of intuitiveness and spontaneity, while undergoing an apprenticeship in the art of cosmic coexistence.

There is, however, another meaning, more secret and yet simpler and more superficial. Diogenes, in fact, having renounced all material possessions and all hierarchy, possesses everything, including the sun—a possession that can be taken away from him and returned to him at any time, depending only on the natural rhythms of the cosmos and the seasons. The truth and intention of his words depend upon this superior form of self-sufficiency. And if Diogenes himself was a pupil of Socrates, it is because the cynic, too, dedicates his life to the search for a 'primal scene', an eternal and essential substrate, capable of founding action in justice and harmony. In this titanic undertaking, sun and steel, training and writing, converge, illuminating the path of one who aspires to the absolute.

Bronze Age Collapse

III

NIGREDO

CULTIVATING DARKNESS

If 'nothing' should detain us, and yet we should suffer delay.

Augustine[1]

Although the world of darkness remains fundamentally alien in essence, the human being is no stranger to its icy touch.

There are moments in life when one realises that one is immersed in a dense darkness, so thick that it seems to preclude any return to the light. These are moments of mourning, despair, or depression; moments suspended over the chasm of madness, when the world falls apart and life seems to have lost all meaning. From a philosophical point of view, this means that the representation of the world that we have received from our loved ones, or that we have constructed along with them—and which we have often shared with an entire community—turns out to be false, limited, or too narrow. As it falls apart, 'our' world, which had until then revolved like a planet around the sun of an I or a We, shows itself to be no more than a collection of fragments from which, like a collage, it had emerged.

If there were a lesson to be learned from such moments, it would consist in the bitter discovery that there is always more than *one* world and that, even from the same fragments, it is possible to construct totally different worlds. Although there is undoubtedly a 'shared world' held in common with others from time to time, it is not hard to see that this one world—a world for all worlds—is always teetering on the edge. The world is like Humpty Dumpty,

1. Saint Augustine, 'The Teacher', in *Earlier Writings*, tr., ed. J.H.S. Burleigh (Louisville, KY and London: Westminster John Knox Press, 2006), II, 3–4, 71–72.

the egg-man in the nursery rhyme and in *Alice Through the Looking Glass*. When Humpty Dumpty falls off the wall, his shell shatters, and even all the King's men cannot put the fragments back together again. We discover that the stories we had been telling about 'my' life, 'our' life, or life in general, have been irretrievably lost.

Having been born and brought up within the reassuring confines of a world, we have at the same time managed to sew a suture between history (that of our country, our era, or even the whole planet) and our own, far smaller biography. Human life consists of a dense network of stories, some of which have been told to us, some of which we have told ourselves; stories from before the disaster in which were contained, like a kind of psychic black box recorder, the direction in which the world, time, and life were headed. 'Meaning' was nothing more than this internal coherence between origin, development, and destination. In moments of fear and trembling, one realises that human existence is similar to that of the scale insect which mummifies on the body of the plant while remaining imperceptibly alive: *we live in the age of technological acceleration, of the Anthropocene, of advanced capitalism.* By drawing these lines, which link the individual to the general, we establish that history is advancing or, on the contrary, that it is standing still and waiting to be set in motion again. But at the height of despair there is neither movement nor standstill. The fragments veer off on their own, each in a different direction. All that remains are indifferent speeds, a world of things that continue to happen, without meaning or reason, without the coherence we had attributed to them (work, study, human relationships, everything seems to emerge from a dream). We have fallen out of time.

Two American psychologists, Lauren Alloy and Lyn Yvonne Abramson, have developed an interesting theory, called 'depressive realism'. While cognitive-behavioural therapy (currently the most widespread therapeutic model) claims that depressed people are plagued by a negative bias (i.e. a chronic and habitual pessimism) which makes them less objective than non-depressed people, depressive realism argues that the depressed person has access to a more objective dimension than non-depressed people. A number of studies show that this hypothesis should be reduced to something less than a theory, although it remains something more than a *flatus vocis*: the depressed are indeed more objective in their perception of the world, evaluate their own performance immediately after completing it, and tend to devalue it more and more over time. Depressed people also seem to have higher expectations for the future than non-depressed people. To some extent, the depressed person is the author of their own defeats, falling from the heights of sincere optimism to the abyss of the darkest despair. What depressive realism has succeeded in showing, however, is that unlike the non-depressed, the depressed person is able to attribute responsibility to themselves where they actually have it, and conversely is able to identify situations that are beyond their control, or anyone else's. Thanks to this special access to a subterranean, indifferent, and uncaring world, the depressive realist casts off the role of the pathological subject, becoming a sort of pessimistic oracle. Unwittingly, Alloy and Abramson have created a conceptual persona, something like Plato's Socrates or Descartes's evil demon.

In Mark Fisher's *Capitalist Realism*—the book of a generation that has decided to patch up the pieces, building a new world and a new meaning—we find the following adage: 'It is easier to imagine the end of the world than it is to imagine the end of capitalism.'[2] As is now well known, for Fisher, capitalist realism is founded precisely on the mantra 'There is no alternative': *There is no alternative*...except the end of the world. The depressive realist would agree wholeheartedly, and indeed, finding himself lost in the darkness of panic and despair, would clearly see that the world has already ended or, rather, that it never existed, or only for a fleeting moment. There is no where and no time to go to or return to. The body of the depressed person is a receptacle for entities beyond time, their voice a channel through which a call is propagated that is both seductive and chilling:

---

2.   Fisher, *Capitalist Realism*, 2.

No flow, no connectivity in the depressive's nervous system [...] His voice [...] sounds like the voice of a man who is already dead, or who has entered an appalling state of suspended animation, death-within-life. It sounds preternaturally ancient, a voice which cannot be sourced back to any living being [...].[3]

The falling apart, the disorientation, is absolute, in the sense that it does not just affect me or other human beings who are my fellow sufferers (as existentialism has taught us), but the whole universe. As we have seen, the research of Alloy and Abramson shows how, following the crisis and the destruction of the world, the depressed person tends to aggravate his or her situation in the long term. This is exactly what happened to philosophical pessimism and nihilism, which gradually turned into eliminativist positions for which consciousness, language, the individual, morality, history, or reality itself do not exist at all.

Compared to many of these new philosophical currents, good old-fashioned solipsism may well seem a moderate solution, somewhat less threatening than an extinctionist programme or a death cult. In exaggerating the depressive position, one fails to realise that what appears during the crisis is not the non-existence of all things but their *inconsistency*, the precarity, fragility, and metastability of the world itself. When the term 'metastability' is used in physics and cosmology, it means that even a slight imbalance would be capable of destroying or altering a system, or even the whole universe. For empiricism (the philosophy of experience), this terrifying inconsistency is owing to the fact that the 'laws of nature' are not real laws. Rather than eternal commandments imposed on matter by the benevolent hand of a creator, they are regularities hanging by a thread, governed by chance—chains of only apparently necessary causes and effects. As the English philosopher David Hume noted, to say that the sun will surely rise tomorrow is fallacious: we are led to believe that it will happen only because

---

3. Fisher, *Ghosts of My Life*, 62.

we have seen it one morning after another, or because it has been marked out for us since childhood; but there is no logical necessity for this to happen. Although it may seem improbable (and here we are forced to employ a whole probabilistic vocabulary!) that the universe will be annihilated at this very moment, there is nothing to prevent it, least of all my expectations and hopes.

The world is suspended over an abyss. Everything is pervaded by nothingness, by a power that extends its tentacles from the heart of the night. A 'hyperdepressive realism' that challenges the very notion of reality. Embracing darkness as a ruinous destiny, starvation, catatonia, and resignation turn into a shapeless, elusive atmosphere with vague and indefinite contours, a field of radical experimentation that may result in self-destruction or in the discovery of unknown pleasures:

> Any symbol is a limitation of belief, or energy, by its own particular form and nature. In order to release the energy of belief, its form or symbol has to be destroyed so that the quantity of belief which it enshrined becomes free to merge with the belief-potential of the believer, which is—ultimately—infinite. When this is achieved, belief becomes free and vast enough to contain reality itself.[4]

Falling into the darkness, we realise that this very darkness is reality in its purest and most uncontaminated state: a black primordial magma, the place of the origin of every world and of all meaning—the grave of every world and of all meaning.

This gloomy depressive world is equivalent to a world devoid of representations and thoughts, to the world before the appearance of the human being or to the one that will follow the disappearance of humans. Realism satisfies its own epistemic conditions through the complete absence of any observers that would restrict and limit its possibilities—a little like what

---

4. K. Grant, 'Austin Osman Spare: An Introduction to His Psycho-Magical Philosophy', *Carfax 4: Austin Osman Spare* (1960).

happens with morality in the case of the promoters of voluntary extinction. If, as David Benatar argues,[5] the lives of human beings are indeed dominated by an optimistic 'Pollyanna principle' (an innate tendency to remember positive experiences more frequently and more easily, and to maintain a fair degree of confidence in the future), then the optimist would not only be immoral—as optimism is designed to indefinitely postpone the good of all living beings, from generation to generation—but would also be the victim of an innate hallucinatory influence. The scientific, technological and social progress of humankind (or rather, a small part of humankind) does not lead toward truth but toward the dead end of extinction. Either we achieve self-consciousness of the real as an absence of teleological representations and orientations (i.e. as an absence of meaning and unity) or we will soon reach the point of no return, at the moment when the tentacles of matter regain possession of this brief moment of awareness that is organic life.

Neither can it be ruled out that these processes might go hand in hand, furiously flushing out our lies and forcing us to abjure them.

Losing hope does not mean sinking into despair—although often there is nothing left but despair. Pessimism and nihilism desert history, narratives, and the future, without realising how the falling apart of the world and its necessities may open up new horizons. Trying to metabolise the lesson of nihilism, one could draw a parallel between this world, absolutely devoid of observers, laws, and directions, and nothingness, that which for us is devoid of all meaning, form, value, and consistency: a concept that is negative in and of itself, escaping every partial perspective (something like the negative God of apophatic mysticism). The world is the totality of things, of facts, of narratives...nothingness is the abyss of the unknown, of the unspeakable, of the unknowable, of absolute unknowing. If everything there is, including the universe, has emerged from nothingness (regularity from chaos, meaning from meaninglessness, comprehensibility from incomprehensibility, melody from noise), and is composed of this same nothingness, then it follows that

---

5.   D. Benatar, *Better Never to Have Been* (Oxford: Oxford University Press, 2006).

nothingness is a plastic and malleable material from which it is possible to extract infinite worlds and infinite meanings. The trick is not to let oneself be captivated by these constructions, not to believe the lies that they whisper in our ears.

In a note dated 8 September 1821, Giacomo Leopardi wrote:

> My system introduces a Skepticism that is not only reasoned and proven, but is such that human reason, according to my system, whatever possible progress is made, will never succeed in ridding itself of this skepticism. On the contrary, it contains the truth [...] but that truth essentially consists in doubt, and whoever doubts knows, and knows as much as one can know.[6]

If classical theory (e.g. philosophies of Socratic or Cartesian inspiration) sees in the suspension of judgement a praxis or, better, a method of doubt, Leopardi's investigation propels thought, at insane speeds, right to the threshold where knowledge crumbles and doubt manifests itself as the absolute unknowability of reality. This limit, which gives onto the unlimited, like a sudden drop into the ocean, is the tangible, material product of a coherent path of rational research; an increasingly desperate, increasingly melancholic progression set out in clear opposition to a hypocritical programmatic *skepsis* (where knowledge is set aside, only to be dogmatically recovered immediately afterwards, perhaps with God as the guarantor of truth). To quote Nick Land, 'suspension is to be discovered, not performed'.[7] It would not, therefore, be a mere question of human limitation or the finitude of knowledge, but of the discovery of an abyss upon which existence itself is founded.

---

6.   G. Leopardi, *Zibaldone*, tr. K. Baldwin et al., ed. M. Caesar (Farrar, Strauss and Giroux, 2015), 760.

7.   N. Land, 'Art as Insurrection', *Fanged Noumena*, 177.

In this sense, Leopardi's work not only stands, as has often been noted, as a continuation of Enlightenment rationalism, but represents its very zenith. Leopardi's adherence to the materialism of his time, in fact, led him to some very peculiar conclusions. Let us start from a datum: since the exercise of reason is an analytical activity, i.e. the breaking down of the whole into simple parts, the result of a rational analysis of the natural world will be to 'resolve and undo nature', in such a way that '[n]ature, thus analyzed, differs not in the slightest from a corpse'.[8]

As we can see from the mere observation of the procedures of medical and anatomical sciences, the absolute simplicity attainable by analysis coincides with the rigidity of the dissected corpse, since the latter is the prerequisite for objective knowledge of the body. Nature, dissected by the scalpel of scientific rationality, passes from a state of dynamic vitality—a constant succession of vegetable and animal subjectivities and sensations—to a condition of inorganic objectivity: the living is manifested as an assembly of limbs, components that in themselves are inanimate.

In fact, one of the most obvious results of the life sciences is that, although they have stubbornly probed every nook and cranny of the body, they have been unable to identify any trace of a soul, spirit, or subject governing somatic matter. With scientific modernity, words, previously understood as an expression of the human soul, became a bridge between the ideas of the mind and the things of the world: material objects (of a sonic-vibrational type) capable of making comprehensible what would otherwise remain empty and indistinct, sensations. It is under the banner of Enlightenment materialism that Leopardi writes in the *Zibaldone*: 'Everything in our mind and faculties is material. The intellect could do nothing without speech, because the word is almost the body of the most abstract idea', and then adds, a few days later: 'The heart may imagine that it loves the spirit, or feels something nonmaterial. But it is utterly deceiving itself'.[9]

---

8. Leopardi, *Zibaldone*, 1329–30.
9. Ibid., 761.

The illusory nature of the immaterial, i.e. of the 'self' and its chains of thought, is a recurring theme in Leopardi's notes, and the reason why his philosophical research can be seen as representing the culmination and, at the same time, the overcoming, of the Enlightenment project. Modern scientific knowledge is indeed based on the clarity of ideas and perceptions of a given observer, as well as on the total self-possession of this same observer. Doubting even the presence of a subject capable of doubt means depriving the scientific method of any cardinal reference—and the paradoxical aspect of the matter lies precisely in carrying out this subtraction according to a rational procedure. Eliminativism is the footstep that precipitates us into the abyss: if only sensory perceptions are considered real, then one must conclude that even the perception of the self, i.e. self-consciousness, is nothing more than a second-level perception—a perception of perceptions—without this global perception necessarily corresponding to a real state of affairs. In this sense, as Leopardi notes, '[a]ppearance not only suffices, it is the only thing that suffices [...]. Because substance without appearance makes no impression at all and achieves nothing and appearance with substance does not do anything or achieve anything more than without it. So you see that substance is pointless, and it all has to do with appearance'.[10]

This spectre of a formless, chaotic world, illusorily ordered by the mind, goes by the name of 'blind brain theory'. According to blind brain theory, the real world is immensely richer and more multifaceted than the one represented in our minds, which, in turn, are merely representations of representations, pseudo-objects that do not exist in material terms. In the words of the neurophilosopher Thomas Metzinger, the crux of the matter is that 'we do not experience the contents of our self-consciousness as the contents of a representational process [...] but simply as *ourselves, living in the world right now*'.[11] Thomas Ligotti approves this disturbing perspective:

10. Ibid., 1754.
11. T. Metzinger, *Being No One: The Self-Model Theory of Subjectivity* (Cambridge, MA: The MIT Press, 2003), 331.

In Metzinger's schema, a human being is not a 'person' but a mechanistically functioning 'phenomenal self-model' that simulates a person [...]. [N]aïve realism becomes a necessary prophylactic in order to ward off the terror concomitant with the destruction of our intuitions regarding ourselves and our status in the world. [H]e pulls no punches when he says, '[T]here are aspects of the scientific world-view which may be damaging to our mental well-being'.[12]

Plunging sensible knowledge—and reason itself—into a limbo of illusions, the path of scientific optimism is obliterated, catapulting the real world into timeless, meaningless, and purposeless darkness. One of the most frequent themes in Giacomo Leopardi's thought is precisely that of the damage done to human life by truth and scientific objectivity; a problem that Leopardi tackles in a way very similar to one of his most famous admirers, H.P. Lovecraft, who, in his *The Call of Cthulhu,* wrote that

the sciences, each straining in its own direction, have hitherto harmed us little; but some day the piecing together of dissociated knowledge will open up such terrifying vistas of reality, and of our frightful position therein, that we shall either go mad from the revelation or flee from the deadly light into the peace and safety of a new dark age.[13]

The senselessness of a cosmos stripped of human meanings, hopes, and goals soon becomes claustrophobic. Ray Brassier states that—having accepted the illusory nature of consciousness and the inevitable extinction in time of all individuals and all species, including the human species—'the subject of philosophy [i.e. the philosopher] must also recognize that he or

12.   T. Ligotti, *The Conspiracy Against the Human Race: A Contrivance of Horror* (London: Penguin, 2018), 95, 96, 98.

13.   H.P. Lovecraft, 'The Call of Cthulhu', *The H.P. Lovecraft Omnibus 3*, 61.

she is already dead, and that philosophy is neither a medium of affirmation nor a source of justification but, rather the organon of extinction'.[14]

Every philosophy, or rather, every idea of philosophy, is inaugurated by a 'decision', by the isolation of one aspect of reality that will subsequently become the foundation upon which thought is able to stand. For example, one might extract becoming from reality, producing a metaphysics of constant transformation, within which it would be impossible to step into the same river twice. Conversely, if we isolate the existence of something—the presence of an object and the truth of this presence before the mind and senses—we would obtain a metaphysical framework In which the change and disappearance of an object would be illogical or unthinkable (nothing is born from nothing, ergo nothing can return to nothing). Between the two positions there is an abyss: the abyss of incommunicability and conflict, the real abyss containing being and becoming, the mixture of these two principles and their absence. Reality escapes and resists all of our decisions to isolate a part of it, forcing us to become aware of the cuts and tears we make in the living flesh of the world.

The senselessness, chaos and non-knowledge that dominate the world of darkness can, however, furnish a practically unlimited supply of materials: real wealth rather than total defeat.

If the sciences already possess a certain claim to objectivity, as expressed in the identification of a whole series of states of affairs (such as the composition of molecules or genetic heredity), philosophy attempts to achieve an even more profound objectivity, asking us to bracket out everything we know about the world, opening us up to new configurations, each contained in turn within this same world: in a way very similar to science fiction, which, in its own way, also demonstrates the groundlessness of the world by exhibiting possible worlds.

More than two thousand years ago, philosophy promised to cultivate doubt and *skepsis*, vowing to destroy the shackles of the senses and of

14.   Brassier, *Nihil Unbound*, 239.

illusion, going beyond what 'appears'. This oath has often been interpreted as a tyrannical injunction to transcendence or a mystical delusion. What it heralded, however, was the coming of an era: the epoch in which shadows would be dissolved and reabsorbed into a blinding ocean of darkness.

But what about the 'real' end of the world? Catalysed by the thought of total destruction, darkness rises to the surface, negating everything. A horror that falls from the sky, like a thunderbolt, that operates on the cosmic scale—from the explosion of the sun to the impact of an asteroid, from elemental catastrophes to invasions by divine or semi-divine creatures—or that insinuates itself silently, flooding into our plane of reality from microscopic or intangible dimensions: epidemics and outbreaks of madness, animal and vegetable revolts, or the gradual accumulation of tiny electronic components that go to make up the new face of God. Each of us knows in our heart the time and destination: the decaying trajectories of a world that has become a reality are already inscribed in its founding axioms. Humankind has narrated its own end for thousands of years, discovering over time a mysterious and yet evident alignment of coincidences, imagining cosmic plots and divine conspiracies. The roads unravel, overlap and intertwine, producing enigmatic labyrinths. Whether or not there are any human beings, outside this maze there are only yet more labyrinths. The mirage dragging the carcass of the world toward the light is a ghostly call echoing from the future.

Total destruction is the maximum limit toward which the thought of reality tends. A proliferation of starry spaces, desolate wastelands, and unperturbed deserts that feed a desire for breadth, openness and vastness. If the world has fallen apart, if the end is already written somewhere between the lines, then we are free: free to go where we want and build what we want, free of the oppressive sense of responsibility with which modern philosophy has burdened us.

'Do what thou wilt' shall be the whole of the law. Our fragile partiality emanates from chaos—matter itself is this chaos and this hidden inscrutability—but multiplicity and lawlessness, hidden in the innermost core of things, also vibrate in the human soul. However frustrating, insubstantial, insane, or laughable all of this may be, there is only this fatality, this concordance between the unravelling of the real and the dissolution of the world. And if there were any teleology, it would only be the passage from a vague foreboding of doom to a scream full of horror.

When one is lost and abandoned in the night, one must learn to cultivate darkness.

CK

MATER DOLOROSA

Thou hast entered the night; dost thou yet lust for day?

Sorrow is my name, and affliction. I am girt about with tribulation. Here still hangs the Crucified One, and here the Mother weeps over the children that she hath not borne. Sterility is my name, and desolation.

Intolerable is thine ache, and incurable thy wound.

Aleister Crowley[1]

I. WORMS

I see now that my terrestrial ur-mother was ravished by something fanged and insane from the wilderness, and that I am a vampire veiled raggedly in humanity, corrupted from birth by an unholy intimacy with death.

Nick Land[2]

In my old school there was what I remember as a large, beautiful garden. My childhood friends and I used to spend long hours of freedom, hidden from the gaze of adults, lost in more or less innocent games amidst the strange, dirty, straggling plant life that often infests city gardens. The vegetation of that garden, along with the small animals that inhabited it, was a source of constant wonder for us: for week upon week we watched how the tender flowers of the sour cherry tree withered only to sprout fruits, which we ate religiously even though they were too tart and often already half-digested

---

1.   A. Crowley, with V.B. Neuburg and M. Desti, *The Vision and The Voice with Commentary and Other Papers* (York, ME: Samuel Weiser, 1998), 140.

2.   Land, *The Thirst for Annihilation*, 206.

by insect larvae. From the neighbouring garden we used to steal the sticky and sweetish berries of the American vine, and dared each other to touch the nettles that grew among its dark foliage. Sometimes, in the midst of the uncultivated bushes and tall grass, someone would find the motionless body of a sparrow or a hedgehog; then, as if in a magical rite to avert its horror, or perhaps just to spend a little longer in the company of the corpse, we would improvise a funeral, adorning the lifeless creature with garlands of flowers and marking the burial place with crooked crosses made of sticks tied up with grass.

In spring, hundreds of small blue *Veronica persica*, one of the most common flowers in the meadows of Lombardy, appeared in the grass between the dandelions and the daisies. Because of their light blue colour and the fine, multi-coloured stripes on their petals, these flowers are known by everyone as 'eyes of the Madonna' and are surrounded by various folk legends associating them with the Blessed Virgin. For me as a child, the idea of Our Lady's eyes took on an extraordinarily material character: I wondered incessantly to what mysterious divine anatomy those innumerable, tiny, faceless irises could belong. Sceptical, like all children, about the possibility of action at a distance, I imagined intricate underground networks of nerves and ganglia that might somehow connect those bizarre sensors to the heavenly abode of the Mother of God. Because their petals are so incredibly delicate that a mere touch is often enough to cause them to fall from their stems, plucking one of those flowers was a crime comparable to the desecration of a sacred relic, the punishment for which was far more terrible than the vengeance of any cruel god. Witnessing helplessly her own horrendous mutilation, the Virgin of Sorrows would burst into an inconsolable cry loud enough to deafen the universe, flooding everything with the desperate pain of those who can do nothing but love their executioner.

One spring afternoon, some of my classmates came to take me to an obscure corner of the garden where they had made a strange discovery. They had found, hidden in the grass, an earthworm with a body deformed by a strange bulge that moved beneath its slimy skin. After a quick consultation, we had no doubt as to the diagnosis of the condition afflicting the wretched invertebrate. The earthworm, we decided, must be a female about to give birth, tormented by a difficult and painful delivery; it was therefore our duty to intervene surgically in order to ease the labour and relieve the pain of the suffering mother. Armed only with a sharp stick, hesitant and full of enthusiastic disgust, we began to pierce the dark, gelatinous flesh of the animal, which twisted furiously around the instrument of its torment. I still remember perfectly the slow, excruciating contortions of its body, and the moment when a legion of innumerable microscopic white creatures swarmed out of its lacerated belly, confused and blinded by the sun. I turned away in revulsion, with the vague consciousness of having committed an ancient and unforgivable crime. As the sacrificial mother continued to writhe desperately, her still-living flesh now reduced to a pulp, fused indistinguishably with the soil, the little parasites scattered haphazardly, ready to infest a new body. The miracle of life was complete.

The spontaneous disgust often aroused by the sight of certain invertebrates seems to increase exponentially when we see them in pain. It will surely be agreed that few sights are more frightening and repulsive than the spasms of a dying insect. Which is strange, because our ancestral evolutionary divergence makes it difficult for us to feel any kind of genuine empathy for these creatures, and even leads us to doubt, on the basis of more or less well-founded speculations on the 'simplicity' of their nervous systems, whether they are capable of any experience equivalent to human pain.

The disavowal of the fact that worms and insects fully belong to the realm of the living is rooted in the ancient belief that they are nothing more than a spontaneous, abiogenetic proliferation of the *dirt* in which they live. The long-discredited notion of the spontaneous generation of some invertebrates survives in our cultural substratum, fuelled by their extraordinary generative capacity, which seems to entirely defy the reproductive economy of ordinary organisms. Think, for example, of the amazing ability of earthworms to regenerate entire segments of their bodies following amputation, which translates into the well-known legend according to which the body of an earthworm, if divided into two parts, will grow back symmetrically from both ends, producing two new identical individuals. Georges Bataille also comments on abiogenesis:

> The generative power of corruption is a naive belief responding to the mingled horror and fascination aroused in us by decay. [...] That nauseous, rank and heaving matter, frightful to look upon, a ferment of life, teeming with worms, grubs and eggs, is at the bottom of the decisive reactions we call nausea, disgust or repugnance. [...] Hence I can anticipate and live in expectation of that multiple putrescence that anticipates its sickening triumph in my person.[3]

This potential for indefinite duplication, which seems to develop exponentially as the organic approaches the inorganic, escapes any principle of the conservation of energy. Rather than a prodigious victory of the organism over death, however, this indefinite reproducibility by splitting, in which the original individual is constantly annulled, seems to bring bodies closer to a perpetual condition of living death. Here is Bataille again on the proximity of asexual reproduction to death: 'There is a point at which the original *one becomes two*. As soon as there are two, there is again discontinuity for each of the beings. But the process entails *one instant* of continuity between the two of them. The first one dies, but as it dies there is this moment of continuity between the two new beings.'[4]

The mitotic proliferation that characterises the hybrid matter of those organisms that inhabit the liminal zone between the organic and the inorganic is thus a process that necessarily depends on 'agony and dissolution': an indefinite multiplication of the potential to suffer, in which life is configured

3.   G. Bataille, *Erotism*, tr. M. Dalwood (San Francisco: City Lights, 1986), 56–57.
4.   Ibid., 13–14.

as a necessary condemnation to be submitted to an automatic, *parasitic* vital

process which proceeds inexorably. While it is not possible to attribute the

human experience of suffering across the board to the rest of the organic

world, it is nonetheless possible to find in the very nature of living matter a

more fundamental form of pain, which seems to be a kind of ancestral wound,

or a sort of original separation from a primitive condition of indistinction.[5]

As Leopardi reminds us in a famous page of the *Zibaldone*:

> The spectacle of such abundance of life when you first go into this garden
>
> lifts your spirits, and that is why you think it is a joyful place. But in truth
>
> this life is wretched and unhappy, every garden is like a vast hospital (a place
>
> much more deplorable than a cemetery), and if these beings feel, or rather,
>
> were to feel, surely not being would be better for them than being.[6]

II. IMMACULATE HEART

> Moreover, I will give you a new heart and put a new spirit within you; and I
>
> will remove the heart of stone from your flesh and give you a heart of flesh.
>
> Ezekiel 36:26

On the morning of 21 May 1972, Laszlo Toth, a geologist of Hungarian origin

naturalised as an Australian, attacked Michelangelo's *Pieta* in St Peter's

Basilica in the Vatican in one of the most infamous acts of vandalism in

history. Armed with a hammer, he repeatedly struck the face and left arm of

the marble image of the Madonna, scarring it beyond repair, shouting 'Christ

is risen! I am the Christ.' Although it may be pointless to look for any trace

---

5.   On the subject of pain in matter, see Nicola Masciandaro's 'Sorrow of Being: In Calignem':
'Suffering, far from being limited to the evolutionary environment of our terrestrial sphere, is more
properly understood as a strange kind of cosmic substance, composed of the rejection of the
whole being of itself, the intrinsic negation of its own event'. Masciandaro, *On The Darkness Of
The Will*, 73.

6.   Leopardi, *Zibaldone*, 1823.

of planning in the absurd gesture of a mentally ill man, the brutality of the assault is representative of the violent materiality so often associated with effigies of the Blessed Virgin. The cult of Our Lady of Sorrows, in particular, revolves around the miraculous events said to have befallen its numerous icons. In almost every Italian province it is possible to find the story of some depiction of the Virgin which, often following a disfigurement inflicted by an unbeliever, shed tears of blood as miraculous proof of her wounded love.

I find this ability to transmute blasphemy into triumph through the alchemical action of suffering to be one of the most fascinating aspects of the cult of the Virgin. Toth's sacrilegious action performed the miracle of making the beauty of the Madonna of the *Pieta*, already considered so sublime as to be almost blasphemous, yet more numinous and dazzling.

In traditional iconography, Our Lady of Sorrows is depicted weeping, her heart exposed and pierced by seven daggers, each of which corresponds to one of the seven sorrows suffered by Our Lady in the Gospels. The number 7 recurs in religious symbolism, and its importance is widely discussed in the Hermetic tradition, where it is almost always associated with the manifestation of divine perfection in matter. From the Christian perspective, though, 7 represents the conjunction of the trinity with the four corners of the Earth, and thus describes the realisation of God's kingdom within this world. In traditional systems of ceremonial magic, the Kabbalistic meaning of 7 is similarly interpreted as the sum of the soul and the four elements, and is thus 'the power of magic in all its force; it is the spirit assisted by all the elemental powers; it is the soul served by nature'.[7] The number 7 has been central to the classification of the natural world since the dawn of the Hermetic tradition in the West, a tradition in which it constantly recurs as a mysterious and pervasive harmonic function underlying the divine order hidden in matter: it appears in the planets as observed by the ancients, in the metals of alchemy, in the colours of the rainbow, and in the notes of the diatonic scale.

---

7.   Lévi, *The Doctrine and Ritual of High Magic*, 95.

References to alternative interpretations of the number 7 are rare and fragmentary in theosophical and esoteric literature, and often shrouded in an impenetrable cloak of mystery. One notable case is the work of Aleister Crowley, in which the number 7 frequently appears in association with the sphere of the divine feminine. In Crowley's work, 7 is unequivocally and recurrently connected to the apocalyptic figure of Babalon, whose symbol is the seven-pointed star that appears in the seal of the A∴A∴ (Astrum Argenteum, the magical order founded by Crowley in 1907), and whose name corresponds to the Kabbalistic sum 7+(7+7)/7+7 (reasonably enough, it is precisely in order to manifest this numerological equivalence that the Greek Βαβυλὼν was transliterated into Babalon).[8] The number 7 is also recurrent in the so-called Enochian system, a complex schema for angelic evocation transmitted to the Elizabethan mathematician John Dee and his assistant Edward Kelley at the end of the sixteenth century. The Enochian system exhibits a structure that might be defined as heptomaniacal: it is centred around complex matrices of letters organised according to multiples of the number 7. Crowley, who was familiar with Dee's angelology through the magical order of the Golden Dawn, included many aspects of it in his own magic, beginning with the word Babalon, which in the angelic language corresponds to the English word wicked.

Babalon is the name given by the religion of Thelema to the Whore of Babylon, the scarlet woman of the Book of Revelation, a necessarily complex and multiform figure that has fascinated esoteric thinkers for generations. It is not the intention of this text to propose an exhaustive exegesis of the symbolism of the Whore of Babylon, upon which much has already been said

---

8.   'In Her wine-cup are seven streams of the blood of the Seven Spirits of God.
      Seven are the heads of THE BEAST whereon she rideth.
      The head of an Angel: the head of a Saint: the head of Poet: the head of An Adulterous Woman: the head of a Man of Valour: the head of a Satyr: and the head of a Lion-Serpent.
      Seven letters hath Her holiest name; and it is BABALON.' A. Crowley, Liber 333: The Book of Lies, Falsely So-Called (Ilfracombe: Haydn Press, 1952), 104.

and written (see the work of Jack Parsons, Peter Gray, and Amy Ireland).[9] There is no doubt that the Whore of Babylon, as presented to us in the biblical text, embodies a sinister and voluptuous femininity, in symmetrical opposition to the pious and sorrowful femininity of the heavenly woman who appears in Revelation 12:1. The same symmetry is maintained, with an additional level of political meaning, in the comparison between the perverse metropolis of Babylon and Jerusalem, the city of God, in Revelation 21–22. The number 7 pervades the whole of the Bible, but, in light of our considerations here, we are particularly interested in its association with the feminine, which recurs on two—again, significantly symmetrical—occasions:

> 1 A great sign appeared in heaven: a woman clothed with the sun, with the moon under her feet and a crown of twelve stars on her head. 2 She was pregnant and cried out in pain as she was about to give birth. 3 Then another sign appeared in heaven: an enormous red dragon with seven heads and ten horns and seven crowns on its heads.[10]

> 3 Then the angel carried me away in the Spirit into a wilderness. There I saw a woman sitting on a scarlet beast that was covered with blasphemous names and had seven heads and ten horns. 4 The woman was dressed in purple and scarlet, and was glittering with gold, precious stones and pearls. She held a golden cup in her hand, filled with abominable things and the filth of her adulteries. 5 The name written on her forehead was a mystery: BABYLON THE GREAT, THE MOTHER OF PROSTITUTES AND OF THE ABOMINATIONS OF THE EARTH.[11]

---

9.   Parsons, *The Book of Babalon*; A. Dimech and P. Grey, *The Brazen Vessel* (London: Scarlet Imprint, 2019); Ireland 'Black Circuit, Code for the Numbers to Come'.

10.   Revelation 12:1–3 NIV.

11.   Revelation 17:3–5 NIV.

The vision of these two contrasting female figures is accompanied in both cases by a demonic creature with seven heads and ten horns, which in the first case plays a role that is antagonistic toward the celestial woman, seeking to devour her child and thus to remove it from the divine light, while in the second case it seems to enter into a sort of mysterious alliance with the scarlet woman. The traditional interpretation of the number 7 as a manifestation of the spiritual order in matter seems to me insufficient to explain the catastrophic scope of these visions, just as it is hopelessly inadequate in the face of the suffering eroticism of the heart of the *Mater Dolorosa* pierced by seven daggers. This reflection, together with the fascination for the figure of the Virgin of Sorrows, has been a stimulus to my research on aspects of the divine feminine in esoteric and Kabbalistic material, trying to understand how to approach it in all its fluidity and complexity, even beyond the strictly numerological considerations that accompany such images.

Let me clarify one point here: in the face of the inadequacy of the interpretations available to us, it is certainly legitimate to surrender to the *contingency of symbols*. On the other hand, we cannot make any claim as to the coherence of the hallucinations of John of Patmos, let alone the legacy of a confused and bastardised tradition such as that upon which Aleister Crowley's work draws. Although our aim is therefore not (and cannot be) to base an historically accurate and simultaneously religiously meaningful exegesis of these ancient and modern revelations in the historical and existential context of those who delivered them to us, we still face the difficult task of receiving and transcribing the voices of symbols that call to us from the depths of the future. The more we succeed in doing this by setting aside man—the *prophet*—the better we will have answered our call.

The typical Neoplatonic reading of the Kabbalistic material proposed by the initiatic traditions, which flowed from Renaissance Hermeticism into nineteenth-century Theosophy and contributed to the formation of a large part of contemporary exoteric doctrines, presents a vision of the cosmic order as a linear and unproblematic emanation from divine unity, overflowing from an original point and spilling over into the manifold aspects of creation, which are then classified according to a descending hierarchy based on their distance from the *source*, the fount of being.[12] The rigidity of this view has been accompanied by an inadequate and inherently oppressive discussion of the role of the feminine, understood simply as a passive and receptive aspect of the process of emanating divine light.[13] On the other hand, Western initiatory paths are profoundly flawed because they neglect the central position occupied by *pain* and *restraint* in the original Kabbalistic material which their tradition purports to draw upon. This is part of the larger and more complex problem of confronting the inability of earlier esoteric traditions to deal with the *processual* and *dynamic* aspects of Kabbalah, which—for reasons that appear immediately obvious when approaching any mystical text—cannot be contained in the immobility of the Tree of Life glyph on which the Right Hand Path has so obsessively fixated.

The need to revolutionise this approach lies not so much in a claim to historical accuracy with respect to the ancient sources of esoteric

---

12.   As an example of this limited view of the Kabbalah I quote a passage from Dion Fortune's *Mystical Qabalah*, still considered a good introduction to Kabbalistic doctrine by many practitioners of different initiatic traditions: 'Let us conceive of Kether, then, as a fountain which fills its basin, and the overflow therefrom feeds another fountain, which in its turn fills its basin and overflows. The Unmanifest for ever flows under pressure into Kether, and there comes a time when evolution has gone as far as it can in the extreme simplicity of the form of existence of the First Manifest. All possible combinations have been formed, and they have undergone all possible permutations. Action and reaction are stereotyped, there can be no new development save the combining of the combinations among themselves. Force has formed all possible units; the next phase of development is for these units to combine into more complex structures. When this occurs, a new and more highly organised phase of existence begins; all that has already been evolved remains, but that which evolves now is more than the sum of the previously existing parts, for new capacities come into being.' D. Fortune, *The Mystical Qabalah* (York Beach, ME: Samuel Weiser, 1999), 40–41.

13.   In this regard, I share the views of Alkistis Dimech and Peter Grey in their text 'My Time is Come: An Erotic Eschatology of Babalon': 'The emanationist God of Neoplatonism remains on his throne. The adept of Thelema lives in a New Age in which the rules have supposedly changed in a fundamental way, but the baggage train of Empire follows closely behind. The goddess does not threaten to descend, as in Dee, but is safely removed into the aethyr whilst the bodies of actual women serve naked on the altar as receptacles for sperm and with no creative potential in their own right.' *The Brazen Vessel*, 419.

thought—a claim that neither we nor anyone else can make—but rather in an understanding of its necessary insufficiency in the face of the fluidity of the symbolic manifestations of the divine feminine. It is our task, as contemporary esotericists, to give voice to the urgency of exploring those conflicting and problematic aspects which the initiatic traditions, whether through superficialism or revisionism, have sought to flatten, transforming the dynamics of the Kabbalistic machinery into what is little more than a convoluted system of lifts and escalators to gnosis.

In the *Zohar*,[14] a fundamental text of the Kabbalistic tradition, there are several moments of nonlinearity in the emanation, moments at which the descent of the divine into matter—and in turn the ascent of matter into the divine—is interrupted and complicated. These moments take the form of *contractions—tzimtzum*—which the divine light imposes upon itself, and which are at the same time indispensable to its manifestation. Any criticism of the structure of the Hermetic Kabbalah as proposed by Western esoteric thought must necessarily begin with a thorough reflection on its points of nonlinearity, which were not included in the dogmas of the initiatory traditions, or if they were, they were carefully concealed.

In particular, it is interesting to note that these processes of *rupture* and *separation* are centred around aspects of the emanation mechanism that are commonly associated with the feminine, and that they are focused in particular on two of the ten *sefirot* or levels traditionally included in the divine emanation process: the sefira Binah and the sefira Malkuth.

These two sefirot appear to be involved in an uninterrupted and symmetrical series of transmutations and movements, both descending and ascending, which lead them to merge and separate from each other several times:

14.   In our research we have made extensive use of Michael Laitman's edition of the *Zohar* and its commentary by Rabbi Yehuda Ashlag. Despite our efforts to give credit to the complexity and depth of the material upon which our research is based, we feel it is important to emphasise that the present essay should not be interpreted as an exegesis or commentary on the texts of Jewish mysticism, any more than it is a commentary on the Kabbalistic writings of Blavatsky, Crowley, Mathers, or Fortune.

'Who is this coming up from the wasteland?' (Shir HaShirim, 3:6). *MI ZOT*— who is this—is the common ground of the two questions, the two worlds, Bina and Malchut, which are bound together. COMING UP—coming up to become the 'Holy of Holies'. For *MI* is *Bina*, called the Holy of Holies. And she joins with *ZOT* (Malchut), so that *Malchut* could come up FROM THE WASTELAND.[15]

It is not our intention here to trace the precise course of these two sefirot in the Kabbalistic 'system', assuming such a system exists. But it is clear that there is a divine feminine aspect trapped within the walls of the architecture of creation which, rather than identifying itself with one or more specific entities, emerges in the form of a dynamic and multiform process. Perhaps the greatest failing of contemporary esoteric reflection on femininity lies in the necessarily unsuccessful attempt to contain it within the rigid schema of divinity as an individual, petrifying the aspects of *transition* and *movement* that are characteristic of it. From this perspective, any form of feminine monotheism—including that of Babalon—is not an adequate response to the problem of the marginalisation of femininity in esoteric traditions, neither is the project of making explicit a divine feminine aspect that is complementary or symmetrical to the divine masculine.

Moreover, the greatest warning against these errors, which has too often passed unnoticed by even the most devout believers, is contained in the very name of the great Babylon, whose antiquated meaning—the *door, passage*, or *gate*—leaves no doubt as to its profound nature: it is something that must be *passed through* if one really wishes to understand it. In this sense, we must move within the Kabbalistic machinery in light of its capacity for the indefinite separation and duplication of feminine identities: not so much by seeking to localise an original feminine principle to replace or oppose the masculine source, but rather by seeking to liberate the feminine in the processual, necessarily delocalised aspects of the divine organism.

15. *The Zohar*, ed. M. Laitman (Toronto: Laitman Kabbalah Publishers, 2009), 347.

Returning to the movements of *tzimtzum*, we can define them as those processes of *separation* within the divinity that are necessary for its manifestation. The process of correction, i.e. repairing the distance separating Malkuth, the creation, from the light of its creator, can only be accomplished through the division of Binah, the heavenly Mother, and the *fall* of her *seven* lower sefirot into corruption and darkness.

The divine light that Binah makes descend in Malkuth to correct it in its darkness is described by the *Zohar* using the image of *tears falling into the Great Sea*:

> He remembers her, He strikes 390 firmaments, and they all tremble with terrible fear before Him. And the Creator sheds tears for the Shechina (Divinity), Malchut that has fallen to the dust. And those tears simmer like fire, and fall into the Great Sea.[16]

This painful process of separation of the original mother, who makes the existence of the world possible, unmistakably recalls the myth of the dismemberment of the draconic Virgin-Mother Tiamat.[17] The celestial symbolism associated with Binah is contrasted with the floral symbolism of Malkuth, which is connected to the image of the *rose among thorns*, illuminated by divine light but soiled with the *red* of the impure and demonic forces that act upon it in its distance from divinity, represented by *exile in the desert*.

This feminine polarity, characterised by the tension between two aspects that are mysteriously identified but at the same time radically distant, when considered together with the symbolism that accompanies the two sefirot, refers us unequivocally to the vision of the two women of the Book of Revelation. In the course of such processes of rupture and estrangement, the decimal structure of the sefirot is decapitated, the chain of emanation is interrupted, and the divine order is subject to the influence of impure forces

16.   Ibid., 200.
17.   See 'Catastrophic Astrology', in this volume.

that fill the *empty shells* of the seven sefirot, once destined to contain the light in creation but which have now been shattered.

According to Gershom Scholem's interpretation, the process of original rupture refers to the root of a primordial suffering in the world, which arises from the necessary distance, or exile, of creation from its creator: 'Thus, since that primordial act, all being has been a being in exile, in need of being led back and redeemed. The breaking of the vessels continues into all the further stages of emanation and Creation; everything is in some way broken, everything has a flaw, everything is unfinished';[18] the three apocalyptic female aspects of the *Dragon*, the *Celestial Virgin* and the great *Babylon* falling in flames must be understood as processes belonging to the same cosmological mechanism of separation.[19] In devising forms of ritual magic capable of sustaining effective occult guerrilla warfare against hetero-patriarchal dogma, it is essential to become aware of the internal mechanisms of the divine architecture in which there occur those phenomena of disequilibrium that secretly make it possible. These moments of disequilibrium are the hidden engines of the process of divine emanation, in which the feminine continually manifests itself as an inexhaustible generative force, a sacrificial victim, and a receptacle for the corrupt dross expelled from the cosmic order. Decoupling these processes from the architecture that produced them yields a monstrous, headless machine which advances irreversibly by mitotic duplication, suffocating the structure that generated it.

III. MIGRAINE

And then I saw a great star, splendid and beautiful, come forth [...] and with that star came a great multitude of shining sparks, which followed the star

---

18. Scholem, *On the Kabbalah and its Symbolism*, 112–13.

19. This tripartite structure is included in our ritual practice and manifested through the use of the tri-triangular seal as a machine for the evocation of the Dismembered Mother Tiamat. On this subject, see the text 'Ritual: Every Worm Trampled is a Star', in this volume.

toward the South [...]. But [...] they were all extinguished and were changed into black cinders [...] they were precipitated into the abyss and vanished from my sight.

Hildegard of Bingen[20]

Sometimes, as I drag myself through the insignificant misery of my life, your beauty pierces me like a dart of tenderness. I see the pale young flesh of your face, brave and desperate like a winter rose, marked by crystals of tears, and your eyes appear to me liquid and frightening like lunar jellyfish luminescent in the abyss. Everything is superfluous and resplendent. The filthy iridescent puddles of diesel, the wreckage plagued by rust, the desperate vegetation crawling with parasites in the cracks of the concrete.

The city is a spiral of nausea. Everything is coming to pieces, falling into a Babel of fragments, in a continuous production of ragged shreds of stuttering, useless matter. In this crumbling and absurd edifice, everyone carries their own stone. My stone is the supermarket receipt that fell out of my pocket and the imprint of chewing gum stuck under the sole of my left shoe. My stone is the fine coal dust that adheres to the train carriage and the half-detached sign that says not to lean against the doors. The city is a sarcophagus of forgotten hieroglyphs.

Pieces of decaying matter rest there, marked with occult ideograms faded by the sun, the Word inexorably breaking down into the primitive alphabet of dust. All things weep toward the ancient heat imprisoned in the heart of the earth. The heart of the earth is a shining wound that bleeds, inconsolably, your name. Migraine is a pain that overflows from the confines of myself, percolating into every last particle of matter; it is a pain without a wound, because it reveals the wound in the heart of the world.

Sometimes I walk through the city in a state of apnoea, as though submerged in amniotic fluid. Pain is a crawling insect that lurks behind the bulbs

---

20. Hildegard of Bingen, *Scivias*, tr. Mother C. Hart, J. Bishop (Mahwah, NJ and New York: Paulist Press, 1990), 309.

of my eyes, injecting them with a miraculous prophetic poison that reveals in everything its blinding aura and the dark spectre of its decomposition.

At first the attacks were brief and sporadic, of tolerable intensity, comparable to any common headache. But with the passing of the years, the crises began to become strangely cyclical and terrifyingly intense, so that I lived, in moments of particular discomfort, with an almost constant sense of anxiety.

I vaguely remember being locked in a hotel room for two days without eating or drinking, wavering between consciousness and unconsciousness, overcome by incessant gagging. My skin trembled, covered with a thick layer of icy sweat. Sleep was a slimy, disgusting substance in which an unknown spectral power constantly forced me to immerse myself, only to emerge increasingly exhausted and drained. My medication is tryptamines, which induce a strange numbness, like a small, localised paralysis around the jaw and at the back of the throat, making me feel almost strangled. When I feel the doses—a few tens of milligrams at a time—wear off and the numbness fades without having relieved the pain, I start to feel afraid.

After twelve hours of vomiting and fasting, one's stomach is empty and all that comes up is bile. One's mouth is so bitter that water tastes like sugar syrup. In the course of these episodes one becomes so close to the floor that its harsh coldness is almost strangely consoling. Some nights I spent screaming. I remember lying in bed exhausted, and in the heart of my absurd grief I was pierced by a vision of luminous nostalgia. The quiet, yearning dream of a primitive motherhood deep in my spasming womb.

Migraine crises pass of their own accord, just as they arrived, without a trace. All that remains is an alienating feeling of a suspicious wellbeing, something for which one feels almost guilty—a little like the miraculous survivors of a massacre must feel. Perhaps precisely because of the absence of any easily identifiable source of pain, the impression is not so much that of an evil that has passed, but rather of having achieved access, by occult spiritual means, to a kind of parallel dimension of the world, which continues to exist independently, hidden beneath the veil of ordinary reality. Because the pain of migraine is not located in a point inside one's own body, but rather emanates like black light from the surrounding matter, emerging from a crisis is like leaving behind the shattered ruin of reality, abandoning it in its secret misery.

In this sense I would say that the migraine attack, as absolutely hateful and revolting as it is, has the character of a sinister unveiling—an experience similar to that of certain dreams in which everyday reality is reproduced with surprising accuracy except for a few misplaced objects, a slightly distorted perspective, an unnatural light as of a black sun in the night; dreams from which one emerges with the persistent suspicion of never having actually awakened. If what manifests itself to the hallucinatory gaze of the migraine sufferer is indeed an arcane substratum of the world, then the comfort between crises is only a temporary deafness to the atrocious and obscene cry that forever courses through creation.

On the subject of the prophetic character of migraine attacks—which in some cases can take on an almost cosmological significance—the neurologist Oliver Sacks reports the following testimony of a patient describing his experience:

> There seems to be a sort of hole in my memory and mind and, so to speak, a hole in the world; and yet I cannot imagine what might go in the hole. [...] I have the feeling that my body—that *bodies* are unstable, that they may come apart and lose parts of themselves [...]. There is still a certain residue of dread, and a fear that the scotoma may go on forever....[21]

The idea of a mysterious and revelatory evil, at once physical and moral, through which the suffering victim achieves the realisation of profound spiritual truths, belongs squarely within the tradition of female mysticism. To quote Sacks again, 'the subject of migraine aura is touched with the incomprehensible and the incommunicable: nay, this lies at its very center,

---

21.   O. Sacks, *Migraine* (London: Picador, 1995), 95.

its heart'[22]—the heart of mystical experience. Sacks himself indicates the similarity of many ecstatic experiences to migraine auras, which 'include not only simple and complex sensory hallucinations, but intense affective states, deficits and disturbances of speech and ideation, dislocations of space- and time-perception, and a variety of dreamy, delirious, and trance-like states'.[23]

Many of the characteristics of the maladies described by the ecstatic seem, in their sudden, devastating, and mysteriously transitory character, to converge with those of migraine or epileptic attacks, two conditions that can often be confused for one another, presenting surprisingly similar symptoms. A case in point, of course, is Teresa of Ávila, who, on 15 August 1539, during what she called her *conversion*, suffered a terrible paroxysm that plunged her into a comatose state for days, and left her almost totally paralysed for three years. In *The Book of Her Life*, Teresa describes the sickness as follows:

> Such were these four days I spent in this paroxysm that only the Lord can know the unbearable torments I suffered within myself: my tongue, bitten to pieces; my throat unable to let even water pass down—from not having swallowed anything and from the great weakness that oppressed me; everything seemed to be disjointed; the greatest confusion in my head; all shrivelled and drawn together in a ball. The result of the torments of those four days was that I was unable to stir, not an arm or a foot, neither hand nor head, unable to move as though I were dead; only one finger on my right hand it seems I was able to move.[24]

Continuing to read Teresa's autobiography, one is struck by the similarity between the description of this terrible illness, which brought her to the brink of death, and the accounts of her *transports* or *raptures*, which are

---

22. Ibid., 52.
23. Ibid., 53.
24. Teresa of Ávila, *The Book of Her Life*, tr. K. Kavanaugh, O. Rodriguez (Indianapolis: Hackett, 2008), 24.

described with the same vocabulary and the same intensity of suffering; the difference is that agony is superimposed here with the joy of ecstasy, in what the saint calls 'an arduous, delightful martyrdom':[25] in the course of the ecstasy, in fact, Teresa reports that 'when the body is in rapture it is as though dead',[26] and that 'even the next day I feel pain in the pulse and in the body, as if the bones were disjoined'.[27] Throughout the different levels of mystical experience classified by Teresa, the idea recurs that the approach to the divine that takes place in ecstasy is essentially an experience that is independent of consciousness and will, and which afflicts the soul like a disease, which it is hopeless to try and bring about intellectually and which it is pointless to try to resist.

It is interesting to compare this kind of ecstatic experience with the meditative experiences commonly sought in initiatic traditions, which coincide with states of absolute *concentration* that obliterate individual consciousness and elevate it to a state of consciousness that we might call cosmic or universal. Here the word *concentration* is not to be understood only in its common sense, that is, as referring to the ability of the intellect to exclude external stimuli and invocatory thoughts in order to focus on a single object or image, but must be understood as a condition that transcends the personal boundaries of the initiate and attains an essentially cosmological scope, indicating a *punctual* state in which the maximum centripetal attraction is realised, and in which the universe manifests itself as emanating from an absolute centre with which the initiate's consciousness comes to coincide. The attainment of such a state of absolute *concentration* is commonly achieved through the constant exercise of meditation practices, almost always borrowed from some 'oriental tradition'. As an example of this approach, it seems significant to quote a passage from *Liber Null* by Peter J. Carroll, considered one of the founders of Chaos Magic:

---

25. Ibid., 125.
26. Ibid., 127.
27. Ibid., 125.

The particular state of mind required has a name in every tradition: No-mind. Stopping the internal dialogue, passing through the eye of the needle, *ain* or nothing, *sama-dhi*, or onepointedness. In this book it will be known as *Gnosis*. [...] In the inhibitory mode, the mind is progressively silenced until only a single object of concentration remains. In the excitatory mode, the mind is raised to a very high pitch of excitement while concentration on the objective is maintained. [...] Thus, strong inhibition and strong excitation end up creating the same effect—the one-pointed consciousness, or gnosis. [...] It is during these moments of single-pointed concentration, or gnosis, that beliefs can be implanted for magic, and the life force induced to manifest.[28]

In the usual universalistic spirit of Chaos Magic, all mystical experiences are thus grouped together under the single goal of achieving the *absolute concentration of gnosis* that brings the initiate into coincidence with God. In fact, what is generally regarded as the most innovative and postmodern current of magic—and which many believe definitely obsolesces any other attempts to build new self-sufficient and separatist systems of magic—is once again manifested in its inherently reactionary intent to reduce all magical and mystical experiences under the single banner of a manic cult of the Centre.

The path traced by the ecstatic indicates an alternative route, radically opposed to those of concentration of consciousness. In approaching this painfully introspective and radically feminine material, it is necessary to be aware that the centrality of *suffering* proposed by the ecstatic is to be understood as a self-sufficient mystical goal, and not simply as another path to the same state of gnosis to which the initiatic traditions aspire. The ecstatic path traced by Teresa proposes suffering itself as *the highest form of gnosis*,[29] the only one in which consciousness can perceive its own

---

28. P.J. Carroll, *Liber Null* (Newburyport, MA: Red Wheel Weiser, 1987), 29.
29. See the 'The Highest Form of Gnosis', in this volume.

necessary separation from the divine light: a prophetic state of 'glorious foolishness, [...] heavenly madness'[30] in which 'the soul [...] is as though crucified between heaven and earth'.[31]

IV. LUNA

> The shadow of the Rock has grown darker and longer. They sit rooted to the ground and cannot move. The dreadful shape is a living monster lumbering towards them across the plain, scattering rocks and boulders. So near now, they can see the cracks and hollows where the lost girls lie rotting in a filthy cave.[32]
>
> Joan Lindsay

I have always lived in cities, of varying sizes, in areas that are highly urbanised and all equally segregated from the wild. On the other hand, since my puberty, I have been strongly susceptible to the idea of having something necessarily wild within me. Such a feeling of radical separation from civilisation was the mark of a hyper-aware femininity, which I portrayed to myself as a kind of untameable natural force. This story, which I kept repeating to myself incessantly, concealed the acute and painful awareness of my unbridgeable insufficiency. What had previously been only the vague consciousness of a female identity (in which—by attitude or education—I found it hard to recognise myself) had suddenly revealed itself as a bodily reality: and while I admired my slender legs growing with vigorous beauty, I realised that my dreams of enthusiastic participation in the world were set to tragically crash against the harsh reality of my female function as a desired object and almost never as a desiring subject.

---

30. Teresa of Ávila, *The Book of Her Life*, 96.
31. Ibid., 125.
32. J. Lindsay, *Picnic at Hanging Rock* (London: Vintage, 2013), 136.

Confronted with the impossibility of participating in the human community in the full and uncompromising way that is granted in its entirety only to men, I withdrew into the comfort of thinking myself entirely other: an force alien to civilisation, if not, in some way, its very nemesis. I dreamt of escaping into the woods, where, amidst the soft moss and lichen-coloured tree bark, to the sound of a clear stream twisting among the rocks, I imagined that I would live forever as a swift and solitary Artemis. The woods and their solitude, however, were always essentially closed to me. That romantic encounter with sublime, unspoilt nature which I so desperately longed for, has in practice always been an experience almost entirely reserved for men. If the supposed weaknesses of my female body and the perpetual threat of rape were not enough to keep me away from any remote, unspoilt place, what oppressed me—even more than the bans and curfews—was a kind of self-imposed responsibility to preserve my feminine nature intact in the face of the wilderness. Any laceration, whether in body or mind, would be a gateway for that wildness to creep up on me and possess me entirely, erasing any remaining traces of my precarious humanity and dragging me into a vortex of orgiastic and self-destructive hunger.

There are those who go into the woods *because they wish to deliberately enjoy the virile privilege of a dialectical confrontation with the uncontaminated purity of wild nature, which qualifies as an absolute outside* from which, through the struggle, a renewed humanity emerges victorious and civilised. 'I scent no compromise in the fragrance of the water-lily. It is not a Nymphoea Douglasii. In it, the sweet, and pure, and innocent are wholly sundered from the obscene and baleful.'[33] But for me the depths of the forest were as obscene and violent as my pubescent body. I found myself so extraordinarily exiled in that same wild strangeness that was necessarily closed to me: no place, human or inhuman, could belong to me.

---

33.   H.D. Thoreau, 'Slavery in Massachusetts', in *The Writings of Henry David Thoreau, Journal, Volume 8: 1854*, ed. S. H. Petrulionis (Princeton, NJ: Princeton University Press, 1981), 195.

Virginity is a blood pact. It is born in the thick blood of the first menstruation and is extinguished in the slimy blood of the torn hymen. However much it may be trampled upon and suffocated in fear, at the root of virginal integrity vibrates a solemn feeling: the consciousness of a warrior power that can sacrifice everything because it can never renounce itself.

Virginity is so intimately entwined with death because it is a brutal sacrament of war: it is the promise to remain true to oneself and the radical refusal to participate in the reproductive order of civilisation, in full consciousness of holding both the key to its maintenance and the key to its destruction. In the eyes of young women there is a hazy Amazonian awareness of their own self-sufficiency—an absolute *self-monotheism* capable of plunging the universe into ruin.

In the face of the violence that creeps into every man's gaze, the fragile beauty of the virgin is transformed into the total, suicidal negation of life itself. On the virginal integrity of the vestal priestesses depended the sacred flame that maintained order in the city of Rome, just as the purity of the holy warrior Joan of Arc, which burned with her in the flames of the stake, kept the destiny of the kingdom of France intact. In the virgin's absolute vulnerability is hidden the unutterable secret of a destructive cosmic power: a shining purity that passes through creation, prophetically flickering like the fire of a meteor. By virtue of its profoundly paradoxical and necessarily elusive nature, virginity is a sacred condition that belongs to the initiatory mysteries of the feminine. In this respect, it is like the Gorgon's gaze, which cannot be described by any human being except by the groan that remains forever choked between the petrified lips of the dying warrior.

Those who approach the bloody purity of Artemis do so with the full knowledge that the price of outrage will be paid in flesh torn by the bites of her dogs, and they offer themselves for food with joy. The intimately paradoxical aspect of virginity, at once guardian of the reproductive order and its absolute negation, is well described by Pierre Klossowski, who in his *The*

Bath of Diana comments on the myth of Artemis and Actaeon as narrated by Ovid in the *Metamorphoses*:

> [Diana] formed healthy young girls in her own image and was nonetheless '*a lioness for women*'; she loosed ravaging monsters across the countrysides of kingdoms hostile or indifferent to her altars, as the hunt became more and more a *game* than an economic necessity, as if to remind men that, being a sign of both the dark and serene aspects of the universe, she presided over her wholeness. Now in what respect did this wholeness coincide with her virginal nature, correspond to her chastity? Why did she renounce the emotions that animate the universe? Was she hiding, from the gods as well as the mortals, her other face eternally? Acteon did not rightly understand that the wholeness of the universe could rest on a *single* deity, nor that a feminine deity, exclusive of any male deity, might express herself in the singleness of a *closed* nature, sufficient unto herself, finding in chastity the fullness of her essence. Goddess beyond destiny, with whom no mortal, even at destiny's behest, could presume to join in union.[34]

This paradoxical aspect of Diana—at once shining and dark, chaste and perverse, protector and destroyer—is reflected in the lunar symbolism associated with the iconography of Artemis, which highlights 'her double nature: murderous and luminous, or rather, luminous because murderous',[35] and which reveals her 'as the principle of life at the core of death or as the principle of death at the core of being'.[36] The moon is a multiform object whose associations are innumerable and often contradictory; the problem can be summed up in the enigma of a star that is both celestial and chthonic, necessarily double, in a reverberation of perpetual self-reflection

---

34.   P. Klossowski, 'Diana at Her Bath', tr. S. Sartarelli, *Diana at Her Bath and The Women of Rome* (New York: Marsilio, 1998), 11–12.

35.   Ibid., 17.

36.   Ibid.

and subversion.[37] In seeking in the moon any familiar and reassuring principle, we find only the disturbing reflection of its perversion, which responds to us with a pale and bleeding smile. The light emitted by the moon is a reflected and diverted light, like a degenerate and impure double of the light of the sun, and emits a spectral radiance tainted by contact with the ancient dust of its craters.

From a Kabbalistic perspective, the moon is associated with the sefira Malkuth, the impure aspect of the divine feminine, because of its property of reflecting light, which is imposed on it by the creator as a primordial *constraint.* To quote Scholem, 'this "lessening of the moon" was interpreted by the Kabbalists as a symbol of the *Shekhinah*'s exile. The *Shekhinah* itself is the "holy moon", which has fallen from its high rank, been robbed of its light and sent into cosmic exile'.[38] More than any other aspect, however, it is the cyclicality of the moon's phases that is ineffable and deeply sinister; it combines the moon's astral and abyssal natures, linking it to the movement of the tides, the reproductive cycles of countless marine animals, and the female menstrual cycle. The cycle evokes the horror of the Flood, incessantly replicated in the sanitary purification of menstruation (the unborn child), which restores the reproductive order while signalling the indifference of the cosmos in the face of its failure. In this respect the moon is a symbol of virginal purity and death, or rather, of cyclical purification through death, and contains all the most deeply disturbing aspects of the divine feminine.

---

37. On this point it seems significant to cite the poem 'I Have Two Moons' by Mahmoud Darwish, quoted by Jason Bahbak Mohaghegh in *Omnicide* (Falmouth and New York: Urbanomic/Sequence, 2019), 107–108: 'We cleanse the moonlight. Your road is long, so dream of / seven women to bear this long journey on your shoulders. / I walk on the lip of the well: I have two moons, / one in the sky, the other swimming in the water. / I have two moons.' As Mohaghegh comments: 'These two, usually conflicting principles of divinity are made to reinforce each other in the fractal mindscape of this author, as the moon is split into two lifeblood counterparts, one flung upwards into a remote unsullied sky, the other parachuted downward onto the moving surface of the water, one forever unreachable and the other immediately touchable [...].'
38. Scholem, *On the Kabbalah and its Symbolism*, 151.

If we wish to understand the moon, we must reserve for it both a maniacal love and a sacred terror. The moon, like the Virgin, like every other aspect of the sacred feminine, embodies a process. It comprises in its very nature everything that human civilisation has ever done to it. It secretes, in the poison that springs from its symbols, all the ancient violence that has been directed at its flesh. The moment we try to strip her of her monstrous mask, telling ourselves that behind her perversion lies an ancient lost harmony, we perform, like the unfortunate Actaeon, a blasphemous and desperately foolish act, presuming to domesticate the divine feminine within our miserable humanity.

Can we be so sure that the face of the unmasked Goddess is more reassuring than the mask we have built for her? In the swollen, bruised surface of the full moon there shines eternally the suicidal laughter of the vestal virgins, buried alive in the viscera of the city, forever suffocated in darkness.

V. MEDUSA

And while I arouse

in secret

those adorned dreams...

in that corpse

is discovered a foetus

thirty days old.[39]

Arrigo Boito

A few steps away from the departments of Mathematical, Physical, and Natural Sciences at the University of Milan where I spent my years of study, there is a square named after Paolo Gorini. The white marble plaques affixed to the corners of the square bear his name, accompanied by a single word: scientist. Arriving at the square from the university buildings, one notices

39.   A. Boito, 'Lezione d'anatomia', Opere (Rome: Garzanti, 1979).

a little further on an anonymous green gate with a rusty iron sign bearing the word 'OBITORIUM'. I remember lingering several times in front of that gate on my way back from exams, perhaps in the secret hope of satisfying my morbid curiosity of glimpsing, between its bars, some piece of a corpse. The fact that the mortuary is located in that very square is no coincidence. Gorini, a scientist from Lombardy and self-proclaimed founder of a bizarre discipline he called 'experimental geology', is known to all as *the petrifier*, because of his astonishing experiments in mummification and the preservation of corpses.

As is well documented in Alberto Carli's monograph *Paolo Gorini, La fiaba del mago di Lodi* [*Paolo Gorini, The Fairytale of the Magician of Lodi*], the problem of the treatment of corpses, in the context of the Italian *Risorgimento*, represented an entanglement of various implications ranging from the necessity of preserving human bodies for anatomical and scientific studies to the political and religious issues at stake in the debates of the period. Moreover, Gorini's strong advocacy of the idea of bringing the practice of cremating corpses back into common use was a virulent challenge to the political and moral authority of the Catholic Church at a time of radical political and institutional renewal. Far from simply representing the curious case of an eclectic scientist marginalised by the academic authorities of the time, Gorini's story—the story of the crematorium he designed and the mysterious *preparation* he used to perform the scientific miracle of petrifying corpses—provides an illuminating insight into the cultural and political ferment of mid-nineteenth-century Italy. The latter was marked by the combined coexistence of the positivist rationalism of the new natural sciences, used as a weapon of rebellion against religious obscurantism, and the underground proliferation of initiatic secret societies, hidden from the control of the Austrian empire and aiming to engineer a more enlightened future for the Italian homeland. In northern Italy, this occult struggle—curiously fought over the putrid flesh of corpses—has left more traces in the necropolises than in the metropolises. Walking along the marble avenues of Monumental Cemetery of Milan, one may see the surnames of the same Milanese notables who appear in Gorini's biography, often as enthusiastic supporters of his scientific endeavours, engraved among the sphinxes, pyramids, squares, and compasses.

Gorini argued that his interest in the question of the preservation and destruction of human bodies stemmed from his horror at the process of their decomposition after burial:

> What happens in burial is incomparably sadder and more repulsive than what would have happened to the corpse if simply left on the ground; and the torment of that wretched flesh, as has been pointed out, lasts for a very long time [...]. It is a horrible thing to realise what happens to the corpse when it is confined in its underground prison. If we could but catch a glimpse through a crack, any other way of treating corpses would be deemed less cruel, and the use of burial would be condemned without appeal.[40]

To respond to this sense of profound horror and indignation, he identifies two possible strategies, drawing, in doing so, upon the great civilisations of the past:

> The ancient Egyptians raised the banner of rebellion and tried to rescue their corpses from the dissolving forces of nature. The Greeks and Romans [...] adopted the ancient oriental custom of consigning corpses to the flames, thus hastening their decay.[41]

Either way, the only salvation from decomposition is to be had through the *mineralisation* of the body, be it through petrification or the transformation of living matter into air and ash by means of combustion. Moreover, Gorini, as an experimental geologist, had developed the idea of cremation

---

40.   A. Carli, *Paolo Gorini. La fiaba del mago di Lodi* (Rome: Interlinea, 2009), 209.
41.   Ibid., 131.

precisely from his research into the *plutonic liquid*, a mysterious incandescent chthonic fluid from whose primordial solidification, according to his theory, mountain ranges and volcanoes originated. This process of mineralisation, capable of restoring to the dead body its lost dignity and, at the same time, raising a Promethean challenge to the natural disintegration of living matter, is of a profoundly alchemical nature. In the words of Elémire Zolla:

> Why should man's passage from life to death be any different from that linking fermenting matter to the ingot, or the plant to its seed, or even to its ash, containing salts charged with the most intrinsic medicinal virtue? [...] The treatment of corpses is alchemical. Embalming, more than any other method, provided the spirit of the deceased with the means to the fulfil the destiny of its body, in a way that was similar to the transmutation of a metal into gold [...]. A corpse that was not treated alchemically and left unsanctified, unpacified, was a dangerous vampire, a wandering poison, fuel for worshippers of black magic.[42]

Whether Paolo Gorini was actually a magician, and what his occult affiliations were, is a question destined to remain unresolved, the answer burned together with his body in the flames of the crematorium. His maniacal dedication to the mission of restoring the bodies of the dead to their original *plutonic* condition nevertheless seems to be an action of great Hermetic significance. Faced with the failure of his attempt to stop time by halting the processes of decomposition altogether, his choice to follow the volcanic path of *returning to dust* is the most desperate and radical attempt to reverse the course of time, returning matter to its original condition of total disarray. In the *bright flame* of this last sacrifice, time is definitively decapitated, leaving only the petrifying gaze of eternity in the eyes of a severed head.

---

42. E. Zolla, *Le Meraviglie della Natura. Introduzione all'alchimia* (Rome: Marsilio, 1997), 419.

VI. STILLA MARIS

Ave, maris stella,

Dei Mater alma,

atque semper virgo,

felix cœli porta.[43]

One of the most curious names of the Blessed Virgin Mary is *Stella Maris*—literally, 'star of the sea'. This name associates her with the North Star, whose inexhaustible rays guide lost sailors through the stormy seas. The origin of the name, however, can be traced back to a transcription error of the more mysterious expression *stilla maris*—'drop of the sea'—used in St Jerome's Latin translation of the *Onomasticon*, a work of biblical geography by Eusebius of Caesarea dating from the fourth century, but which has since been lost. This appellation is in turn a translation of the Hebrew form of Mary's name, *Myriam*, whose controversial etymology has engendered various hypotheses; among them the hypothesis adopted by St. Jerome was most probably the one that traced the name Myriam back to the combination of the Hebrew words *mar*, 'drop', and *yam*, 'sea'.[44]

As in all such stories of the propagation of errors, it is not known whether there was any form of intentionality in the choice to transfer one piece of information to future memory rather than another. Certainly, today we are more inclined to associate the image of the Virgin Mary with the bright vault of heaven than with the unexplored depths of the ocean. Like a code irreversibly encrypted in its ancient names, the Immaculata silently reproduces the secret of its abyssal nature, overflowing like a poisonous sea from the openings of its beautiful weeping eyes.

---

43.   'Hail, star of the sea / Nurturing Mother of God / And ever Virgin / Happy gate of Heaven.' Mediaeval hymn.

44.   See A. Maas, 'The Name of Mary', *The Catholic Encyclopedia* (New York: Robert Appleton Company, 1912).

In his book *Thalassa*, psychoanalyst Sándor Ferenczi sets out to provide as scientific a foundation as possible for the age-old link between motherhood and the ocean. To this end, he elaborates a theory of thalassal regression, i.e. 'the idea of a [...] striving towards the aquatic mode of existence abandoned in primeval times' and its 'continued operation in the sphere of genitality'.[45] For Ferenczi, it is not so much that the ocean is a symbol of the womb, but rather that the womb is an ancient reminder of the ancestral ocean from which mammals were torn so as to adapt to life on land. According to his Lamarckian perspective, human beings bear upon their bodies, like bizarre living fossils, the traces of all the ancient catastrophes that life on earth had to go through in order to reach its present stage of development. Among these ancient geological traumas, the most important for understanding the sexual and reproductive development of the human being would be the drying up of the primordial sea in which our aquatic ancestors lived. If the trauma of birth is merely a repetition of the more ancient trauma of the emergence of life from the sea, the primary objective of human genitality would therefore be to return, through the penetrative sexual act, to the original waters, in a true regression to the ocean.

The sexual differentiation of human beings would thus have emerged from the struggle for the possibility of immersing their gametes in the other, for which the woman, defeated, acts as a receptacle, carrying within herself the traces of that ancient lost ocean. To quote Ferenczi:

Individual observations of the symbolism of dreams and neuroses reveal a fundamental symbolic identification of the mother's body with the waters of the sea [...]. Now such symbolism might be expressive of the fact not only that the individual lives on the mother before birth as a water-inhabiting endoparasite [...] but also that sea and earth were actually the precursors of the mother in the development of the species, and at this stage took the

45. S. Ferenczi, *Thalassa: A Theory of Genitality*, tr. H.A. Bunker (New York: Norton, 1968), 52.

place, in that they protected and nourished these animal ancestors, of the maternal protective adaptations which were acquired later.[46]

Ferenczi's idea, in its bizarre originality, contains some interesting insights. After all, the notion that ontogeny—the development of animal individuals—is a recapitulation of phylogeny—the development of the species through geological eras—fascinated biologists from the late nineteenth to the early twentieth century. At that time, it was not entirely absurd to think that such an idea could also be extended to human psychological development.

What is most interesting in Ferenczi's thesis is precisely the theory that absolutely inhuman, even geological, forces of a necessarily catastrophic nature are at work in the development of subjectivity. Beyond its semblance of scientific rigour, *Thalassa* is a catastrophic *cosmogony of separation*, in which the human individual emerges not so much as the apex of a developmental process, but rather as the ultimate receptacle for universal suffering, accumulated over millions of years of phylogenetic trauma. Pain pervades the development of human subjectivity in its entirety—from mating, understood as a spasmodic search for the *moisture* of the other, to pregnancy, in which the embryo becomes a parasite and is tragically transformed from a beloved object into a source of horror:

> It is also possible, however, that the greater part of the arrangements for the protection of the embryo do not represent precautions on the part of the maternal organism simply, but are rather, perhaps, at least in part, the product of the vital force inherent in the germ cells themselves—much in the manner of certain animal parasites which can make use of the originally purely defensive reactions in the body of the host [...] to create for themselves a protected place of abode, usually a vesicle or pustule filled with fluid.[47]

---

46.   Ibid., 47.
47.   Ibid., 64.

Humanity's drive to emerge from the abyss, understood both as the primordial oceanic abyss and as the condition of primitive inorganic indistinction, is therefore not a creative urge, but always a catastrophic urge for separation and estrangement. Evolution, rather than a drive to rise to the top of the natural order, is the result of a continuous propagation of *traumas*, to which life responds with an ever-increasing *regressive* drive: plunging into the future with its gaze always turned back toward the ancient ocean from which it continues inexorably to move away.

VII. MY SON, DO NOT ABANDON ME

At other times I cry inconsolably. And afterwards, sometimes I become so angry that I can hardly keep from tearing myself to pieces; at other times, the anger is so intense, I can't stop beating myself horribly until my head and other parts of my body become swollen. And when my soul begins to see all its virtues falling and withdrawing, I am overcome with fear and grief; and I cry out to God shouting to Him over and over again almost continuously: 'My son, my son, do not abandon me, my son!'

Angela of Foligno[48]

Do not abandon me.

Everything plunges into darkness. All is lost, forever faded away into the chasm of your absence. As the sun is swallowed up in a black light, the sky reveals itself as a desperate vertigo. The stars are hideous worlds, lost forever in the empty depths of the universe that stretches out until it tears itself to pieces. The moon is pallid and weeps over us the vermilion sea of your massacre.

In the west, dawn rises with a desperate, indefinable colour. In the fading cosmos I understand that behind the blinding rays of day there has never

48.   Angela of Foligno, *Angela of Foligno's Memorial*, tr. J. Cirgnano, ed. C. Mazzoni (Cambridge: D.S. Brewer, 1999), 65.

been anything but ocean. Dreadful speeds force us apart in an inexorable light; everything rotates madly in a vortex with no centre.

The impaled sun sinks into the whirlpool of the sky. The naked earth is a dismembered animal vibrating with silent screams. My hands are red with blood. *It seems to me that I blaspheme.*[49]

The shreds of your disembowelled body continue to writhe in despair on the cross of creation, repeatedly pulsating in their dance of death as the eggs of countless parasites hatch, burrowing into the swellings of your belly.

Ecce vermis: the dust has become flesh.

LT

---

49.   Ibid., 69.

SOLARISATION

So the Ancients feared visions at noon no differently than they feared them
at night. [...] At noon, even the shadows of the dead were reputed to appear
and go wandering, as we can see in the cited verses of both Statius and
Philostratus, who tells that the shepherds did not dare to approach Pallene
at noon, or Phlegra, where lay the bones of giants, for fear of the ghosts that
appeared in that place making a frightening noise.

Giacomo Leopardi[1]

BLACK SUN

Three silos stand out in grey against the earth, ashen as if covered by a
layer of radioactive dust. Threatening undergrowth punctuates the rough
surface, while the dark silhouette of a cabin watches silently from the
distance. High above, against the backdrop of a milky sky that looks as if it
has the consistency of semen, looms a dark sphere, austere and terrifying.
A circular shadow that seems to hail from some remote and hostile galaxy, a
sun that declares itself to be what it should not be, a star that neither shines,
illuminates, nor radiates heat—*Black Sun*.

Minor White chose this title for one of his most iconic photographs, taken
in 1955 in an anonymous corner of the American provinces. If we didn't know
that the photo was taken in a remote part of the Pacific Northwest (Oregon,
according to the sources), upon studying the landscape we would say that it
was a typical Southern Gothic scene: the kind of desolate, derelict rural hell
described by Flannery O'Connor and William Faulkner in their novels set in

---

1. G. Leopardi, *Saggio sopra gli errori popolari degli antichi* (Firenze: Le Monnier, 1846), 94.

the South. For once, however, it is neither geography nor place names that convey the feeling of the shot. What does it matter where the image comes from? The ash-coated undergrowth and the black sun towering above it, if anything, tell of another world, at once familiar and alien: a world equal and opposite to the one we know, totally indifferent to stable comprehensible coordinates and known latitudes, as if the darkness that dwells in the light of things had been brought to the surface.

If we then want to investigate *how* this world managed to imprint itself on the medium that is conventionally considered the most neutral, reliable and realistic of those available for presenting what exists—photographic film—we would have to resort to a technical explanation: the process employed by White is called 'solarisation' and has been known since the dawn of photography. To achieve it, nineteenth-century daguerreotypists simply overexposed sensitive materials to sunlight, thus producing what is known as 'tonal inversion': black becomes white, white becomes black, the negative becomes positive and vice versa. Starting in 1929, the same technique was famously employed by Man Ray and Lee Miller to produce those typical snapshots of the subconscious that constitute one of the most famous examples of Surrealist art.

The appearance of photography is the moment in which techné is established not only as a human artefact and, where necessary, as an instrument of investigation, but also as a representational and cognitive filter between the human being and the reality around them. It is therefore curious that, despite the fact that the camera was presented as the first device capable of finally providing a faithful mirror of the world around us, it was almost immediately used to immortalise ghosts, spectres, and ectoplasmic presences intent on inhabiting the interstices between the visible and the invisible.[2]

2.　Our purpose here is not to investigate the relationship between the birth of photography, spiritualism, and the first attempts to capture spectres and mysterious presences on film. The bibliography on the subject is vast, but for a first brief examination of the link between the two, the Wikipedia entry 'Spirit photography' provides a good summary.

Machine civilisation opened up its portals and immediately announced that this filter, if properly activated, was potentially capable of overturning the principles upon which the empirical experience of human beings is based. An instrument that was the child of the great ultra-rational epoch that would see the nineteenth century described as the 'age of wonder', photography was nonetheless (as Man Ray would understand) the apotheosis of the purely irrational, in the sense that its particular kind of rationality did not coincide with that inscribed in the synapses of the human brain—at least in its waking state.

From this point of view, solarisation is an initial moment of vertigo on the edge of the precipice that separates the quest for knowledge from an excess of awareness. Both in the pioneering experiments of Ray and Miller and in the black sun of Minor White, there is proof of a paradox which, in the midst of the rational and mechanised twentieth century, announces itself as mysterious precisely because of its technical nature, reaffirming that technology is first and foremost the realm of the phantasmal and the unfathomable: because, logically speaking, if it is the sun that illuminates the reality around us, then more sunlight should automatically translate into more reality—for only sunlight makes it possible to focus on the most infinitesimal details of a world that finally finds its incontrovertible representation in photography. But instead, excessive exposure to the sun unexpectedly reveals a counterintuitive, disorienting, 'incorrect' truth: solar disk turned black, skies milky, positives and negatives changing places, the nemesis of the world as we know it. With solarisation, what remains fixed on the film is an occulted repression, hitherto trapped in some unmentionable recess of the lens-eye: more sun does not mean more reality—more sun means an inversion of visible reality.

In the alchemical tradition, the black sun is one of the symbols of nigredo, the process of putrefaction in which matter disintegrates and is reduced back to primordial chaos. This is the initial stage of the Great Work, the one in which the alchemist's conscious self is called upon to abdicate itself until it disappears into the deepest of inner chasms—a sort of indistinct and horizontal degree zero, seething with pustules that erupt like poisonous lava. From an alchemical point of view, solarisation should therefore be read as a sort of mechanical nigredo capable of making the cosmic power of the sun explode to such an extent as to translate it into its apparent opposite: the non-visible, the unnameable, the unknowable emerge from the shadow zone in which the veil of phenomenal reality had confined them. And the primordial chaos finally appears in the guise of an uninhabitable planet, indifferent to the human gaze. The fact that this unveiling takes place through the filter of a machine (in this case a photographic camera) seems entirely logical: the dimension revealed by solarisation is an extra- (anti-?) human dimension, and it is therefore perfectly natural that the human eye cannot grasp it.

The darkness of the black sun is not the darkness of those who have seen too much and know too much. The darkness of the black sun is at most the reflection, the approximate and imperfect representation, of a world so far beyond human gaze that only recourse to occult witchcraft (in this case technology) allows us to grasp its vague contours. The same sun that saves the world by warming it with the sacred fire of reason and knowledge, is a sun that rises from the underworld where everything falls into a cold spiral of alien fury.

MERIDIAN DEMONS

In ancient Mediterranean civilisations, it was at midday that the demons of the underworld materialised in the world above. When the sun is at its highest, when the scorching disc is at its zenith and the shadows dwindle until they disappear, the world of the living and the world of the dead come into mutual contact, that 'sacred and terrible noontide' of which Leopardi speaks.[3] In turn, Roger Caillois described midday as the '*hour of transition*' when the sun 'divides the day into equal parts, each governed

---

3.   G. Leopardi, *Saggio sopra gli errori popolari degli antichi* (Firenze: Le Monnier, 1846), 94.

by the opposing signs of rise and decline'. It is here, in this by definition liminal moment burdened by the overwhelming power of the sun at its peak, that according to Caillois 'the dead make their appearance: *they who cast no shadow'*.[4]

The deadly qualities of the sun at its brightest are confirmed by the link between midday and states of melancholy and depression, as summed up in ancient times in the by no means coincidental formula *daemonium meridian*.[5] Is it not surprising, then, that the adjective 'sunny' is commonly used to describe a person with an optimistic and jovial manner? Or that the Mediterranean peoples, constantly kissed by the sun at these latitudes, are by convention associated with moods such as good humour, cheerfulness, and expansiveness?

That the sun, is, on the contrary, in the words of Artaud, a powerful messenger of the 'principles radiating from the depths of the Breath of Chaos' was perhaps intuited by those authors who originated the forms and stylistic features of so-called Gothic fiction.[6] Prior to its now traditional association with the misty atmospheres of its native Northern Europe, the Gothic novel was in fact baptised in the waters of a Mediterranean which, to these authors, who grew up in a cold and not particularly sunny eighteenth-century England, must have appeared to be an indecent repository of irrational superstitions and malignant ravings. The novel to which the birth of the genre is usually attributed, *The Castle of Otranto* by Horace Walpole, is set in a depressed Puglia marked by intrigue and guilt. The rapes, incest, demons, and torture that punctuate *The Monk* by Matthew Gregory Lewis unfold in an equally sunny Spain. A corrupt and sexually morbid Venice is the backdrop for

---

4.   R. Caillois, 'The Noon Complex', in *The Edge of Surrealism: A Roger Caillois Reader*, tr. C. Frank, C. Naish, ed. C. Frank, (Durham, NC and London: Duke University Press, 2003), 125.

5.   The relationship between depression and midday (or more generally the summer season) deserves far more in-depth study. A classic on the subject is A. Solomon, *The Noonday Demon: An Anatomy of Depression* (New York: Scribner, 2001).

6.   A. Artaud, *Heliogabalus or, The Crowned Anarchist*, tr. A. Lykiard (London: Creation Books, 2003), 15.

Charlotte Dacre's *Zofloya*. In William Beckford's bizarre *Vathek*, the action shifts to an unspecified Middle Eastern location oppressed by the stifling heat of the desert. And as for an author like Ann Radcliffe, the mere titles of works such as *The Italian* and *Sicilian Novel* say it all.

At the height of the Age of Enlightenment and at the dawn of the Age of Reason, the noonday demons spawned by the incessant solarisation infesting the Mediterranean took shape in the fantasies of a handful of writers who projected Horror into a sultry and blinding Elsewhere. Their works were a mixture of exoticism and an attraction-repulsion for the regimented, antiquated, and very Catholic Southern Europe, which in turn overlooked the equally premodern southern edge of a former *Mare Nostrum* now dominated by a mysterious and bloody Islam. But it would take some time for those demons to be actually awakened. And for this to happen, it would be necessary to wait for the intervention of yet another visitor from the south, from the outside, since those who used to frequent these demons would never, ever have dreamed of declaring them to a world where the sun does not shine.

ITALIAN SOUTHERN GOTHIC

It was in 1954 that Alan Lomax arrived in Italy for what would prove to be one of the most important stages in his research career. Accompanied by his colleague Diego Carpitella, a thirty-year-old fellow ethnomusicologist of Calabrian origin, Lomax, the greatest scholar of American folk music, spent nine months exploring the music, sounds, and traditions of the most remote corners of the peninsula, from the fishing villages of Liguria to the marble quarries of Carrara. Almost immediately, however, his attention was drawn to what lay buried beneath the ruins of the devastated and still remote South—that outcrop of rocky land planted in the centre of the Mediterranean that goes by the name of *Mezzogiorno*.

Lomax knew that, in 1954, Italy was about to take the final leap that would transform it from a backward and still essentially peasant nation into a great industrial power finally at ease in its longed-for modernity. The small old world of rural villages lost amidst a countryside dotted with olive trees was destined to succumb under the weight of the new, winding motorways and the consumerist race that would soon be dubbed Italy's 'economic miracle'. In short, there was no time to lose: this already archaic world had to be documented before it vanished into a confused pool of memories.

What Lomax could not have suspected was the power of solarisation. If, in the photographic medium, this took the form of an inversion that revealed the occult reality hidden in the shadows of things, the presences imprinted on the magnetic tape carried on the researcher's back were quite inhuman, their phantasmal qualities amplified by the spectral properties of recorded, dematerialised and disembodied sound—once again, by the interaction with technology.

Beastly noises, guttural sounds, shrill voices, aberrant lamentations: far removed from the festive atmospheres that had always been associated with the folk culture of Southern Italy, the music and voices captured on tape by Lomax were immoral, sounding as if they had been worn away by dust and carried off by the nagging breath of an implacable sirocco. They told of a socially and sexually manic world, inhabited by irrational feelings, demonic fantasies, inexplicable fears, and guilt so excruciating that it overflowed into insanity. What emerged was a piece of the Mediterranean that no longer had anything in common with the typical postcards that made southern Italy look like a folkloric succession of beaches and typical dishes, full of 'bella vita' and 'dolce far niente'. Rather, the Mezzogiorno acquired the threatening characteristics—in the words of the documentary La Taranta which followed shortly afterward—of a land 'cracked by sun and solitude', where 'man walks on mastic bushes and clay'.[7]

During his mission to the countryside of regions such as Lucania, Salento, and Campania, Lomax had uncovered the black soul of Southern Italy, bringing to the surface a tangle of archaic traditions, pagan Christianity, and ritual practices that seemed to go back centuries. The recordings collected in the

---

7.   La Taranta, dir. Gian Franco Mingozzi, 1962.

field shocked him so much that he formulated a 'New Hypothesis' according to which the music of Southern Italy should be analysed not in conformity with classical notation systems, but as an immaterial clash between the human body, the social context, and memory. This latter was, however, a memory capable of regressing infinitely into the past, so much so as to suggest a spiral temporal trajectory in which the category of the present collapsed under the weight of ghosts hailing from an unstable chronology; Lomax would never have admitted it, but his endless collection of tapes was host to exactly that music of the spheres innervated with alchemical elements that was being hypothesised during the same period by Harry Smith and his *Anthology of American Folk Music*. Only, instead of reflecting the cosmic harmony that regulates the proportions of the universe, it was a music of repugnant spheres whose motion was capable of freeing the nefarious forms at the centre of the universe itself.

When confronted with Lomax's discoveries, Italian cultural circles initially reacted with horror: instead of the bucolic snapshot of some pleasant, still uncontaminated countryside just outside the city, they outlined a portrait of a South suspended in a limbo that seemed to refer to an ancestral, cruel, and malignant world rather than to a pre-modern one. The anthropologist Ernesto De Martino deciphered the complicated occult geographies of that world in studies with explanatory titles such as *Sud e magia* [*The South and Magic*] and *La terra del rimorso* [*The Land of Remorse*]: true examples of Gothic essays in which chilling stories of abuse and abomination come one after the other, in between magical formulas and sinister rites that would have delighted the ancient mad emperor Heliogabalus. The 'scientific' veneer and materialist approach employed by De Martino—a Gramscian intellectual who, for his research on tarantism in Salento, also drew on funding from the Parapsychology Foundation in New York—give way before a narrative which perfectly reflects a solarisation raging through the folds of a society domi-nated by blind divinities that blaspheme and bubble at the centre of infinity. In the choked screams, in the ranting glossolalia of the magical rites of the

South, there lay the extreme warning of the noonday demons who had come to announce a perpetual apocalypse without eschaton—a theme that De Martino would explore in his last, testamentary work *The End of the World*.

Like the horrifying music of the spheres taped by Lomax, the end of the world that De Martino sensed in Southern Italy arose from the conflict between the aberrant eternity of a present without telos and the forced linearity of a machine civilisation crashing down from the future, trapped in the spirals of an essentially achronic past. Once subjected to the power of solarisation, the delirious results of such a conflict were translated into an unprecedented form of *Italian Southern Gothic*: the crude and hyperrealist heir to the fantasies that had troubled the dreams of English writers at the end of the eighteenth century, and the dark negative of the romantic hagiographies of which the Mezzogiorno had been the subject since the age of the Grand Tour. Once a placid symbol of a relaxed 'endless summer', the sun was now confirmed as a tyrannical presence capable of confusing reality and transforming every single shadow into a violent hallucination. The languor of warm days by the sea was replaced by an oppressive heatwave. The endless silences of the countryside, populated by nothing but drystone walls and dessicated olive trees, became an omen of generalised madness. The religiosity in which millenarian cults and invasive visions commingled acquired heavily occult, esoteric, if not outright luciferous overtones. Even Punchinello's indolent and farcical mask ultimately betrayed all the signs of an intimately diabolical presence. In his empty, idiotic gaze lay the darkest underworld of the Mediterranean psyche.

ACID (NEO)REALISM

At the end of the 1950s, the pioneering investigations of the Mezzogiorno by Lomax and De Martino inspired a small group of directors—principal among them Luigi Di Gianni, Gianfranco Mingozzi, Vittorio De Seta, and Cecilia Mangini—to initiate the brief season of so-called 'Italian ethnographic documentary'. In a desolate black and white that seemed corroded by the heat, titles such as *Magia lucana* [*Magic from Lucania*] (1958), *La Taranta* [*Tarantula*] (1962), *I dimenticati* [*The Forgotten Ones*] (1959) and *Stendalì* (1960) brought to the cinema the oppressive atmospheres of a nascent Italian Southern Gothic; but instead of being accepted for what they really were—sulphurous examples of the prevailing solarisation—they were automatically catalogued under the heading of 'documentary denunciation'. This was only to be expected: since they portrayed conditions of extreme hardship and had no qualms about bearing witness to a social reality exhausted by poverty, the ethnographic documentaries quite naturally ended up being ascribed to the generalised *engagé* climate prevailing in the 'neorealist' Italy of the period. And in some ways the two were indeed linked. We just need to understand which 'reality' lies at the heart of the *realism* that follows the prefix *neo*.

Born directly out of the rubble left by the Second World War, neorealism was the founding act of modern Italian cinema; according to the *Enciclopedia Treccani*, its distinctive feature was 'the need to know and to modify reality'.

> Hence the choice of events and characters from humble contemporary
> everyday life; the preference [...] for non-professional actors; the rejection
> of the studio and the prevalent choice of natural settings and natural speech.

As with all forms of artistic and literary realism, the declared mission of neorealism was to provide a portrayal of the existing world with as little artifice as possible, and directors of proven moral rigour such as Roberto Rossellini, Luchino Visconti, and Vittorio De Sica applied themselves fully to the task; no oneiric flourishes, no cryptic metaphors, no obscure symbolism: neorealism made it a point of honour to show the viewer reality *as it is*, even in its most unpleasant aspects—poverty, indigence, abuses of all kinds, political and social backwardness.

Once again, however, solarisation leaves no room for doubt. The first indication of how impossible it was to separate the self-styled 'reality' from the noonday demons stirring within it already came from the novels that antic-ipated and expanded the new realism to which post-war cinema would refer. In *Conversations in Sicily*, Elio Vittorini subtly allows the documentary inten-tions of his travel literature on the Mezzogiorno precipitate onto the sloping plane of a feverish oneiricism, in which everything appears in the light of day and yet nothing is as it seems. And the witches, cemeteries, drunken priests and invisible brigands that populate Carlo Levi's memoir *Christ Stopped at Eboli* are, in the words of the author, nothing more than the still image of a land in which 'time has come to a stop', a world where 'there is no room for reason [...] and history', announced in the novel by one of the most classic representations of the Black Sun: the solar eclipse.[8]

In turn, neorealist cinema, devoted to shooting in the open air and traditionally filmed (in black and white) on long summer days, seemed to capitulate before the same inescapable atmospheric conditions that were soon to be condensed into Italian Southern Gothic. After all, in many cases the tales told by neorealism were nothing more or less than horror stories. In *Appunti su un fatto di cronaca* [*Notes on a News Story*] (1951), Luchino Visconti focuses on the Roman suburbs which, as in the worst nightmares, 'besiege the gold of the city with their inertia and starvation'.[9] In the 'sunlit squalor' of one of these suburbs, twelve-year-old Annarella Bracci was kid-napped, raped, and murdered on 18 February 1950. In the short film Visconti devoted to the story, the outskirts of Rome become a sun-drenched desert where human and non-human rubbish is dumped, and in the final shot a road lost in the middle of nowhere seems to connect the humble blocks of flats in the Primavalle district to a sky which, rather than smelling of salvation, seems to be an omen of eternal damnation. Hell lies in the celestial vaults: what better representation could there be of solar inversion?

With its slow rhythms, its rarefied aesthetics, and its narratives plagued by the cosmic fatigue of living, neorealism ended up dilating even the driest

---

8. C. Levi, *Christ Stopped at Eboli*, tr. F. Frenaye (New York: Time, 1947), 70, 117.
9. *Appunti su un fatto di cronaca*, dir. L. Visconti, 1951.

narration of the crudest news story into an alienating metaphysical-psyche-delic dimension, immediately confirming that, even if it does not sink into the ultimate abyss of solar chaos, an excess of sunlight can lead to visions and hallucinations. When Italian cinematography switched to the use of colour and more commercially profitable tendencies took over, the intrinsically *acid* properties of neorealism were transmitted, not to the so-called auteur cinema, but to the two main 'B-movie' schools of the sixties and seventies: the spaghetti western and the giallo. The former, by transferring the action to an imaginary America dominated by stylised violence and the long silences of its protagonists, would find its greatest fulfilment in clearly lysergic films such as Giulio Questi's *Se sei vivo spara* [*Django Kill... If You Live, Shoot!*] (1967) and Cesare Canevari's *Matalo!* [*Kill Him*] (1970). As for the giallo, whose very name (literally, 'yellow') already evokes the blinding tyranny of the Mediterranean sun—it drowned Northern European horror in a riot of erotic deviance, black esotericism, and insanity, direct heir to the *furor solis* documented twenty years earlier by Lomax and De Martino, and recon-necting with its unconfessed ethnographic roots already as Brunello Rondi's pioneering *Il demonio* [*The Demon*] (1963), to finally arrive at classics such as Lucio Fulci's *Non si sevizia un paperino* [*Don't Torture a Duckling*] (1972).

Among the various strands of post-neorealist Italian cinema, the giallo is the one which, from a visual point of view, most blatantly embraced the pop and psychedelic culture of the period. It is also a consistently 'acid' genre, in the sense that it was born of the perfect combination of parasatanic esotericism, extreme sex, and LSD. Yet not even its bright colours manage to emancipate themselves from a gloom, from an underlying opacity, that always seems to want to lead back to the depressed *nigredo* that broods at the centre of the Mediterranean. Solarisation does not merely burn colours. Solarisation turns colours off, alters their flows, inverts their wavelengths to the point of transforming every chromaticism, every sensation of brilliance and vivacity, into the dull exhaustion of a life that once was and that perhaps somewhere still intones its curses.

WHITEOUT

The filmic-initiatory work that will most of all succeed in fully activating the inversion mechanisms produced by solarisation is that of Pier Paolo Pasolini. His 1961 film *Accattone* is in some ways the defining neorealist film, the one that not only closes a season of Italian cinema, but also definitively lays out its intentions. On the one hand, if—to return to *Enciclopedia Treccani*'s definition—the distinctive trait of directors such as Roberto Rossellini and Luchino Visconti lay in 'the need to know and to modify reality', then 'knowing and modifying reality' should be understood as an essentially magical gesture, according to the classic Crowleyian description of magic as 'the Science and Art of causing changes in conformity with the Will'.[10] On the other hand, the hallucinatory bath suggested by the first neorealist films is to be taken to its extreme consequences, revealing the power of solarisation without any 'natural' filter and indeed amplifying its occult characteristics.

From the point of view of both content and style, *Accattone* seems to start out once again from Visconti's *Appunti su un fatto di cronaca*: a desperate portrait of the Roman suburbs which, in its representation, opens up to a parallel dimension inhabited by the nothingness of the inhuman and the end of the world. But while it is true that much neorealist cinema had investigated the hallucinatory qualities of the sun, inadvertently inaugurating a primitive form of black-and-white psychedelia, it is only with Pasolini that the dazzling voids of acid neorealism become a complete form of abdication of the Euclidean logic of space, so much so as to produce what we shall call here 'Mediterranean whiteout'.

Whiteout, reports the *Cambridge Dictionary*, is the 'meteorological condition in which snow and clouds alter the way sunlight is reflected, to the point that only extremely dark objects are visible'; in short, it is a winter

---

10.   A. Crowley, *Magick Without Tears*, ed. I. Regardie (St. Paul, Minnesota: Llewellyn, 1973), 27.

phenomenon, typical of high altitudes, northern regions or polar areas where blizzards rage. Conversely, the Mediterranean whiteout is a phenomenon whereby the sun at its brightest causes the power of its light to become so excessive that it turns the field of vision into a single expanse of dazzling white—a condition of blindness born of the liquefaction of existence rather than its blurring

In *Accattone*, the use of whiteout is so insistent that it is almost difficult to keep one's eyes open: everything is played out in the starkest possible contrast between whites and blacks ('only extremely dark objects are visible'), with these latter floating phantasmagorically in an endless and heavy sea of light. A grim reflection of the Eternal City that once was, the outskirts of Rome become, for the protagonist of the film, a R'lyeh melted by the sun, with geometries 'too great to belong to any thing right or proper for this earth', declaring itself to be a city 'built in measureless aeons behind history by the vast, loathsome shapes that seeped down from the dark stars'—in a word, from the Black Sun.[11]

THE EXTERMINATING ANUS

The Italian Southern Gothic, variously announced by Lomax's songs, De Martino's essays, and Carlo Levi's novels, with Pasolini detonates into a sunlit nightmare in which the Noontime Demons are openly evoked, infecting a reality reduced to a death rattle, devoid of moisture and fresh air. Their presence betrayed by nothing more than the scrubland from which rises the simultaneously fragile and penitential threat of the 'whip of Christ'—the fields of broom that Giacomo Leopardi described as surrounding the 'empty places' of a troubled Rome, and which he met again a little further south, on the 'arid slope' of Vesuvius, 'formidable mountain, the destroyer'.[12]

This brings us back to Visconti's *La terra trema* [*The Earth Trembles*] (1948) and, with it, Rossellini's *Stromboli terra di Dio* [*Stromboli, Land of*

---

11.   Lovecraft, 'The Call of Cthulhu', 93, 92.

12.   G. Leopardi, 'Wild Broom (XXXIV)' in *The Canti*, tr. A.S. Kline <poetryintranslation.com>.

God] (1950)—both films which have volcanoes as their backdrop, in which the protagonists succumb almost by inertia to the geotraumatic forces brooding beneath layer upon layer of craters, calderas, and lava. Etna, Stromboli, Vesuvius, and the Campi Flegrei remind us that Southern Italy is not only a land of the sun but also a land of volcanoes. Georges Bataille sensed that there was a direct relationship between the two elements, to the point of coining the neologism *Jesuve*—a cross between *je*, 'I', and *Vesuve*, 'Vesuvius'—as a 'filthy parody of the blindingly hot sun'. For Bataille, both the sun and the volcano are elements linked to the anus, site of unproductive coitus, of the sterile expenditure of energy: on the one hand, 'the *solar annulus* is the intact anus of her body at eighteen years to which nothing sufficiently blinding can be compared except the sun', a source of energy that cannot be penetrated by a human's binocular gaze without blinding them forever; on the other hand, volcanoes 'serve as [the] anus' to a globe that 'eats nothing' but which nevertheless 'violently ejects the contents of its entrails', their essential function being to spread 'death and terror everywhere'.[13]

'Death and terror' is the final outcome of Pasolini's solarisation, which began with the whiteouts of *Accatone* and ended with the coprophagous ramblings of *Salò or the 120 Days of Sodom* (1975), the film that encapsulates Pasolini's entire initiatory journey, presenting itself as the *summa* of the Bataillean equivalence between sun and asshole, and consequently between the disk of the sun and its inversion. Just as it is impossible to rest one's eyes on the noonday sun, *Salò* is conceived as a work that is clearly unbearable to the eye, so brutal, so atrocious, so *unwatchable* are its visions. The anus-oracle is shown everywhere in its capacity to receive streams of infertile sperm and at the same time to return nothing but shit, waste, the lifeless detritus of a sacrificial abortion. The inversion of the biological function to which male coitus responds in nature (the sowing of life) merges with the inversion of the mandate given by the earth to the sun (the illumination of the world). Sodomy, anal intercourse, the *unnatural* qualities of

13. Bataille, 'The Solar Anus', *Visions of Excess*, 9, 8.

anal penetration, become instruments for reconciling oneself to that reality which is equal and contrary to the world above, that reality revealed by the blinding shadows of the Black Sun.

In this sense Pasolini's method is identical to that which the English occultist Austin Osman Spare introduced with his concept of the 'new sexuality': the obsessive practice of any form of 'unnatural' sexual act in order to penetrate the innermost layers of the psyche and thus trigger what he called 'Atavistic Resurgence', i.e. the awakening of the 'ancestral states of the subconscious mind'. Atavistic Resurgence blurs temporal planes and connects the individual with what Spare called 'spaces beyond space'. Biographer Kenneth Grant recalls how, through such practices, Spare was able to visit 'fantastic cities constructed of lines and angles that bore no semblance to anything earthly', a description that seems to echo the exact words Lovecraft used for his R'lyeh and which fit perfectly with the lunar Roman suburbs portrayed in *Accattone*.[14]

After all, Spare and Pasolini were two priests who, on different fronts, presided over an identical initiatory ordeal—as was understood by Coil, the British post-industrial music duo, direct heirs to the chaos-occult tradition inaugurated by Spare himself. And if their first album *Scatology* (1984) already bore on its cover a reference to the binomial ass and shit over which towered unmistakably the silhouette of the Black Sun, it is in the following *Horse Rotorvator* (1986) that the overlap becomes total. Because it is on that album, set between death disco anthems such as 'Penetralia' and 'The Anal Staircase' (further essays on the alchemical properties of anal inversion), that there appears a sorrowful ballad dedicated to Pasolini and to the place upon whose beaches the director of *Accattone* and *Salò* was killed: 'Ostia'.

14.   K. Grant, 'Austin Osman Spare', *Encyclopedia of the Unexplained: Magic, Occultism and Parapsychology*, ed. R. Cavendish (New York: McGraw-Hill, 1974), 224.

RETURN TO REMORIA

The sacrificial aspect of Pasolini's death and its connection to the abject forms of the Black Sun cult become clearer if we consider the place where his body was found in November 1975, just a few weeks before the announced release of *Salò*. The outermost of the Roman suburbs, perpetually beaten by the waves of a Mediterranean Sea reduced to a filthy dump, crushed to the ground by the sun that transforms Rome into a flat expanse of rough, horizontal roofs, Ostia bears in its name a direct reference to the circular—and therefore solar—wafer of the Catholic liturgy; the term retains within it an undeclared yet unredeemable blasphemy. On the one hand, in Latin *hostia* means 'victim'; on the other, its root is the same as that of *hostis*—'enemy', 'adversary', or in other words 'Satan'. Within the consecrated wafer of the Christian religion there lies the ghost, vainly exorcised, of the ancient cult of Mithras and of the double nature, salvific and terrifying, of the first solar mysteries.

The true origin of the name Ostia, however, is to be found elsewhere: the district, which lies nearby to where the Tiber flows into the sea, takes its name from the Latin *Ostium*—'mouth', 'river mouth'. It is a place where foul effluvia from the city's digestive tract spill out: literally the asshole of the metropolis. That this asshole carries the same name as the Mithraic disc trapped in the Christian host is perhaps no casual irony; it refers once again to the processes typical of inversion triggered by solarisation—which confuses and overturns everything. The ultra-periphery, with its urban waste and its dejection, gnaws at the edges of the metropolis. It becomes the place where the city's hierarchies themselves are upended: the outside engulfs the inside, the edgelands swallow the centre. The Mediterranean R'lyeh shown in *Accattone* divests itself of the metaphysical filter of the Mediterranean whiteout to reveal itself not as a hypothetical alien city 'out of space', but as equal and opposite of the everyday city.

From this point of view, the suburbs of Rome portrayed in *Accattone*, and in which the director of *Accattone* himself died, are the perfect spectral substantiation of Remoria: the city that would have been born *if*, in the ancient fratricidal legend about the origins of Rome, Remus had won instead of Romulus.[15] The myth of Remoria dates back to the birth of what was to become the city symbolic of the entire Western world, and is indicative of how the very foundation of Rome took place through a sacrifice under the auspices of the Black Sun. According to Plutarch, the ritual murder of Remus by the first king, Romulus, coincided with a solar eclipse—an event which we can interpret as full of omens and which invites us to look behind the sun, temporarily obscured by the moon, for *another sun* capable of illuminating a different reality, an alternative to the one we know.[16]

We know that Romulus's gesture is responsible for the birth of the *Urbe* par excellence, the city that, in the West, sanctioned the dominance of the vertical ideology based on hierarchy, order, and discipline—a traditionally 'square' city in which the continuous conquest and production of what exists betrays a quintessentially phallic movement, and in which no waste of energy is tolerated or even contemplated. What the city of Remus would have been, on the other hand, we can deduce from the myth and the legendary associations that have accompanied Remoria since ancient times. We know very little about Remus: in legend he is described as an unstable and irrational personality, quite the opposite of the calculating Romulus, founder of the long tradition that would lead to the Rome of the *rex*—the Caesars and the emperors. Remus's Remoria can therefore be imagined as a sort of twin city with inverted features compared to the one that actually rose on the banks of the Tiber, and at the same time as a latent spectre of a city born already dead, whose poisonous breath blows over the world of the living as a perpetual reminder of the *what if*.

---

15. I have written on the myth of Remoria and its link with the modern Roman periphery in *Remoria. La città invertita* (Rome: minimum fax, 2019). Many passages in this chapter (as well as the following one on the dark continuum) are dealt with more fully in that work.

16. On the relationship between the Black Sun and Nemesis, the second sun, responsible for cataclysmic events and mass extinctions, see 'Catastrophic Astrology', in this volume.

Already, according to Ovid, the name Remoria is at the origin of the term *lemures*, 'ghost'. From the outset, the city of Remus is identified as the incarnation of the beyond-threshold and of the inversion of above and below. This spectral nature also means that, if the Rome of Romulus is the city in which energy is put to good use so as to continually fertilise and reproduce what already is, Remus's Remoria must be the city of expenditure, of *dépense* and the sterile sacrifice of what will never be because it never really was. Finally, if the Rome of Romulus is a 'square' city whose ditch clearly delimits what is inside from what remains outside, the Remoria of Remus must be, on the contrary, a round, circular city, tracing out once again the features of the sun-anus couplet which, rather than establishing certain boundaries and impassable lines, welcomes the effluvia of the world of the living, returning nothing but scraps and deformed copies.

It is (also) from this point of view that Remoria finds its full representation in the endless suburbs that, with their chaotic and senseless sprawl, have made modern Rome one of the largest and at the same time least densely populated cities in the West. The only identifiable form in the interminable alternation of full and empty spaces that connects neighbourhoods like Ostia to the monumental Rome of the ancient city centre (the city of Romulus) is, not by chance, a circle: the ring road called the *Grande Raccordo Anulare*, which for seventy kilometres winds its way through the neighbourhoods that make up the ragged edge of the metropolis. There is much speculation in local folklore on the *Grande Raccordo Anulare* as a magic seal which, in the acronym GRA, bears the name of its creator, the engineer-magus Eugenio Gra. But what is of interest here is the GRA as a circle that replicates the features of the solar disk on the ground, that mimics the circumference of a volcano crater, and that declares its anal nature in being an engineering work incapable of connecting anything because its beginning does not exist and its end is nowhere to be found.

Symbol, fetish, magnet, and principal (horizontal) monument of the outskirts of Rome, the GRA brings us back to the original meaning of the name Remo: 'flowing'. The blood of the brother killed by the first king of Rome flows, and so does the blood of the poet whose sacrifice spills across the already filthy beaches of Remus's suburbs. The sperm that spurts into the rectum, so refractory to any breath of life, and the desire that, for Deleuze and Guattari, is as much a yearning for life as it is a longing for death. And lastly, the cars go round and round along the seventy kilometres of the GRA, and with their annular movement announce, on this immense uranium anus that solarisation projects in a spiral between the bowels of the Earth and the great stars of the cosmos, the coming of a new presence: that of the automobile.

DARK CONTINUUM

Muta is an album by Leo Anibaldi from 1993, one of the masterpieces of Italian techno, together with the coeval works of other protagonists of the 'sound of Rome' such as Lory D and the D'Arcangelo brothers. From the end of the eighties, a new era characterised by machines and the cold touch of cybernetics found its haptics on the relaxed shores of the Mediterranean, which was suddenly infected by the technoid virus originally born in the laboratories of large—and cold—industrial cities such as Detroit, London, Manchester, and Berlin. *Muta* is at the same time a summary, an overcoming, and an epitaph for Roman techno: you can't even dance to it, so resigned are its atmospheres, closer to those of an old giallo movie than futuristic snapshots of some cyberpunk metropolis.

And after all, it could only have been that way: not only has Rome never been a cyber-metropolis—it has never even been a punk city. Even at the turn of the seventies and eighties, the subculture that most fascinated the young working class children of Remus's sprawl was, if anything, a different one: goth. Imported from England, the goth aesthetic celebrated the blackness of the night, the long sunless winters, and the cadaverous pallor of flesh resistant to any tan. Here, instead, it became the style of reference for hordes of curly-haired, dark-skinned post-adolescents, the children of former peasants, descended from the asphyxiating heat of southern Italy. The Mediterranean origins of the Gothic novel have little to do with it. Coil's ballads dedicated to Ostia are already more fitting: after all, the death disco to whose rhythms post-industrial music moved betrayed a strange association with the 'disc of death' that is the Mediterranean sun.

In these conditions, it is hardly surprising that what Leo Anibaldi and the other DJs and producers of the *Suono di Roma* had in common was an acid, strident, and irremediably *dark* sound: a kind of gloomy industrial techno in which, behind layers of obsessive drum machines and Roland 303s gone mad, one seemed to perceive the sound, at once grandiose and tormented, of the ruins that still dot the outskirts of the former Eternal City. In other words, the sound of Remoria. But more generally, we can take *Muta* as a pivotal moment in the 'dark continuum' that binds together five decades of music in Rome, and whose initiators were Goblin, who in the 1970s created the haunting soundtracks to Dario Argento's giallos. There is in fact a direct thread linking the horror rock of Goblin to the modern depressed aesthetics of trap collectives such as Dark Polo Gang, one which passes through the techno years and those annular sabbaths that were rave parties.

To summarise the key moments: at the end of the seventies, Goblin's Claudio Simonetti became an Italo disco producer, authoring a series of dancefloor hits under the moniker Easy Going. The project was born in the gay club of the same name in the centre of Rome, decorated with frescoes by Tom of Finland and twinned with another club called Much More. In Easy Going and Much More, the main local DJs who had played at the clubs in the 1980s transmigrated from Italo disco to house. And it was in this atmosphere that the apprenticeship took place of the first DJs who, with the discovery of techno, would give birth to the dark atmospheres of the Sound of Rome. Their activity suddenly intensified in the early nineties, when the rave parties organised around the GRA attracted audiences that could easily reach 20,000. This gave rise to a culture that for the whole decade transformed the Remorian suburbs into a sort of perennial psycho-urban laboratory where electronic music, acid esotericism, substance abuse, and deviant practices of all kinds and degrees converged. When that season came to its natural end, a small collective of musicians emerged from the remains of the rave civilisation, made up of unredeemed former ravers, drug-addicted rappers, and producers with a passion for old giallo films. They called themselves TruceKlan, and took it as their mission to exacerbate the dark tones of Lory D and Leo Anibaldi's techno in a rap format, infusing them with B-grade Satanism, psychic suffering fuelled by synthetic drug abuse, and homages to the acid neorealism of the films about the Roman suburbs. Despite the almost total indifference of the rest of the nation, their impact on the city was enormous for much of the 2000s and beyond; but even their saga was destined to end, albeit not without yet another passing of the baton. Around the mid 2010s, from the circle of producers within TruceKlan, a very young Sickluke, the man to whom we owe the first mixtape of the trap collective Dark Polo Gang, emerged. Entitled *Full Metal Dark* and entirely devoted to imagery that transforms the psychic discomfort of TruceKlan into a cosmic hyper-depression without redemption, it was the record that reaffirmed the Roman musical underworld's obstinate adherence to the myth of Remoria and the pitch black of the blinding sun.[17]

In the dark continuum that leads from the Goblin of the Dario Argento soundtracks to Dark Polo Gang's hymns to depression, there is a series of elements which, superimposed one on top of the other, make up one of the most complete portraits of Italian Southern Gothic. The morbid sexuality described by Lomax and De Martino on their missions in the Mezzogiorno—and which furnished the background to the giallo cinema baptised by Dario Argento himself at the beginning of the 1970s—is transformed, in the passage

17. For obvious reasons of space, I avoid going into detail and examining in depth the various moments that marked the passing of the baton mentioned here. I will limit myself to emphasising that the Roman dark continuum is not simply a speculation of my own but takes concrete form in a series of real personalities and figures who materially acted as a bridge between the different periods—from the rave organisers who would go on to become full members of the TruceKlan to Lory D's role in the birth of Roman trap.

from Goblin to Easy Going, into a discovery celebration of the 'inverted' sexual act and of the reproductive *dépense* represented by anal intercourse. The disco-sodomite orgies of Easy Going, in turn, announced the Sabbathic roundabouts that would be the great techno gatherings around the GRA ring road. In fact, the legacy of the witches' sabbath resonates in the rave parties not only because of their shared illegal and Saturnian nature, but above all because of the 'horizontal movement' of the dances which, as Luciano Parinetto recalls, makes the sabbath an eminently anal ceremony, committed to *inverting* the existing regime so as to reveal—in the words of Silvia Federici—'the living symbol of the "world turned upside-down"'.[18]

On the other hand, the dark tones bordering on the pathological that unite such apparently very different records as Leo Anibaldi's *Muta*, TruceKlan's albums, and Dark Polo Gang's *Full Metal Dark,* testify to the fact that this upside-down world is nothing other than the world in which noonday demons rage. The apparently 'nocturnal' qualities of the Roman dark continuum cannot be separated from the context in which these experiences were born—a sunburnt city whose periphery is bathed by the Mediterranean, under which invisible volcanoes still smoulder, ready to be reactivated with their payload of extermination. The blackness sung of by the dark continuum is therefore that of Leopardi's 'sacred and terrible noontide' and of that of Italian Southern Gothic's world in which 'there is no room for reason [...] and history' of course; but above all it is a lifeless darkness, completely deprived of any vital impulse. Alan Lomax's recordings retained a spectral quality because they captured on the icy support of the magnetic tape the songs and screams of a world populated by the living dead; in the Roman dark continuum, however, everything is *synthetic*, just like the drugs so dear to the old ravers of the nineties and to the rappers of TruceKlan and Dark Polo Gang. The rubbery coils of Goblin's synths, Leo Anibaldi's artificial rhythms, TruceKlan's samples, Dark Polo Gang's robotic autotune—all are examples of a surrender to the inhuman that is not reducible to a mere 'adaptation to

---

18. S. Federici, *Caliban and the Witch* (Brooklyn: Autonomedia, 2004), 177.

technical progress'. If anything, in the marriage of artificial sound and sun-kissed depressed aesthetics there lies the realisation that—as Minor White had already suggested—'the sun is not fiery after all, but a dead planet'.[19] The memory of how too much sun ceases to mean an increase in illumination and begins to mean a cessation of life resonates in the undead touch of the dark continuum. An excess of sun is deadly; too much heat yields a heap of cold bodies.

ARCANA

Of all the films ascribed to the giallo genre in the 1970s, none better captures the power of solarisation than *Arcana*. Filmed by Giulio Questi in 1972, it is the story of Mrs Tarantino, a widow from the south of Italy who emigrates with her son to wealthy Milan, the foggy capital (at the time) of northern Italy. Having found lodgings in a squalid working-class neighbourhood while the city is busy with the construction of a new metropolitan subway, Mrs Tarantino earns her living by organising seances thanks to her alleged knowledge of the occult arts, a direct legacy of that 'Lucanian magic' which not even Ernesto De Martino's investigations had managed to banish once and for all to the dustbin of superstition. The last representative of a forgotten world governed by a matriarchal society, Mrs Tarantino has an incestuous relationship with her son, who takes advantage of this to steal the secrets of magic arts from his mother and spread panic in the neighbourhood.

The entire film is based on the unresolved conflict between an indus-trialised Milan, fully integrated into modernity, and a South that is by now exhausted but still full of occult presences, which Questi depicts with a paroxysmal use of whiteout, with overexposed yet extremely dark images of a South condemned to remain forever in the past.

As if in a dream, these images underpin the portrait of a glowing Milan, in which the underground construction sites seem to have the unwanted effect

19. Quoted in H. Blau, *The Dubious Spectacle: Extremities of Theater 1976–2000* (Minneapolis: University of Minnesota Press, 2002), 250.

of reawakening long-buried chthonic powers, uncovering the unspeakable load of irrationality that smoulders at the centre of the earth as well as in the bright sunshine of Southern Italy, and pouring out onto to the surface a monstrous array of amputees scarred by their labour.

A sort of surreal posthumous appendix to the original acid neorealism, directly inspired by the *furor solis* of the Italian ethnographic documentary, *Arcana* is perhaps the true masterpiece of Italian Southern Gothic, but not even its fame as a lysergic, cursed, rambling film has saved it from a regrettable and embarrassed oblivion. Because, despite the overtly fantastic register used by Questi, *Arcana* is really a realist film in the purest sense of the term: the great emigration that has seen Southern Italy slowly depopulate since the Second World War, as its inhabitants continue to abandon in droves every year a land 'cracked by sun and solitude' to pour into the rich and industrious North, has also been an emigration of ghosts. Rational, enlightened Milan, comfortably ensconced in the midst of the sinuous currents that govern Capital, the hypermodern Milan that has replaced the ancient fog with a grotesque skyline of skyscrapers redolent of Shanghai and Dubai, the Milan which, from the heights of the Po Valley, distils the poison of protestant ethics, adulterating them with the pragmatism of the Catholicism of noble civil sentiments, sinks its bowels into that same underworld of old subterranean construction sites in which immigrant workers from the South lost parts of their limbs, their hands, their toes—but also memories, spells, ancient curses, new curses. Every city contemplates its nemesis, every city preserves the deformed negative of what it could be but is not, every city conceals within the folds of its geography a latent Remoria that pushes for the inversion to take place. The solarisation that presses from the bowels of Milan, left buried there by the children of Lucanian magic who built, with their own bare hands, the modern metropolis of today, can be triggered at any moment, and perhaps it has already begun to demonstrate its exterminating power.

When, in March 2020, Milan became the global epicentre of the new pandemic that revived the memory of ancient plagues and pestilences in the

West, benign observers from the healthy sectors of society were shocked by the mass flight of children of the South, who unrepentantly left the city where they had found work, home, and affection, to find refuge in the land from which they had originally fled. This escape was interpreted as a betrayal, an act of irresponsibility toward the metropolis that had welcomed them: but in fact it had the flavour of a mission accomplished. For they were also children of the rituals set up by Mrs Tarantino half a century ago, when she arrived in Milan, apparently to feed the engines of that omnivorous machine that is Capital, reminding the world that there is no such thing as consumption without waste, that there is no such thing as nourishment without the production of excrement, that somewhere there is always an asshole. Abandoned to itself, reduced to a ghost town, Milan found itself held hostage by noonday demons. The Black Sun glimpsed under the manholes of *Arcana* was beating down on the city of neo-Gothic spires and hi-tech skyscrapers, and from there it was preparing to blind the entire West with its darkness.

CANICOLA

From a hundred and fifty million kilometres above, a ray shoots down murderously. Its intensity is a hundred thousand kilolux. It radiates such light that all shadows evaporate. It melts knowledge of things in its heat.

The parched earth is a bitter desert: the fire of the sun is the fire of hell! Death falls from sidereal distances: it does not illuminate but blinds, because too much light means darkness ('you cannot look the sun in the face'). Lucifer is the bearer of light, yet his is the domain of shadow.

One hundred and fifty million kilometres to ascend to the underworld beyond the surface. Source of life, bringer of death: source of the life of death. Principle of delusions, hallucinations, and abnormalities. Cause of the abysses of the human psyche.

Sunstroke: pathological effect of too prolonged an exposure to sunlight, causing meningeal and cerebral congestion. Manifests itself in fever and mental disorders. In exceptional cases, coma and death.

VM

THE HIGHEST
FORM OF GNOSIS

Every species can smell its own extinction. The last ones left won't have a pretty time of it. And in ten years, maybe less, the human race will just be a bedtime story for their children; a myth, nothing more.

John Trent

Monstrosity—'properly understood'—says much about the path to the *unnameable*.

Nick Land

Something is causing Pain and something energizes the Agony: may it not be caused through the latent Idea of Supreme Bliss? And this eternal expectation, this amassing of ornament on decay, this ever-abiding thought—is coincidental with the vanity preceding death? O, squalid thought from the most morbid spleen how can I devour thee and save my Soul?

Austin Osman Spare[1]

I was standing in the middle of a field in a remote and unknown area of northern Italy, located on the outskirts of one of the meaningless little towns gracelessly crammed into that part of the world. In the centre, right in front of me, stood a high-voltage electricity pylon, larger than Christ on his bare cross. There I stood, struck by the overwhelming realisation that there was

---

1. *In the Mouth of Madness*, dir. John Carpenter, 1994; N. Land, 'Abstract Horror', *Phyl-Undhu, Abstract Horror, Exterminator* (Shanghai: Time-Spiral, 2014), §105; A.O. Spare, *Ethos: The Magical Writings of Austin Osman Spare* (Thame: I-H-O Books, 2001), 53. This work was born with the full moon in Aries, after a prolonged sabbatical while Venus did her drunken dance over Scorpio.

no reason why we, as a sentient species, would want it to be there. It wasn't transmitting any electricity, and it certainly wasn't a segment of the long electrical artery that turns earth into energy. It was not connected, it was not transmitting life to anyone.[2]

It was a ganglion cyst—not cancerous, not fatal, but malignant enough—growing in the flesh of an absolutely insignificant city: a city like the one I was born in. It was one of the many fruits of forgotten post-industrial putrescence, just like me, and its function was also the same as mine: to be an antenna for the land that generates us. Unlike other pylons, this one functioned as a *spirit box*, using its incomprehensible tangle of cables and metal rods to capture and crystallise those stifled voices that weave a black market of sighs[3] in these outlands that make up the 'provinces'. It was a dark tree, narrating the lies and deceptions, the angelic and demonic choruses sung by the ruins of the wastelands of Italy.[4] It was a messenger of the chthonic neuroses of this city, a symptom emerging from the inversion of an involuntary *psychoanalysis of the flesh of that part of the world*, the referent of an unpronounceable *lalangue*.[5] It was 'a rat-body' with its 'activity,

---

2.   From a strictly ritualistic point of view, the most appropriate and practical definition of this phenomenon would be a phallus separated from any organic body, used for necrophilic couplings with a vast surface, which rejects any descent into its bowels, protecting within itself the dark exchanges and secretions of its own nigredo. Choose your instrument accordingly. The location of the phenomenon: 45.800037, 8.741641.

3.   In this respect, we fully agree with Elytron Frass that the nocturnal underbelly of the earth should be described as a Faustian market, with its occult logic of psychic warfare tactics of an anti-Feng Shui. E. Frass, 'Alt Economy of Inner Night', *Vast Abrupt* (2019), <https://vastabrupt.com/2019/10/21/alt-economy-of-inner-night/>.

4.   A similar phenomenon was described in 'The Tower', *Vast Abrupt* (2018), <https://vastabrupt.com/2018/06/12/the-tower/>.

5.   The Lacanian concept of *lalangue*, introduced in Seminar XX, refers to a Real which is unspeakable, disrupts language and representation, and appears through scars and involuntary incisions in the symbolic order—the spontaneous growth of strangeness within the realm of the signifiant. As the psychoanalyst August Ruhs says In his endorsement of Florian Hecker's *Inspection II*, 'By transcending the unique authority of Freudian discourse, by alienating and synthesizing the dialogue of analyst and analysand, by penetrating the realm of that babble that is the obvious origin of human language and communication, designated by Jacques Lacan as "lalangue", [it] discloses a space beyond representation, and hence beyond sense, intelligibility

its networking, its paradoxical proliferation, its selfdigestion, its eructations, its necroticness, its hunger, and its hole making'.[6]

The role reversal embodied by this pylon within this world should come as no surprise. Italy is one of the most haunted places on the planet. Its plains are drenched in the blackest bile the earth has ever produced, its houses and monuments overflow with an inorganic minerality capable of transmitting syphilitic paralysis everywhere.[7]

It is a site of spiritual possession on a national scale, a possession which can take the most diverse forms: both in the shadowy realm of the provinces and in the schizoid, chaotic urban planning of its gigantic, feral cities.

From the striking public humiliation of Venice, condemned by the sea to be wiped from the face of the planet, to the 'Remorian' sprawl of Rome, condensed, like the gurgling of a muttering corpse, around the saturnine pulsating anus of the GRA (*Grande Raccordo Anulare*), magnum opus of the sorcerer Eugenio Gra;[8] from Etna, which continues to erupt bronze sandals, testimony to the irrational and arbitrary asymmetry that carves out the boundaries of the works produced by the bowels of the earth, to the deadly psychedelic sun that ceaselessly beats down on the fringes of the Mediterranean, annulling all reason and disarming all logic; from Milan, bastard daughter of neo-Chinese hypercapitalism, besieged by the *mould-ridden*

and significance. [...] Closing the screen of the cerebral computer, psychoanalysis emerges as the hard disk's synaptic music, echoing the big bang of our psychic genesis' (F. Hecker, *Inspection II*, Editions Mego, eMego 268 [2019]). My electrical pylon reveals another, more sickly genetic origin.

6.   J. McSweeney, *The Necropastoral* (Ann Arbor, MI: University of Michigan Press 2015), 3.

7.   According to many alchemists, melancholy was caused by an excess of black bile which caused a spike in the mineral content of the blood. This should be an indication of the type of materials that might be used during the ritual.

8.   Both the Spareian genealogy of the creation of the GRA and the Dionysian dynamics of the Remorian sprawl (see 'Solarisation' in this volume) are essential to understanding this national catastrophe. The anal ring of the GRA is so obviously a magical signature of its creator, Eugenio Gra, that we see no reason to tear off its highway disguise in order to prove its infernal nature. We take it for granted that the cancerous outflow of the borgatasphere, which extends around the sabbatical circle of the motorway, is a prime example of the bilious wound through which we were brought into this world. See Mattioli, *Remoria. La città invertita* (Rome: Minimum fax, 2019).

drug forests that devour its suburbs, punctuated by autonomous zones of luciferous anti-oedipity,[9] to the provincial *Choronzonianism* that reigns supreme over that imaginary region that goes by the name of Padania, with its fascistoid excesses and its futuristic will to massacre, the entire body of this land is contorted by painful, unreal spasms.

This too is an ancient phenomenon. It may sound banal to recall the phantasmagorical Otranto, gigantic severed-head without a vital organ in sight, which established the motif for that poetic cosmic flatline known as the 'Gothic novel'. And it may sound trivial to recall Cefalù, Aleister Crowley's temporary toxic utopia, a tiny example of heterotopic witchcraft wielded against the 'Human Security System' embodied in a secluded patch of the horrid peninsula. Perhaps then we should go back to figures of Roman decadence such as Caligula and Nero, and to the suicidal joy of Heliogabalus, all exemplars of a jouissance that is so profound, innate, and omnicidal that history books can barely bear to mention it. The examples are manifold; let us just reiterate that the possession we are talking about here is nothing more than a secret hidden in plain sight. Only the foolish or the blind would ridicule it or deny its self-evidence.

The origins of this possession, this pestilence, this demonic biliousness, this excess of alchemical minerality, are perhaps diverse. In the pathetic words of Sigmund Freud, 'society [is] based on complicity in the common crime',[10] but, as far as *Weird Italia* is concerned, the possible crimes that may have precipitated this terrifying situation are many in number, and all equally suitable candidates as the culprits of such a massacre.[11] Giordano Bruno's *ligatures*, among the favourite topics of many influential tamers of

---

9. The forest that grows on the outskirts of Milan is a ghostly rendezvous for all the heroin-addicted vampires and methamphetamine zombies—wilderness-catalyst for the synthetic K-death of the whole province. Milan emerges from these crypts, and all who dare enter must know that they are headed for the heart of darkness.

10. S. Freud, *Totem and Taboo*, tr. J. Strachey (Routledge: London and New York, 2004), 170.

11. Let us point out, *en passant*, that we do not seek to identify the crime so as to contain it, but to celebrate it and enjoy and participate in its majesty.

pagan cultures and semiotic domesticators of savagery, may have been some kind of Faustian pact,[12] generating a cosmic inversion that now engulfs us all. Or perhaps Galileo's scientific revolution inflicted such a deep wound upon the anthropocentric body that by its own strength alone it has forced the earth into premature damnation. Or maybe the asymmetrical satanic warfare of many witches,[13] such as those found in utterly insignificant places like Venegono, is still ongoing to this day.[14] Or, finally and most straightforwardly,

---

12. At least that's what the patron saint of our spiritual insurrection, Luciano Parinetto, seems to suggest: 'For Bruno, a magician is someone who, operating on nature, in practice reverses the knowledge he has acquired of the descending/ascending connection that ties together all the entities of the infinite cosmos in the equally infinite tangle of ligatures that constitute it.' L. Parinetto, 'Bruno pro nobis', *Giordano Bruno, La magia e le ligatures* (Rome: Mimesis, 2000), 11–12.

13. 'Being to be defined but constitution of the idea of Being, which is negation rather than affirmation, when we exasperate it, attack on the anthropomorphic idea of Being, solution of antinomies, doubts, worries, problems, through this dramatic account of the disappearance of the notion of Being in which, moreover, Satan appears.' A. Artaud, *The Death of Satan and Other Mystical Writings,* (London: Calder & Boyars, 1974), 9.

14. A.M. Castiglioni, *Streghe e roghi nel ducato di Milano. Processi per stregoneria a Venegono Superiore nel 1520* (Rome: Selene, 1999). It should come as no surprise that the most widely read book in Italian high schools is Manzoni's *I promessi sposi*, in which girls and boys witness the cadaverous hand of Divine Providence dragging a couple of poor idiots across a literally pestilential land, where the Catholic Mass is a rite of collective infestation, and mass paranoia and perennial witch hunts tear the land apart. This same pestilential landscape is the incarnation of Italy in the Decameron. We might hypothesise that, as in Artaud's poetics, the plague indicates an acceleration of the material subconscious of human society (or any human structure, for that matter) toward desecration and thermodynamic laceration. The plague is the provincial social manifestation of the miasma at the centre of the earth upon which we stand, the uncontrollable draining of bodily fluids that erodes society until all that remains is an archipelago of disfigured humanoids at war with themselves and with everything. Some have called this pestilential trend, based on a cascade of putrid slime, 'patchwork', and have tried to construct a positive vision of the anarchy to come. We absolutely approve of this adventurous anti-politics and we encourage the reader to dig deeper into this noble endeavour. In the words of Artaud:

'But from this spiritual freedom with which the plague develops, without rats, without microbes, and without contact, can be deduced the somber and absolute action of a spectacle which I shall attempt to analyze.

Once the plague is established in a city, the regular forms collapse. There is no maintenance of roads and sewers, no army, no police, no municipal administration. Pyres are lit at random to burn the dead, with whatever means are available. Each family wants to have its own. Then wood, space, and flame itself growing rare, there are family feuds around the pyres, soon followed by a general flight, for the corpses are too numerous.

this may be only the local manifestation of a more general planetary tendency—one aspect of the worldwide annihilation we have called *modernity*, an era that claims to be 'progressive, innovative, irreversible, and expansive'.[15] Whereas *pre-modern*s lived in a world 'marked by dogmatism, a drive towards unity, verticality, the need for transcendent rule and the symbol of the sun', moderns live in a catastrophic miasma that can only be characterised as 'lunar, secular, horizontal, multiple and immanent'.[16] This national nigredo could simply be a particularly virulent manifestation of a disintegration and lunacy that is taking place everywhere in the world at various speeds. It could also be that, even more brutally, as Nick Land recently argued, the universe itself is nothing more than a disintegrating machine; we are simply witnessing our own peak *laceration*, our own private martyrdom.[17]

The dead already clog the streets in ragged pyramids gnawed at by animals around the edges. The stench rises in the air like a flame. Entire streets are blocked by the piles of dead. Then the houses open and the delirious victims, their minds crowded with hideous visions, spread howling through the streets. The disease that ferments in their viscera and circulates throughout their entire organism discharges itself in tremendous cerebral explosions. [...] Over the poisonous, thick, bloody streams (color of agony and opium) which gush out of the corpses, strange personages pass, dressed in wax, with noses long as sausages and eyes of glass [...] chanting absurd litanies that cannot prevent them from sinking into the furnace in their turn. These ignorant doctors betray only their fear and their childishness.

The dregs of the population, apparently immunised by their frenzied greed, enter the open houses and pillage riches they know will serve no purpose or profit. And at that moment the theater is born. The theater, i.e., an immediate gratuitousness provoking acts without use or profit.

The last of the living are in a frenzy: the obedient and virtuous son kills his father; the chaste man performs sodomy upon his neighbors. The lecher becomes pure. The miser throws his gold in handfuls out the window. The warrior hero sets fire to the city he once risked his life to save. The dandy decks himself out in his finest clothes and promenades before the charnel houses. Neither the idea of an absence of sanctions nor that of imminent death suffices to motivate acts so gratuitously absurd on the part of men who did not believe death could end anything.' A. Artaud, *The Theatre and its Double*, tr. M.C. Richards (New York: Grove Press, 1958), 23–24. These notes should inform the setting and atmosphere of the ritual. Read Artaud religiously.

15. Ireland, 'The Poememenon: Form as Occult Technology'.
16. Ibid.
17. N. Land, 'Disintegration', *Jacobite* (2019), <https://jacobitemag.com/2019/07/15/disintegration/>. For those who are not yet convinced, and insist on considering the hypothesis of this infestation an exaggeration, we recall the words of one of the most important scholars

Yet the phenomenon is, let me repeat, clearly evident, and perhaps too widespread to study analytically or even significantly. Its scale and violence are so enduring, all-encompassing, and cryptic that any sensible approach would be doomed to failure. Those who would document this mass infestation would have to return to the parabola of the electrical pylon and assume its position. They would, in other words, have to listen to the bazaar of horrible howls that incoherently narrate the pain of this part of the world. They would need to turn themselves into a howling spirit box, joining us and all the people of this part of the world, the other fruits of this rotten belly, and surrender to the impetuous chthonian *lalangue*. Emptied of everything, they must try to transmit the inverted wisdom.

This is what we shall try to do—we shall do what we were born to do, and we shall report what we record, without making any claim as to its clarity or coherence. Our transmission will report the voices of a few deceased people, conveying to the reader the wisdom of a small part of a *black and subterranean canon* which, in this ocean of bile, is the only thing within our power. Our only guiding principle will be *masochism*.

---

of Hamid Parsani's occultural work, a clear demonstration that demonic infestation finds its privileged tactics in the excess of destructive power: 'Modern criminology refuses to acknowledge the presence of demons, in the same way that secular disbelief condemns the inanity of a demon possessing a helpless human: if demons exist and are that powerful then why would they possess a wretched anthropian? Such an objection misunderstands the mechanisms involved in the communication between xeno-agents and the human security system. For demons maintain their outsideness precisely through a power of overkilling (sheer exteriority of a force), inflicting more power than is needed just to unlock a gate. Demons simply crack open the prey. The overkilling power effectuates an openness outside the system's capacity to afford it. Once openness cannot be afforded by the system's capacity, it turns into an instance of butchery rather than an act of emancipation characterized by human "access" to the outside. Overkill is a spectacle staged on the fundamental incapacity of the system to cope with the outside. Through overkill, the xeno-agent performs its demonic spectacle and effectuates its exteriority which the system cannot afford. The exteriority of the demon cannot be captured by the desire of the system for openness, and for this reason such exteriority overkills (butchers open) the system. To possess a strong man is certainly enough to flaunt the demon's power, but all the better if the possessed is a child or old woman, to signify the outsideness of the demon through which overkilling power is generated.' R. Negarestani, *Cyclonopedia: Complicity with Anonymous Materials* (Melbourne: re.press, 2008), 118–19.

I have chosen this category because it is the only weapon destructive enough to deal with the subject and survive the gnosis we shall encounter along the way. Anyone wishing to approach such a generalised *demono-mania* should take into account Gilles Deleuze's definition of masochism: an 'ice age', an expiation of our humanity. This category will be thoroughly explained through the figures we shall conjure up along the way, the voices we will extract from the *free black market of ideas in the world below*—but first, allow me to scribble, with trembling hand, some preliminary notes on the concept of masochism.

MASOCHISM AS INVERTED WISDOM

'Healthy' sex and its consequences have been a disaster for the human race. The abandonment of the fetish—or at least the reduction of fetishism to the stale pantomime of the *servant-master dialectic*—has had a terrifying effect upon our ability to think speculatively.[18] Libidinal security, the goal of society's sexual sovereignty, has hampered our ability to speculate meaningfully about our own dissolution and unconditional liberation as a species, about the inhuman forces that plunge us into our inner Hades. Stubbornly locked within the sharp distinction—which functions, de facto, as a unity-within-separation—between the subject-father and the object-slave, we have stifled the call of the depths, whose lament we hear even in the most superficial forms of unrestrained, xenophilic fetishism. If only we could once and for all disentangle the dialectic, free ourselves from the BDSM romantic comedy in which we find ourselves trapped, and see our desires for what

---

18. 'Alienness—and the alienation that results from a confrontation with alienness—is the genesis of novelty and change. Wherever one encounters the alien, a mutation or a transformation isn't far behind. And yet, because alienness involves an aspect of unknowability and unpredictability—an erasure of the familiar and the homely—it is also one of the things in the world which makes us most afraid. We fear the different and the strange, yet we require these things in order to evolve. This makes for a paradoxical affective relationship with the notions of otherness and difference that alienness encompasses—a bizarre and complex orientation unifying dread and desire.' A. Ireland, 'Alien Rhythms', *0AZ* (2019), <zinzrinz.blogspot.com/2019/04/alien-rhythms.html>.

they really are, then we would finally feel in touch with a universe penetrated by an infinite love of its own dissolution.[19]

This was, more or less, the simple insight that moved a young Gilles Deleuze as he wrote arguably his most useful book, *Coldness and Cruelty*. For Deleuze, the word *sadomasochism* was a perverse psychoanalytical joke designed to convince us that there is only one form of sexual deviancy. There is only one two-headed beast, repeating the tired game of masters and servants ad nauseam.[20] But this is a lie, we know it, we have always known it.

Deleuze begins to slay the dragon by considering sadism and masochism as two distinct entities, each with its own economies, its own pains and pleasures, its own catastrophic ends. He then divides these two forms of massacre into two elements: a personal one, representing the experience of desire *for us*, and an impersonal one, tracing the movements and exchanges of unconscious libidinal forces *without us*.

---

19. 'Thus insofar as Xenophilia is satisfied it cannot be. Insofar as Xenophilia is, it cannot be satisfied. Xenophilia is doubly unconditional. Lacking satisfaction conditions, it 1) does not represent a goal state and 2) cannot oppose a present state on the grounds that it fails to realize those goals. Finally, if *per impossibile*, the posthumanist could envisage satisfaction conditions of her desire she would no longer be motivated by xenophilia. Xenophilic futurity need not be posed as radically incomprehensible but its adequate conceptualization must await the event of its construction or disconnection.' D. Roden, 'Xenophilia', *Enemy Industry*, 2019, <http://enemyindustry.wordpress.com/2019/05/02/x-phi-or-alienation-is-not-correlation>. Keep these two conditions in mind while performing any kind of ritual following our doctrine. Once you cross the threshold, they may save your soul and prepare you for what awaits you on the other side.
20. This opening up of the vast horizon beyond the sovereign sexual deficiency is probably one of the best ways of conceptualising the pagan explosions of sunlight that thundered through Mark Fisher's later work. *Acid Communism*, another form of adventurous anti-politics that we strongly support, involves recovering the communitarian experience of outsideness of the tribes that inhabit the desert on the outskirts of the City of Man. 'A new humanity, a new seeing, a new thinking, a new loving: this is the promise of acid communism, and it was the promise that you could hear in "Psychedelic Shack" and the culture that inspired it. Only five years separated "Psychedelic Shack" from the Temptations' early signature hit "My Girl", but how many new worlds had come into being then? In "My Girl", love remains sentimentalised, confined to the couple, in "Psychedelic Shack", love is collective, and orientated towards the outside.' M. Fisher, 'Acid Communism (Unfinished Introduction)', in *K-Punk: The Collected and Unpublished Writings of Mark Fisher (2004–2016)*, ed. D. Ambrose (London: Repeater, 2018), 793.

The sadist is embodied, even more than by Sade himself, by the figure of Spinoza. The desire of the sadist is a tome produced *more geometrico*. Body is piled upon body, every pore is sexualised and libidinised only to be mercilessly wounded over and over again. Every bodily fluid is calculated, classified, and defined so as to force a more complete dispersion. The human body becomes a pure trunk of barely contained blood, an enormous digestive tube endlessly vomiting and shitting out precise and ordered quantities of unstructured matter, a pure distributor of tears. The sadist is thus driven by a deeply annihilating desire, a fervour that burns with an eternal will to be the horribly precise right-hand man of the foetid God of the Old Testament.

> We have therefore to distinguish two factors constituting a dual language. The first, the imperative and descriptive factor, represents the personal element; it directs and describes the personal violence of the sadist as well as his individual tastes; the second and higher factor represents the *impersonal* element in sadism and identifies the impersonal violence with an Idea of pure reason, with a terrifying demonstration capable of subordinating the first element. In Sade we discover a surprising affinity with Spinoza—a naturalistic and mechanistic approach imbued with the mathematical spirit. This accounts for the endless repetitions, the reiterated quantitative process of multiplying illustrations and adding victim upon victim, again and again retracing the thousand circles of an irreducibly solitary argument.[21]

Sadism is thus the *apotheosis of separative wisdom*, which seeks the dissolution of the self and the world through the full use of its power to categorise, calculate, expose, and dictate. For us, this is no insignificant clue. However, it serves no practical purpose in our demonomaniacal descent into the web of terrors that curse the land that spawned us. While we undoubtedly encourage our reader to go deeper and indulge in the annihilation of

---

21.   G. Deleuze, *Masochism: Coldness and Cruelty* (New York: Zone Books, 1989), 19–20.

the world so as to reach the pulsating pinnacle of their intelligence, we are looking for something else.

According to Deleuze, masochism has a very particular nature, a nature that makes it a completely different beast from the economy of sadism; it is not the dialectical negative of the latter, but something completely different. It is a '"black" theology'[22] or a 'perverse mysticism',[23] an *obscure wisdom*, a *supra-sensual and superior sentimentalism-as-pure-gnosis* which operates through depersonalisations and inter-purifications. While the sadist enjoys an amplified form of wisdom—a wisdom that precisely divides, categorises, disembowels, pierces, lacerates—the masochist draws upon a different wisdom which, from the point of view of 'sanity', appears as the absolute enjoyment of running backwards toward the black heart of one's inner steppe, toward the centre of the earth itself. While sadism is the pleasure of surgically tearing apart the unity of the world and self, the all-devouring apotheosis of wisdom, masochism is the forbidden enjoyment of descent and immersion, of getting lost in the cosmic labyrinth, of freezing to death in the return to the infinite Night, full of agonies. It is, to recall the Thing from which we started, the becoming-spirit box, faithful receiver of the voices of the dead, of the Outside and of the aeonic massacre of the cosmos; it is the becoming-steppe of the world and the immersion in its bowels. Deleuze writes:

> Like Sade, Masoch distinguishes two natures, but he characterizes them differently. Coarse nature is ruled by individual arbitrariness: cunning and violence, hatred and destruction, disorder and sensuality are everywhere at work. Beyond this lies the great primary nature, which is impersonal and self-conscious, sentimental and supersensual. In the prologue to Masoch's *Galician Tales* a character known as 'the wanderer' indicts Nature for being evil. Nature replies in her own defense that she is not hostile and does not hate us, even when she deals death, but always turns to us a threefold face:

---

22. Ibid., 120.
23. Ibid.

cold, maternal, severe.... Nature is the steppe. Masoch's descriptions of the steppe are of great beauty, especially the one that appears at the beginning of *Frinko Balaban*; the representation of nature by the identical images of the steppe, the sea and the mother aims to convey the idea that the steppe buries the Greek world of sensuality and rejects at the same time the modern world of sadism. It is like a cooling force which transforms desire and trans-mutes cruelty. This is the messianic idealism of the steppe.[24]

Masoch is a great inverted climber who ascends to the heights of the supra-sensual only to fall deeper into the geotraumatic core of sexuality,[25] the pulsating heart of the earth that opened up and, through desiccations, ice ages and other instruments of aeonic torture, forced the living to become a sensual entity. While sadism is the libidinal economy of violent separation and destruction, masochism is the enjoyment of regression, self-negation, determination from outside, and disappearance.[26] The masochist is the

---

24.   Ibid., 55

25.   'The theory of trauma was a crypto-geological hybrid from the very start. [...] Abandoning the circumspection with which Freud handles what he still supposes to be 'metaphorical' stratal imagery, Dr Daniel Barker's Cosmic Theory of Geotrauma, or Plutonics, flattens the theory of psychic trauma onto geophysics, with psychic experience becoming an encrypted geological report, the repercussion of a primal Hadean trauma in the material unconscious of Planet Earth. Further developing Professor Challenger's model of 'generalised stratification', Barker ultra-radicalises Nietzschean genealogy into a materialist cryptoscience. [...] Resident Alien; The Insider. Trauma is at once a twisted plot, a geological complex, and a heavily-encrypted file-system. The archives come to the surface only to be churned and folded back into the detritus of their own repression. The tendrils of the 'pathogenic nucleus' merge imperceptibly with 'normal tissue'. And every living individual that ever existed is a playback copy, drawn from the recording vaults, trapped in a refrain that sings the glory of Cthelll.' R. Mackay, 'A Brief History of Geotrauma' (2011) <https://readthis.wtf/writing/a-brief-history-of-geotrauma/>.

26.   This cyborgian character of masochism was lucidly observed by Theodore Reik. For Reik, the paradoxical structure of masochism so clearly reflects the humiliation of Prometheus (defier of the gods and the thief of fire, tied to a rock and eaten alive for all eternity), which is so gloriously—at least from an unconditional accelerationist perspective—endemic to technocultural enhancement, that he sees in the masochist the epitome of modern humanity: 'All the different and frequently discordant tunes we heard in masochism, finally united in a full and sonorous accord: to uphold oneself despite all force, and where this is not possible, to perish in spite of all force. That is the grim tragicomedy of the martyr-attitude of modern man or at

master of the art of making inner demons speak through the devious use of prostheses, contracts, and bindings.[27] He becomes a cold steppe where no one has ever set foot but where, against all forms of stable organisation, geotrauma-tics still resound loudly and clearly.[28]

The forms and particularities of this *catabasis through ascension*, which makes the masochist a libidinous desert tuned to the cries of the planet, are well documented. It could be said, for example, contrary to what Bataille seems to imply in some of his writings,[29] that masochism, in this absolutely cosmological and self-destructive sense, has served as the total consummation of and the impetus behind most mystical experiences in Christian theology.

---

least of its essential characters. Here is a tale of human frailty and sorrow which is at the same time a tale of human force and lust'. Note the clear anabatic-katabatic structure of this passage, an indication of the validity of our description. T. Reik, *Masochism In Modern Man* (New York: Farrar and Rinehart, 1941), 433.

27. In its purest forms, masochism is a deadly addiction, the deadly injection derived from the radiation secreted by the Black Sun, which unlocks the ossified energetics of the repressed inorganic, forcing us to descend completely to the non-sexual, tectonic roots of our sexuality. These are the terrible psychotic tremors that generated our '"perversion," in the sense of a drug that allows [us] to ensure a narcissistic homeostasis by means of a nonverbal, unnamable (hence untouchable and omnipotent) hold over a nonobjectal Thing.' J. Kristeva, *Black Sun: Depression and Melancholia* (New York: Columbia University Press, 1992), 48.

28. Let us pause for a moment to recognise once again the basis of all of our ritual practice and magical thinking: catastrophe will always be the principal engine of the universe. As clearly stated in 'Catastrophic Astrology', we side with the intellectual tradition that has explicitly promoted this ontological position: Sándor Ferenczi, Sigmund Freud, Daniel Barker, Georges Bataille, Zecharia Sitchin, Immanuel Velikovsky and, more recently, Thomas Moynihan (*Spinal Catastrophism: A Secret History* [Falmouth: Urbanomic, 2020]). Keep this genealogy in mind when imagining the universe in which your ritual should take place.

29. 'In its cruelty, eroticism brings indigence, demands ruinous outlays. Moreover it's too expensive to be thought of in relation to asceticism. On the other hand, mystical and ecstatic states (which don't entail moral or material ruin) can't do without certain extremes against self. My experience with the latter of these as well as the former makes me aware of the contrasting effects the two kinds of excess have. To give up my sexual habits would mean I'd have to discover some other means of tormenting myself, though this torture would have to be as intoxicating as alcohol.' G. Bataille, *Guilty*, tr. B. Boone (Venice, CA: The Lapis Press, 1988), 22.

Let us take Henry Suso, one of the most misunderstood doyens of Christian mysticism. The peculiarity of his character lies in the fact that he took our understanding of mysticism to its highest level. His holiness is characterised by cool, cenobitic behaviour. He was in the habit of constructing his instruments of torture in order to understand more fully the self-immolation of God himself, taking the idea of the imitation of Christ to a whole new level. His writings are imbued with the will to become-desert, to ascend catabatically toward the highest form of knowledge, toward the gnosis of the tectonic rocks of the bowels of unconscious desire.

A striking example of this is his notoriously masochistic and pornographic imitation of Jesus's crucifixion, in which God unfolds before his grieving eyes the paradoxical structure of the masochistic anarchic complex. Let us quote it in full:

After the Last Supper, when in the anguish of my meek heart, and in the pain of my whole body, I resigned myself on the mountain to the bitter death, discovering that it was near, I was covered with sweat and blood. I was captured by my enemies, severely tied up, meanly carried away. At night I was abused vilely; they scourged me, spat on me and blindfolded me. Early in the morning I was brought before Caiaphas, accused, found guilty and condemned to death. An unspeakable pain was visible in my pure mother, from the first glance she had of my anguish, until I was nailed to the cross. I was shamefully brought before Pilate, unjustly accused, condemned to death. They stood before me with terrible looks, like cruel giants, and I stood before them meekly, like a lamb. I, the Eternal Wisdom, in white robes, was mocked as a madwoman before Pilate. My beautiful body was painfully torn and tortured by the cruel blows of the whip. My tender ears were pierced by the cries of 'Hang him, hang the criminal!' resounding in the air.

THE SERVANT: Ah, Lord, the beginning is so painful, how will the end be? If I saw a wild animal so mistreated in my presence, I could scarcely bear it; so, then, your sufferings would have pierced my heart and soul, and rightly so! But, Lord, there is a great wonder in my heart. My beloved Lord, I seek your divine nature in every place, but you reveal only your humanity. I seek your sweetness, you express your bitterness. I wanted to suck your breast, you teach me to fight. Ah, Lord, what do you mean by this?

ETERNAL WISDOM'S ANSWER: No one can attain to the divine majesty nor to the extraordinary sweetness if he is not first drawn to the image of my human bitterness. The higher one ascends, without having crossed my humanity, the lower one falls.[30]

Here we can clearly see the (un)structure of masochistic desire, we can breathe the unspeakably frail air at the height of loving despair. Henry Suso's omniscient and ineffable God speaks of the dark theology that Deleuze saw in Masoch's work: true supra-sensual transcendence is a fall into humiliated immanence, it is a downward ascent that empties the masochist of everything, aiming at the cold core of his desire. The masochist is the explorer of the steppe that is at the origin of Love, the chilling and inhuman desert from which sexuality is descended.

Mysticism, then, is the closest approximation to an extremely geo-traumatic sexuality, a sexuality that abolishes humanity and lets the Great Inorganic Outside speak, personified by an Unmanifest and Unnameable God. Accelerate mystical theology and you will hear the earth scream....

But that's enough; you will have already grasped the concept we wanted to sketch out.

Let us then proceed to explore this terrible Italian affliction, making use of a tiny black canon of heterogeneous voices that offer testimony to the spiritual infestation that possesses us and the land from which we come. To this end, we will use the concept of masochism in two specific ways: first, we will report only the voices of the Great Masochists, masters in the art

---

30. E. Suso, *Libretto dell'Eterna Sapienza* (Rome: Paoline, 1992).

of geotraumatic masochism. Second, we will use masochism as a guiding thread, a recurrent theme that unites the different voices we bring together in our exploration. We will question those who, to varying degrees and in this blighted land, have embodied the pleasure of enduring the horrific shrieks of tectonics tearing apart the Unity of the World, who have forced themselves to become hyper-Schopenhauerians by exploring the inorganic laws of massacre and desire, who have seen God, the Creator of the Cosmos, as the ultimate impaler and desecrator, who have wanted so badly to become inorganic that they have decided that the entire human race must disappear, once and for all. We will do this by looking for masochism everywhere, like mad detectives, and in our turn masochistically endure this parade of lost souls. Now, please, turn around and go away.[31]

THE BLACK CANON

You are one of the only vivid memories of my first adoption and I hardly knew you. The voices came fast, not knowing how to articulate what you had done or why. The first voices were shouting SUICIDE, saying you were dead.

Soon afterwards they changed the story, found better informants, made sure you were still alive. You cut your wrist in front of a church, spilling blood on the white stairs that lead to God's putrid kingdom.

You were not trying to die out of despair, that's what upset them. You were enjoying it, they said incredulously. You were trying to impress someone, you were humiliating God and all creation for no reason, laughing all the way to the gates of Hell. Your act was without reason, or was motivated by futile

---

31.   The shadow-text ritual ends here. Following the detailed instructions in this anthology should give you a fairly precise idea of what you should do when engaging in ritual practice. In the following pages you will find a few more details, i.e., the coordinates for the pilgrimage, but consider them as external and somewhat preliminary information. Read the canon in a paranoid fashion. Within it you will find other important associations that will inform your ritual practices. Some are obvious (such as the ritual symbolism of The Child, The Empire, The Decadence, The Two Mothers, The Armies, or even the number of the last footnote of the shadow-text), others not so much. Pay attention.

motives, which was even worse and more unbearably shocking than your supposed death.

They would have accepted you as a dying, adolescent idiot, bleeding out on the church steps,[32] in the arms of God, forgiven and soon forgotten in the rotten belly of Heaven. They would have liked to say that you were depressed, that it was society's fault, that it was sex, drugs, and their capitalist-realist complements, that it was a protest against the slow erasure of your future, that the culprit was the end of the old traditions.

But you were rebellious, you declared with all your heart that you wanted it badly and that you would do it again and again, opening up for them the sterile anus of your desire. In the face of your willingness to publicly extinguish yourself, in the face of your blood ritual, the public discourse and the structure of the *polis* became, as it always had been, the containing structure for a dastardly, descending hunger, the exile of the Primordial Masochist. We talk to each other, we form communities, we build cities and states and nations to drive a stake through the heart of Love, which is always virtually a death drive and a form of suicidal passivity, an already accomplished anti-politics.

They were so shaken up that they put the most ridiculous band-aid on your desire to regress beyond and below the organ: as they continued to search for better words and appropriate descriptions, they said you were 'emo'; you had done it, they said, because every teenager was fascinated by this aberrant fashion trend, one of many barbarities in a country inhabited by assholes and junkies, with someone always hanging from the branch of a tree in some forest never far from where you were. All the cool kids cut their wrists, you were no different.

And after all, this last one wasn't such a bad assessment; you did it for some stupid and insignificant reason, as is the case with all the best blasphemous acts. This description, at least, with its embarrassed incredulity, barely able to be spoken, highlighted two fundamental tendencies of the obsession you embodied.

---

32.   45.818544, 8.827224.

Firstly, it showed that your gesture was the epiphenomenon of a much wider headless movement, a collective, non-local but nevertheless somehow provincial tendency of anti-human, cultural consumption. You were following the long shadows of limitless modernity, of the erosion of all solidity, of the endless, unstoppable and continuous joke of human extinction and erasure, of that Thing that so many scholars have desperately tried to tame and sociologise. You were the puppet of a frenzied cosmic liquidation and its parade of universal idiocy—of the terminal form of the blind, stupid, obtuse, and uncontrolled process of *K-death*.

Secondly, it expressed in a somewhat sublime way the absurdity of your act. Rather than trying to turn it into a social, ethical gesture, a reasonable, rational protest, it described you as an antisocial thrillseeker. You were following the ephemeral enjoyment of death, the unmediated joy of suddenly regressing back to the erupting womb that gave birth to us and executing the whole of society and the self. Beneath the surface of this world, you discovered the mechanisms of massacre and enjoyment, you climbed the blade to the mall-goth heart of the universal death drive.

You, two-headed monster, suicidal and provocative. Co-spiritual hand behind my armies; mother, unsatiable and insatiable, of the desire to mourn my death. Giulia Mesa and Giulia Domna.

§ 01 The first theoretical guide we can identify in this obsession is another teenage suicide. There is a pathetic story that Julius Evola tells in his biography. He recalls an extremely desperate time in his life in which he lost the will to live. He felt as if possessed by a very negative interpretation of Nietzsche, an interpretation that had come to him from an author who he first described, in order to distance himself from him, as 'Jewish'. This depressive reading of Nietzsche had spread through Evola's life like black bile, paralysing him to the point of being unable to be or do anything. His whole macho-Aryan pose collapsed miserably as the result of a confrontation with the words of a teenager.

The account of this author's work in Evola's *The Path of Cinnabar* reads like a typical Lovecraftian story. We have the protagonist who comes across a terrifying text and, word by word, begins to understand the unthinkability of human existence. Finally, he accepts the idea that reality is more monstrous and icy than he could ever have thought. The terrible text appears as the pinnacle of a masochistic prosthetics, a machine that wounds the mind endlessly, that drives you toward a mortal apotheosis until you plunge into the bowels of Hell.

Only an encounter with the quietism of Buddhist extinctionism saved Evola from madness and suicide. Only a newly acquired fascist spirituality, with its humanist and supremacist dream of material acquiescence and subjective indestructibility, could put a stop to the madness of the metaphysical masochism that he had been facing. This is how Miroslav Griško recounts Evola's torment and his recovery:

> Recounting in his memoirs an intent to commit suicide and thus follow the pattern of his influences [...] the seemingly haphazard discovery of a fragment from the *Majjhima Nikaya* spares Evola's terrerstrial life: 'He who takes extinction to be extinction and, having taken extinction to be extinction, thinks of extinction, thinks of extinction, thinks of extinction, thinks "Mine is extinction", and rejoices in extinction, such a person, I say, does not know extinction.' Extinction must always be deferred, continually pushed towards the most extreme exterior point. Suicide and non-suicide form the same gesture from the perspective of the remoteness of the higher form of extinction. In this conception of extinction's remoteness, the unmappable model of inner war nevertheless yields the minimal form of a praxis, which infers in its performance the prosecution of a mission.[33]

But who was this boy who brought Evola to the brink of death? What sort of inhuman metaphysics had he conceived?

---

33. Griško, 'Operation Eukaryotic Cell'.

Carlo Michelstaedter died in his native Gorizia on 17 October 1910: he shot himself after an argument with his mother. He was 23 years old.

Michelstaedter left behind him a heap of writings and poetic texts, as if he had exploded into a million pieces, all pervaded by the hyper-Schopenhauerian-Nietzscheanism that had almost killed Evola. Together, these writings form a labyrinth of masochistic ramblings against an indifferent universe. The only complete work, the only real book he left us is his university thesis, entitled *Persuasion and Rhetoric*.

It is a book that truly seems like an alien artefact, and one that resists all forms of categorisation and temporal analysis. It is clearly the work of an angst-ridden teenager, angry at the world and at himself, locked in his isolated room writing clumsy anathemas; but at the same time, paradoxically, it is a rigorous treatise on a higher form of black physics, a deeper and more disturbing form of entropy. It is an essay written in a language that is a pidgin of dead and living languages schizophrenically blended together, addressing a deeper gnosis of the fundamental laws of nature.

While it has often been read as a quasi-existential book celebrating finitude, suicide, and the inevitability of our individual death, the text should instead be regarded as a precursor of the entropic Love described by the Gruppo di Nun in its *Dogma*. This book, in other words, is a kind of long presocratic fragment that anticipated our own understanding of nature and of this collapsing universe. Michelstaedter's black physics is our physics.

The central thesis of Michelstaedter's work is a radicalisation of Schopenhauer's idea that '[t]he parts of the body must correspond completely to the chief demands and desires by which the will manifests itself; they must be the visible expression of these desires. Teeth, gullet, and intestinal canal are objectified hunger; the genitals are objectified sexual impulse; grasping hands and nimble feet correspond to the more indirect strivings of the will which they represent'.[34] According to Schopenhauer, every organ can be imagined and constructed according to the purposes of the desires it embodies. Every

---

34.   Schopenhauer, *The World as Will and Representation*, vol. 1, 108 [§20].

part of us is the realisation of some Final Attractor, a final satisfaction that forms us from the beginning. For Schopenhauer, each organ is an independent little teleoplexic creature driven by a congenital and primordial hunger.

For Michelstaedter, Schopenhauer's idea is fundamentally correct, but he does not fully grasp the implications of his own theoretical statement. Primordial hunger is not simply the way to explain and analyse some particular teleoplexic circuits, but it is the key to understanding the cryptic and telic structure of reality itself. The Real is this hunger and it is this descending drive, this corrupt carnage that forces everything to its terminal state and finally to its expulsion:

I know I want and do not have what I want. A weight hangs suspended from a hook; being suspended, it suffers because it cannot fall: it cannot get off the hook, for insofar as it is weight it suspends, and as long as it suspends it depends.

We want to satisfy it: we free it from its dependence, letting it go so that it might satisfy its hunger for what lies below, and it falls independently for as long as it is content to fall. But at none of the points attained is it content to stop; it still wants to fall, for the next point below continually overtakes in lowness that which the weight has just attained. Nor will any future point be such as to render it content, being necessary to the weight's life insofar [...] as it awaits below. But every time a point is made present, it will be emptied of all attraction, no longer being below; thus does it *want at every point the points below it*, and those attract it more and more. It is always drawn by an equal hunger for what is lower, and the will to fall remains infinite with it always.

If at some point its will were finished and it could *possess* in one point the infinite descent of the infinite future, at that point it would no longer be what it is—a *weight*.

Its life is this want of life. If it no longer wanted but were finished, perfect, if it possessed its own self, it would have ended its existence. At that point, as its own impediment to possessing life, the weight would not depend on what is external as much as on its own self, in that it is not given the means to be satisfied. The weight can never be *persuaded*.

Its life is this lack of its life. When it no longer lacks anything, but is finite, perfect, possesses itself, it will have ceased to exist. The burden is to itself the impediment to possessing its life, and it no longer depends on anything but itself in what it cannot satisfy. The weight can never be *persuaded*.[35]

This is the expression of a terrifying metaphysics, a philosophy built on the thirst for the *annihilation* of matter. Michelstaedter radicalises Schopenhauer and transforms his thought into a depressive realism which pierces the veil of human cognition and penetrates the fundamental cryptic laws of nature. Michelstaedter's black physics is the physics of a dying cosmic fire, a runaway entropic process that we can feel in our bones as our lives slowly shatter toward its Heart of Darkness. This is what terrified Evola: the absolute obliteration of this world, the transformation of knowledge into the arid, masochistic, and ever-so-useless dowsing in the ashes of a cosmos burning to the ground.

Clearly, Evola's response to this cosmic massacre was fascist self-deification, isolation, and the symmetrical stasis of meditation. Michelstaedter, on the contrary, does not offer the reader an easy way out, nor any hope of individual salvation. He proposes to those who follow his inverted wisdom to practise what he calls, perverting the very word, *persuasion*: a destruction of the veil of reality that unleashes the world's true, hideous nature. Against Evola's fascist rigidity, Michelstaedter proposes an openness to *abandoning the familiar in order to accommodate inorganic desire*, even if this means a masochistic and mystical surrender to the laws of massacre and the abyssal circuits of jouissance. Michelstaedter tears the cosmos apart

---

35. C. Michelstaedter, *Persuasion and Rhetoric*, tr. R.S. Valentino, C.S. Blum, and D.J. Depew (New Haven, CT and London: Yale University Press, 2004), 8–9.

and peremptorily demands that you leave everything behind, once and for all. The putrid gospel of this teenage Antichrist is *do what you will*, let the impersonality of your entropic desire burn you to ashes.

> *Doing* is not for the sake of having done; having done does no good. You do not have in the present what you have done, and yet you want to retain it. In order to have it you must *do it again* like anything else: and you don't reach an end. *Performing a beneficence* is not doing unto others or giving them what they *believe they want*: giving alms, healing the sick, feeding, giving drink, clothing—these are *allowing others to take*, not giving or doing but *suffering*.[36]

§ 02 A hyperentropic physics is not enough, we need to impale God himself. We need a cosmology, even a theology, to get to the heart of this abysmal spiritual infestation.

Andrea Emo was a loner all his life. He never published anything in his lifetime, yet he scribbled his curses endlessly. He wrote the most terrifying of all theologies. For Emo, God is the unstoppable arrow of time that abolishes all that is. The Lord of this World is the inner and occult temporal warfare that ravages and annihilates meaninglessly. *God consists in his own annihilation* was Emo's motto. And it will be our theology.

Emo was a disciple of a peculiar school of Italian Hegelianism called *actualism*. The main proponent of the actualist reinterpretation of Hegel was Giovanni Gentile, one of the most important intellectual figures of the fascist regime. The main theoretical outcome of this form of Hegelianism, to simplify it to an almost embarrassing level, is that Hegel's philosophy should be thought of as a philosophy of the *act as it unfolds*. Dialectics should be read as a perpetual motion through which everything constantly develops and leaves behind any given form. A thing, whatever it is, should be considered as a perpetual action, which, through its pauses, its contradictions and its

---

36.   Ibid., 49–50.

wounds is constantly moving away from its inner potential toward its outer consumption. According to Gentile, everything that exists is to be equated with a 'fire' that 'burns its fuel to extract light and heat'. Everything exists because it burns, and exists only through its own combustion.

Here again, the voices of our black canon know the foundations of fascist dreams and ideas of a completely and definitively ordered world through violent amplifications, accelerations, and radicalisations of the defective organs of their frightening house of cards. Emo pours petrol on the fire of the actualist forest, turning actualism into the expression of an unqualified Heracliteanism, an *all-consuming war.*

Emo's philosophy derives from a simple awareness: if the dialectical process is this burning up of everything that exists, then everything that exists is simply always already a form of cosmic consumption, of useless slaughter. Every last little thing in the universe is its own massacre and abolition. Being is synonymous with losing blood, in a haemorrhage that will not end until the whole universe is nothing but blackness. If for Gentile the theory of the primacy of the dialectical act was an ontological foundation and the constitution of everything, for Emo it is, for reasons that lie at the limits of the logically stringent, its opposite: it is the demonstration of the lack of any basis or foundation, and is the ontological dismissal of everything that exists, now and forever; even God himself is nailed to the cross just to show us the way to self-consumption.

Emo crystallises this idea in his philosophy of time. Time, according to Emo, is nothing but the formalisation of this crypto-tendency toward total consumption. Time is the vector that transforms the constant death that we are at every moment into an ordered diagram: a simple arrow toward the Ultimate, the Final Attractor. Emo is a thermodynamic supremacist, a fanatic of the eternal trajectory of the universe.

For such acosmic pessimism, the only acceptable form of knowledge, in the face of an evanescent universe, is that of masochistic regression. The only healthy form of knowledge is that accessed through the return to the

Heart of Darkness, a sinking into the inner logic of a terrible war. The only worthy form of gnosis for this submerged dialectic is attained via a return to the beginning, before creation, through a becoming as cold as the perpetual march of temporal massacre itself. It is to abandon everything and go back to the impassive circuits of Gnon, free of all human assumptions and prejudices. Emo writes:

If science could discover the 'virus' of immortality and inject it into the veins of man, would the disease of the absolute be cured? The absolute ruler cures his illness by accepting the absolute negation which is the absolute purification, and which is the actuality of a faith. History is a series of horrors, like time; time that supplies the cemeteries with ever new victims. Although we see time as progress, it leads man back to the nothingness from which he emerged. Time can also be a regression; the triumph of regression. But Clio, the Muse of History, turns this series of horrors into a magnificent poem; destructive time becomes divinity, *logos*; ferocity and its series become Providence, chance and arbitrariness become necessity, a universal idea. Why does History, a history of tragedies, appear to us as a wonderful world, a tale that brings peace to our spirit? What is the catharsis, the purification, that makes the historical poem so beautiful, indeed sublime? History is the purification of the absolute because it is its continuous resurrection from its continuous negation. Perhaps, like memory, it is the only way to know actuality, pre-actuality; it is the miracle of the actuality and diversity of a long negation. Progress is always a progress towards presence; memory is presence in the form of images—that is, it is the present in the form of resurrection. Time is the triumph of regression; but our triumph is the actuality of regression; the actuality that is known in regression, like memory. Every vanishing instant is a regression, like memory. Every vanishing instant is a regression, but that is the actuality of regression and it can only be known in regression. Actuality can only be known in regression, can know itself as actuality only in regression, in memory, and only memory can give this actuality the name of progress. Actuality is saved from regression, which is 'only' by being its actuality. Memory is knowledge of regression, that is, the actuality of regression and therefore the form of our salvation.[37]

Salvation lies in drowning in the merciless arms of our own slaughter and suffering its terrible sights.

§ 03 A man descends into the depths of a cave. He wants to die: this world is too much for him. In the belly of the cave there is a small lake. The man sits beside it, pondering and asking himself whether dying is really worth it, only to realise that perhaps he is slowly but surely changing his mind on the matter.

In the end, he makes a decision. Life is worth living if only for the comfort of its useless inertia. The man gets up and bangs his head against the ceiling. The world is eclipsed by this descent.

He wakes up and comes out of the cave. The world that greets him outside has been transfigured. To be precise, it is exactly the same as it has always been, but there is not a human being in sight. His suicide has turned out to be an extinction.

This is *Dissipatio H.G.* by Guido Morselli, a luciferous remake of the *Twilight Zone* that haunts every reader who comes across it. It certainly haunts me.

As a boy, I used to go to Morselli's villa on the shore of a dead lake, surrounded by the rotten stench of one of the deepest scars of Italian post-industrialisation. His villa was a surreal pink building, now turned into a public park, and my friends used to sneak in to smoke cigarettes. We dreamed of desecrating the place and using a spirit box in the depths of this pink cave where Morselli had lived out the last years of his life.[38] We wanted to ask him whether the afterlife was that vast dehumanisation, that deep emptiness

---

37. A. Emo, *Supremazia e maledizione* (Rome: Raffaello Cortina, 1998).
38. 45.845264, 8.723498.

he had described in the book that was parasitising our hormone-driven fantasies and the miasma of our homeland. Was it as serene and neurotic as the misanthropy that oozed from its pages? Was it that little chamber produced by endless inner monologues that he had imagined?

Morselli's novels, especially *Dissipatio H.G.*, are patient novels, lullabies sung by an elusive universe, but they are also ruthless in their aversion to humanity. In one book, a uchronic reconstruction of the Italian psychic landscape, Morselli describes society as a 'cathedral of spiders'[39], and in reading *Dissipatio H.G.* one cannot help but be persuaded by the idea that he is having a great time crushing them all, one by one. Any reader, faced with the endless stream of thoughts of the novel's protagonist, the last man on Earth, will recognise the prolonged enjoyment Morselli draws from describing a world that has rid itself of every living human being. The author relishes every opportunity to mock the now defunct and vanished human race. He feels no shame or remorse in laughing at our hopes and dreams, which, against the backdrop of this dying and inhuman world, now look like a ridiculous farce. Morselli is the patron saint of the feverish joys of omnicidal vision. Morselli is the man who put down on paper the masochistic love for the disappearance of humanity, for the emptying out of everything human. It was he who realised this deep need to see the whole world disappear. Morselli was also the living demonstration of how terrifying these joys could be. Can the homicidal dream have a different purpose? Can we be masochists, emptying our bodies of the human and seeing the world in its a-human grace without giving up our own lives, at least for a moment?

Standing in the garden of his house, I felt a slight desolation that I have never felt again, an intoxicating proximity to my joyful misanthropy that made me wonder how long I could bear this state of absolute solitude, this distance from the world of states, nations, egos, and humans, that poisonous freedom which seemed the only true form of freedom, the only true approximation to absolute and final formlessness. *Do what you will*, at last.

---

39. G. Morselli, *Contro-passato prossimo* (Rome: Adelphi, 1987).

I remember the story a friend of mine wrote while he was there with me. It was told from the point of view of a heroin addict. It was a long and rambling metaphor that spanned at least five pages with a certain naive grace. The gist of the story was that the substance, descending through the needle, symbolised the addict's descent, his uncontrolled spiral beyond the human, toward a form that I would call demonic. The whole story revolved around the paradox that the addict was enjoying his personal descent into hell, his separation from humanity. I think the story was some kind of coping mechanism or something. We were all recovering from Morselli's syndrome, his questions, and the discovery of the desecrating and descendent character of nature.

Thinking about Morselli, I feel as if I am going round and round in circles, as if my life is a dirty joke. Here I am, again, reflecting on the same disappearing world, making sense by myself, once again, of the iron laws of thermodynamics and the infinite Love I feel for them. Gruppo di Nun was touched by the gnosis that Morselli glimpsed in his suicidal words, but we formalised it further, I think. We made it a doctrine, so as to teach you the pleasure of living without your humanity. See these atrocious sights with us.

The highest form of gnosis coincides with the spiral: infinite reflection on dissolution.

EM

CATHOLIC DARK:
TO RISE OR FALL IN
HYPER-ALIEN SILENCE

Anything that can be reached with a ladder does not interest me.

Ludwig Wittgenstein[1]

Neither by land nor sea shalt thou find the road to the Hyperboreans.

Pindar[2]

A certain Christina, born in 1150 in the village of Brustem in Flanders to a
humble shepherd couple, dies in her early twenties—possibly from an epileptic fit. During the funeral rites, however, Christina's body opens its eyes
and rises up to the beams supporting the church roof. After convincing her,
not without difficulty, to leave her refuge, the family and the priests present
at the ceremony listen in terror to the story of Christina's journey from
the abysses of Hell through the circumvolutions of Purgatory to Paradise,
meeting God face to face and receiving from Him the ability to return to
Earth, temporarily sacrificing eternal life so as to atone for the sins of the
souls in Purgatory.

Soon, the joy of Christina's 'return' transforms into a serpentine wave
of terror. What if she is just a rotting body infested with demons? Or what
if, even worse, she is one of the living dead? Christina's behaviour changes
from day to day, becoming more and more ambiguously inhuman. She can

1.   *Culture and Value: A Selection from the Posthumous Remains*, tr. P. Winch, ed. G.H. von
Wright, H. Nyman (Oxford: Blackwell, 1998), 10.
2.   Quoted in Nietzsche, *The Anti-Christ, Ecce Homo, Twilight of the Idols*, §1, 3.

smell the sin that plagues human beings, and intuitively knows their inner desires. Disgusted with humans, Christina spends hours and hours in solitude, wandering in the forest, climbing nimbly up barns, bell towers, and roofs, or soaring into the air spontaneously (so much so that her biographer, Thomas of Cantimpré, did not hesitate to call her a 'shadow' and a 'bird-woman'). Her mother and father try to chain her up to keep her at home, but Christina breaks the chains with superhuman strength. Fire does not burn her, water does not drown her; her body seems to be totally immune to corruption, illness, and pain. When she speaks, her words sound distant and frigid, as if they came from some remote and inaccessible place. It gets to the point where, in order to experience for herself the suffering of those condemned to death, Christina hangs herself on the gallows in the middle of the village square, among the corpses of criminals.

The villagers begin to call her 'Christina the Savage', 'Wild Christina', and 'Crazy Christina', initiating a spiral of violence and abuse that she bears patiently until the day she is fiercely chased from her house. After a period of wandering, she reaches the city, where she settles among criminals and murderers, sharing in the spoils of their crimes. Amongst these outcasts, she finds generosity, mercy, and pity.

Throughout the rest of her unlife, and even during her subsequent time in a convent, Christina will continue to transgress every boundary, bending the laws of nature to her will, occasioning shame, horror, and disgust, and dying twice more, only to rise again and again—waking as if from a dream the first time, emerging from the grave the second time. On the day of her second death, Christina desperately asks the nun who finds her body and causes her to wake up: 'Why are you disturbing me, why are you forcing me to come back?'[3]

---

3.   T. de Cantimpré, *The Life of Christina the Astonishing*, tr. M.H. King (Toronto: Peregrina Publishing, 1999), 53, 153–54. For the original text in Latin, see <https://monasticmatrix.osu.edu/cartularium/vita-de-s-christina-mirabili-virgine-life-christina-mirabilis>.

Christina's body is inhabited by an alien power, a power of which, however, she is but an obscene appendage, a shard of the absolute night of Paradise lodged in this worldly Hell. Her obsessive search for a vertical line of escape, her contempt for humans, and her constant provocations are the conse- quences of a profound love of anti-gravity. Christina defies death in order to fall back into its embrace and be rid of her body, she eagerly seeks its icy touch and cannot bear to be separated by darkness and silence. When she is not being mauled by dogs or drinking the water of lepers, Christina spends her time gazing at the sky—peering enigmatically beyond the clouds, beyond the atmosphere, into deep space.[4]

THE DARK INFLUENCE OF THE UNNAMEABLE COSMIC ATTRACTOR

The Christian tradition has built its nest on the most inaccessible of peaks. Even the earliest anchorites felt the overwhelming urge to soar, not only spiritually but also physically, above the world—to the tops of trees, moun- tains, and pillars. Between the fourth and fifth centuries AD, after being expelled from his monastery because of his extreme fasting practices, Simeon, in his early teens, decided to occupy a small space on the slopes of a plateau. A few years later, annoyed by the constant visits of worshippers and pilgrims who flocked to the foot of the rocky outcrop in search of advice, blessings, and prayers, Simeon decided to abandon all vestiges of horizon- tality and embrace radical verticalism. After climbing a pillar, he installed a small platform on its top, dedicating a handful of hours in the afternoon to his 'public' without ever descending from the pillar, and making himself accessible only by means of a ladder. Year after year, the pillar upon which

4. All of these biographical details are drawn from A. Bartolomei Romagnoli, 'Christina l'Ammirabile', in *Scrittrici Mistiche Europee*, vol. 1, eds. A. Bartolomei Romagnoli, A. Degl'Innocenti, F. Santi (Firenze: Sismel, 2015), 152–85, and A. Bartolomei Romagnoli, 'Christina l'Ammirabile', *Nuovo Dizionario di Mistica*, eds. L. Borriello, E. Caruana, M. Rosaria Del Genio, R. Di Muro (Vatican: Libreria Editrice Vaticana, 2016), 590–93.

Simeon meditated in partial isolation was replaced by ever taller pillars, rising from the initial four metres to fifteen in the year of his death.

By disdainfully fleeing upwards, Simeon makes a twofold break with the logocentric Hellenism of the Church Fathers, the irreverence of the 'fools for Christ' (the ultra-cynics) and the suffering horizontalism of the Desert Fathers. Rejecting public dialogue, rational argumentation, confrontation, irony, lamentation and even the paradoxical argument for humour, the 'stylite' (one who lies in contemplation on a pillar) formulates a science of elevation: a discipline totally different from the ancient mysteries or shamanic practices, culminating in the return of the initiate to a world shared even with the unini- tiated. Moving away from the primitivism of the dendrite (the tree dweller) and the mountain hermit, the stylite brings together technique and anthro- potechnics, ascension and asceticism, within one and the same paradigm. The pillar is a constantly rising Tower of Babel, or a rocket pointing straight up to the sky (a sort of minimal anticipation of the minaret). Interpreting the Platonic analogy of the vertical line to the letter—which from the world of illusions and shadows passes through the world of the senses and the world of geometric-mathematical entities, until it reaches the unspeakable supreme forms—the ascetic makes use of the tools offered by this world, but discards them as he or she goes, as one does with a ladder. '[A]nd, behold, a ladder set up on the earth, and the top of it reached to heaven; and, behold, the angels of God ascending and descending on it.'[5]

The cathedral will be the logical continuation of this progressive elevation: a project which, through architecture, becomes collective and metropolitan. In the structure of the cathedral, the spire and the pinnacle represent the last remnants of asceticism, beneath which the heavy bulk of European society swells abnormally and parasitically. The spirit of gravity (the 'prince of this world'), with its nefarious levelling effects, opposes the lightness of the mystic, their desire to leave the ground and rise ever higher, beyond the atmosphere. One example is Joseph of Cupertino, whose sudden and

---

5.   Genesis 28:12 (ASV).

abrupt flights forced the Friars Minor to anchor the saint to the ground. The story of this saint 'of the flights' shows how, for the spirit of gravity, there is only one time and place propitious to the journey: death and the grave; until then, light spirits must keep their feet firmly on the ground. Paraphrasing Carlo Michelstaedter,[6] one could compare the mystic to the inventor of an air balloon that can rise indefinitely: the further the balloon gets from the ground, the more anxious and impatient its crew becomes—so oppressed by the thinness of the air, so confused by the lack of visibility, that they refuse to continue their journey. The prominence of verticalism in religious architecture only reiterates the concept by means of a humorous contrast: it is easier for a cathedral to levitate spontaneously toward the moon than it is for the Church to levitate toward heaven.

The cathedral's institutionalisation of the heights is immediately transformed into a game of escapes and captures: the supplicating masses thronging under the stylite are mineralised into the rocky body of the Church (the foundation stone), while the column, absorbed by the crowd and becoming its centre, is transformed into the cathedral (the vertical stone). Access to a summit that is never absolute, but always relative to the valley, is mediated by ladders: hierarchies and infrastructures, doctrines and teachings, sacraments and ordinances. These two communicating devices, in turn, include within their system an 'altimetrical' function: the idea that there is a limit beyond which one is nothing more than a madman in the grip of perdition, or a pioneer capable of conquering new limits.

It was perhaps this total saturation of the horizontal to which we owe the spread of the impulse to found hermitages and monasteries: places dedicated to a peaceful search for silence and autonomy, often gravitating around the figure of a hermit. What is certain is that this tendency toward vertical flight led to 'earthly' institutions attempting to delegitimise and annihilate it, or else to incorporate it, raising the threshold even higher and welcoming it

---

6.   Michelstaedter, *Persuasion and Rhetoric*, 77–84. The reference is to the famous parable of 'Plato's balloon'.

into the body of the Church. In the midst of such an atmosphere of teeming business (all rules and time scales), anchorites and anchoresses, driven away once again from the city and the crowds, rose above the monasteries and convents, on vertiginous rocky ridges, at the top of peaks, in all those places where human beings are but a rare presence—making themselves light and unencumbered enough to escape a congested planet.

In the age when stone is gathering momentum, the stylite returns to confront the mountain heights, climbing the terrifying natural spires in search of an original place: a launch pad toward unlimited altitude. This upward journey turns philosophy into a 'high mountain road which is reached only by a steep path':

> It is an isolated road and becomes ever more desolate, the higher we ascend. Whoever pursues this path must show no fear, but must leave everything behind and confidently make his own way in the wintry snow. Often he suddenly comes to a precipice and looks down upon the verdant valley. A violent attack of dizziness draws him over the edge, but he must control himself and cling to the rocks with might and main. In return for this, he soon sees the world beneath him; its sandy deserts and morasses vanish from his view, its uneven spots are levelled out, its jarring sounds no longer reach his ear, and its roundness is revealed to him. He himself is always in the pure cool mountain air and now beholds the sun when all below is still engulfed in night.[7]

In order to obtain a distance from all interference, in an attempt to access the clarity of the inner conversation, this desire for silence and solitude is ready to sever all ties with humanity and earthly life. Traditionally, it is in this absence of shared stimuli and representations that the soul, suddenly realising that it has neglected itself and devoted too much time to the veneration of the cathedrals of humankind and those of nature, turns to its

---

7.   A. Schopenhauer, *Manuscript Remains, Volume 1: Early Manuscripts (1804–1818)*, tr. E.J.F. Payne, ed. A. Hubscher (London: Bloomsbury, 1988), 14.

inner Highness—the supreme altitude, towering above even the highest of mountain ranges. In the *Ascent of Monte Ventoux*, having been shamed by his selfish passion for climbing, Petrarch descends from the summit in spiritual torment:

> How many times I turned back that day to look at the mountain top which seemed scarcely more than a cubit high compared with the height of human contemplation, unless it is immersed in the foulness of earth? As I descended I asked myself: 'If we are willing to endure so much sweat and labour in order to raise our bodies a little closer to heaven, how can a soul struggling toward God, up the steeps of human pride and mortal destiny, fear any cross or prison or sting of fortune?'[8]

The mountain, however imposing and inhospitable it may be, reveals itself as a continuation of the mineral body of society and the Church. It is no coincidence that every day, in Japan, numerous individuals at the height of despair, in search of silence and clarity, travel to the foot of Mount Fuji, in the spectral forest of Aokigahara, to take their own lives. It is in places like these that the spirit of gravity concentrates and thickens, crushing all vertical flight with its oppressive atmosphere, saturated with suffering. In the 'sea of trees' the corpse of the hanged man, dangling from the rope like the needle of a horrifying compass, points to the source of all human ills, located a little lower down, in the settlements beyond the valley, and even further down, toward the centre of the earth. A force so imposing that not even the soul of the suicide can rise up to the sky but remains confined in a spectral prison.

The stratification of the planet, conventionally subdivided into three realms—inorganic, organic, and noetic, according to a supposed progression whose ascension and transcension is only apparent—merely serves to

---

8.   F. Petrarch, 'The Ascent of Mount Ventoux', *Selections from the Canzoniere and Other Works*, tr. ed. M. Musa (Oxford: Oxford University Press, 1999), 18.

dissimulate the fundamental centrality of the planetary nucleus, the gravitational attractor that anchors everything firmly to the ground. The hermit
is constantly threatened by something akin to an epidemic of petrification
gradually spreading across the planet, taking hold of even the lightest of
human beings. This tendency to escape, in some senses misanthropic or
rather anthropophobic, is what endows the vertical ascetic with inhuman
and anti-terrestrial characteristics, which become more and more intense
as the altitude increases and the oxygen decreases. On the way up, the heat
poured out of the earth's core is dissipated, and thought, decontaminated
of mineral waste, becomes icy—being pervaded by a feeling of delight and
detachment, 'the by-product of pain and danger'.[9]

As the poet Pascoli warns, this desire for constant surpassing does not
originate in an athletic feeling, a 'spirit of climbing', but in a drive for lightness, devoid of all intentionality and conflict. The will to fly does not consist,
therefore, in a positive will, but in a negative will: not in a negation of the will
but in a negative will, which goes so far as to negate itself. The obstacles that
present themselves before the ascending soul are not rungs (the overcoming
of which would allow it to acquire greater propulsion), but weights from which
it must free itself as fast as possible. The vertical ascension of the body is
something that must be overcome, for the body itself is an obstacle: 'St Paul
[...] during the time he was enraptured [...] his soul remained in his body [...].'[10]

When, around 1100, the young Cleridonia left her home to go into the
mountains, she changed her name to Chelidonia, from the Greek *chélidon*,
'swallow', identifying herself with the animal's rapid and graceful flight. It is
thanks to this spirit of lightness that asceticism, understood as dominion
over oneself and one's carnal desires, shows the way to a vertiginous ascent,

---

9.   A. Lunn, 'Alpine Mysticism and Cold Philosophy', in *For Hilaire Belloc: Essays in Honour of His 72nd Birthday*, ed. D. Woodruff (London: Sheed & Ward, 1942), 71.
10.   Eckhart, 'Sermon 54', *The Complete Mystical Works of Meister Eckhart*, 287.

up to the farthest, highest peak

of mystic scripture,

where the mysteries of God's Word

lie simple, absolute and unchangeable

in the brilliant darkness of a hidden silence.

Amid the deepest shadow

they pour overwhelming light

on what is most manifest.

Amid the wholly unsensed and unseen

they completely fill our sightless minds

with treasures beyond all beauty.[11]

If the earth's atmosphere no longer poses any limit, it is because the alien attractor, capable of reversing gravity, is the blinding cosmic darkness. Seduced by the prospect of absolute isolation and inhuman silence, the soul (the swallow) leaves behind the umpteenth stairway to Paradise that is the physical body, rising on the ascending currents of levity.

AGAINST GRAVITATION, AGAINST FREE WILL

God is the purest naught, untouched by time and space;
The more you reach for Him, the more He will escape.

Angelius Silesius, *One Cannot Grasp God*

During the second half of the sixteenth century, Juan de Yepes Álvarez, known as John of the Cross (Juan de la Cruz), composed the *Ascent of Mount Carmel*: a treatise on the stages leading to the summits of the Highness, with advice and explanations on how to deal with the 'luminous darkness' that awaits the traveller there. John writes:

---

11.   Pseudo-Dionysus, 'Mystical Theology', 135.

For this path ascending the high mountain of perfection leads upward, and is narrow, and therefore requires travellers that have no burden weighing upon them with respect to lower things, neither aught that embarrasses them with respect to higher things. [...] Oh, who can explain the extent of the denial our Lord wishes of us! This negation must be similar to a temporal, natural, and spiritual death in all things [...].[12]

Since God is incomprehensible and inaccessible, the will, if it is to center its activity of love on high, must not set itself on what it can touch and apprehend with the appetite, but on what is incomprehensible and inaccessible to the appetite. Loving in this way, a soul loves truly and certainly [...] also in emptiness and darkness concerning its feelings.[13]

The negative will that permeates ascension is exemplified by the style of apophatic mysticism. Where positive theology produces a whole series of affirmations concerning God (such as 'God is good' or 'God is just'), negative mysticism—well aware of the impossibility of attributing human attributes to an inhuman and otherworldly entity—extinguishes the divine attributes one by one, patiently performing their negation ('God is not good', 'God is not just') until it reaches a dimension in which emptiness and darkness reign: a dimension saturated by the very means through which the act of negation was performed, the 'not'. This is a real operation of psychic alleviation, culminating in silence and stupor, a further suppression of what has traditionally been considered the lightest part of the soul: the intellectual soul, from which ideas, thoughts and words emanate.

---

12.   St. John of the Cross, 'Ascent of Mount Carmel', *The Collected Works of St. John of the Cross*, tr. K. Kavanaugh, O. Rodriguez (Washington DC: Institute of Carmelite Studies, 1991), Book 2, Ch. 7, §3, 169; Book 2, Ch. 7, §6, 171. [E.A. Peers' translation (<https://sourceoflightmonastery.tripod.com/webonmediacontents/1950901.pdf>) has been substituted for the translation of the quotation from §3—trans].
13.   St. John of the Cross, 'Letter 13', *The Collected Works of St. John of the Cross*, 748.

In the soul thus pervaded by negativity, emptiness is an effect of sensory deprivation, the darkness of the mind's emptiness, the silence of the annihilation of the very matrix of every thought: 'When God is seen in this way, in darkness, he neither brings laughter to my lips, nor devotion, nor fervour, nor burning love; for neither body nor soul trembles or moves [...]. The body sleeps and the tongue is cut out.'[14]

To deny the chain of attributions and predications, to unlearn what has been learned thus far, is not merely an individual practice, but a cosmic one, consisting in freeing oneself not only from the environmentally induced conditioning that has been enforced over the course of one's life, but even from what billions of years of gravitation have produced in matter itself—from the extension that defines a body, from the appetites of the living, from the data of the senses upon which animals draw, from the representations upon which human beings base their conscious experience. '[M]y argument now rises from what is below up to the transcendent, and the more it climbs, the more language falters, and when it has passed up and beyond the ascent, it will turn silent completely, since it will finally be at one with him who is indescribable. [It] is not inexistent, lifeless, speechless, mindless. It is not a material body, and hence has neither shape nor form, quality, quantity, or weight. It is not in any place and can neither be seen nor be touched. It is neither perceived nor is it perceptible.'[15] The negation proceeds unceasingly, until the most volatile of all concepts makes its appearance: 'But if God is neither goodness nor being nor truth nor one, what then is He? He is pure nothing: he is neither this nor that.'[16]

Nothingness—the negative concept par excellence, devoid of any empirical, logical or semantic consistency—is all that remains once the world has been diligently annihilated, piece by piece.

---

14. A. da Foligno, *L'Autobiografia e gli Scritti della Beata Angela da Foligno* (Castello: Il Solco, 1932), 176–177 [I–106].

15. Pseudo-Dionysus, 'Mystical Theology', 139–141.

16. Eckhart, Sermon 54, *The Complete Mystical Works of Meister Eckhart*, 287.

There is nothing lighter than nothingness itself—and yet foolish is he who believes that ascension ends in the darkness of nothingness. Voiding (*kenosis*) is the culmination of a positive feedback process in the course of which God, stripped of all human attributes, recedes into an alien anonymity, while the seeker is stripped of all the characteristics that make them not only human, but even 'material'. The more the one is lightened, the more the other becomes abstract and intangible. What binds divinity and the soul, beyond the relationship between God and human, or Creator and creature, is precisely the volatility of nothingness: 'If I were not, God would not be either [...] if I were not, then God would not be God.'[17] Light is the being that wants for nothing, wanting only nothingness and the nothingness of not wanting—the annihilation of all difference between God and creation, their equalisation in the void.

There is no love more ardent, no passion more intense, no affection more tormenting and unquenchable than this desire for dissolution, through which God loses his creatures and creation its creator. If there is no intentionality or conflict in ascension, it is because the mystic, by abjuring his own free will, wisdom, and all faculties of discernment, has surrendered to divine rapture, giving himself up to the anti-gravitational force that claims everything for itself. The ascent has no end, nor can it be interrupted by a decree of consciousness; it is not a spatiotemporal process that transits from point *a* to point *b*, but an inscrutable perpetual motion that finds less and less friction along its path, accelerating indefinitely:

> At the hour of death, the decision is made whether man falls back into the womb of nature, or else he no longer belongs to her [...]. However, he will be least afraid of becoming nothing in death who has recognized that he is already nothing now [...] since in him knowledge has, so to speak, burnt up and consumed the will.[18]

---

17. Eckhart, 'Sermon 87', *The Complete Mystical Works of Meister Eckhart*, 424.
18. Schopenhauer, *The World as Will and Representation*, vol. 2, 609.

That which is vain and can be swept away in a breath—like God and the creature—is inherently light. Vanity of vanities, all is vanity! And vanity is the first principle of divine grace, and it is precisely by virtue of it that everything can soar toward heaven, like dust carried by the wind.

'Therefore let us pray to God that we may be free of God',[19] writes Meister Eckhart, since such a distinction between God and the creation is bitter and unbearable. We pray to be set free of God and, at the same time, we pray to be *raised up* by God, never to return to earth. As that which ends the journey, return means the death of the traveller. In fact, interrupting an act of pure transition, every return implies a corresponding replenishment, a weighing down of the soul.

To refill is to satiate, to quench a desire (the word *fill* derives from the ancient North European terms *fyllan*, *fulljan* and *fylla*, indicating not only filling but also satisfaction). *Desire*, in turn, derives from *desiderium*, a word composed of the negative prefix *de-* and the word *sidus*, which literally means 'to miss the stars'. This 'cosmic nostalgia' implies a fundamental distinction between a mysticism of return and a mysticism of non-return. The mysticism of return is like bracketing out the world, representations, knowledge and individual consciousnesses. As with methodological doubt, all one need do is remove the brackets to get the world back again, safe and sound. Having abandoned the journey or, even worse, having been grabbed and brought back down to earth, the returning mystic resembles someone going out for a walk: they go around the block and return immediately. The returning mystic is satiated: although he has only had a taste of the immense light of the stars, his heart has become so small that it is already full (which, after all, is what one would expect of a rigorous ascetic).

The mysticism of non-return, on the other hand, is more like stumbling, like putting a foot wrong and, instead of falling to the ground, paradoxically, beginning to plummet upwards. There is no confirmation of any prior certainty, only astonishment and rapture; no satiation, no possible satisfaction.

19. Eckhart, 'Sermon 87', *The Complete Mystical Works of Meister Eckhart,* 422.

The mystic of non-return has nothing to say, nothing to do, nowhere to go—his words are identical to those uttered by all those who, like him, continue to ascend without pause.

Three times, before expiring, Angela da Foligno cried out 'Oh, unknown nothing!', only to slip into a succession of cries before abandoning earthly life forever. The mystic is a channel through which the boundless night emits signals from deep space. Indecipherable cryptograms that only hint at their occult nature.

If the world is what is *mundus*—what is bright and in full view—worldly asceticism is a climb to the peak of the visible (again, the English word *world* indicates precisely the dimension in which human affairs take place, if not the human species itself). The mystic-of-return struggles in a constant pilgrimage to the threshold of gravitation, failing each time:

> [H]ardly had we left that rise when I forgot all about the circuitous route I had just taken and again tended to take a lower one. Thus, once again I found myself taking the easy way, the roundabout path of winding hollows, only to find myself soon back in my old difficulty. I was simply putting off the trouble of climbing; but no man's wit can alter the nature of things, and there is no way to reach the heights by going downward.[20]

In the mysticism of non-return, on the contrary, the soul, stripped of the body and of the causal chains of nature—lifted beyond the atmosphere by the enigmatic alien attractor—is projected into an unclean ascension: denying the world, it proceeds at increasing speed into the darkness, following an abyssal verticality that plunges into an aggressively inhuman region.

---

20.   Petrarch, 'The Ascent of Mount Ventoux', 13.

All angels, all saints, and everything that was ever born must keep silent when the wisdom of the Father speaks: for all the wisdom of angels and all creatures is pure folly before the unfathomable wisdom of God.

Meister Eckhart[21]

In coelo quies. Tout finis ici bas.

Arthur Schopenhauer[22]

Around 1950, eight hundred years after Christina the Savage's levitations, Enrico Fermi, abruptly interrupting a lively conversation about extraterrestrial life and interstellar travel, asked his guests: 'Where, then, is everybody?'. The only answer to this question is the deafening silence of the cosmos: the source of Christina's nostalgia, the hope that the universe is nothing more than an immense tomb, ensconced among the stars. This silence, however insignificant and overflowing with desolation, is the most alien thing there is. It is the supreme *xenos*, 'the "wholly other" (*oateron, anyad, alienum*), that which is quite beyond the sphere of the usual, the intelligible, and the familiar, which therefore falls quite outside the limits of the "canny", and is contrasted with it, filling the mind with blank wonder and astonishment'.[23]

A foreign and estranging ocean, superhuman and indifferent, from which there emanates, like a sort of disquieting cosmic background radiation, a seductive and obsessive call. To the *mysterium tremendum* is added the *mysterium fascinans*, the magnetic influence that captures the spirit. In non-return, the heart overflows with xenophilia—a passion that becomes

---

21. Eckhart, 'Sermon 87', *The Complete Mystical Works of Meister Eckhart*, 420.
22. The final entry in Schopenhauer's diary, August 25, 1804. Quoted in R. Safranski, *Schopenhauer and the Wild Years of Philosophy* (Cambridge, MA: Harvard University Press, 1990), 52.
23. R. Otto, *The Idea of the Holy*, tr. J.W. Harvey (Oxford: Oxford University Press, 1958), 26.

more and more intense along the way, and which can be allegorically divided into degrees of altitude.

A few metres above sea level, the wonder still concerns one's own body, the excellent forms of things and the natural order. '[O]ur love shall have its beginning in the flesh.[24] In fact, '[t]hat we may arrive at an understanding of the First Principle, which is most spiritual and eternal and above us, we ought to proceed through the traces which are corporeal and temporal and outside us, and this is to be led into the way of God.'[25] The mind ranges from the most common to the most unusual forms, exploring possible combinations and configurations. In this first phase, the alien is the organism—or rather, the merely possible, non-actualised terrestrial organism: a positive nothingness, as embodied in flocks of unicorns, dragons, zoomorphic plants or anthropomorphic creatures, and objects of bizarre or perturbing form.

The divine power is manifested here as an 'imprint', since the living form bears within itself a spark of anti-gravity: a faculty of ascension which (with the passage from the inorganic to the organic dimension) enabled it to emancipate itself, albeit minimally. It was while she was in the grip of this fury that it was revealed to Hildegard of Bingen that 'God, Who made all things by His Will, created them so that His Name would be known and glorified, showing in them not just the things that are visible and temporal, but also the things that are invisible and eternal'.[26]

'We ought next to enter into our minds, which are the eternal image of God [...] to pass over into that which is eternal.'[27] At this height, the vanity of things reveals a boundless horizon of possibilities: if there is no limit to form, there is no limit to matter either—everything that is, could have been otherwise. 'Different worlds [...] may be created by divine power, but not by natural power. [...] God can create many other worlds'.[28]

---

24. St. Bernard of Clairvaux, *De Diligendo Deo* (Vancouver: Eremitical Press, 2010), XV, 39.

25. St. Bonaventura, *The Mind's Road to God* (Boston: Wyatt North, 2020), Ch. 1, §2.

26. Hildegard of Bingen, *Scivias*, 94.

27. St. Bonaventura, *The Mind's Road to God*, Ch. 1, §2.

28. I. Buridani, *Quaestiones super Libris quattuor De Caelo et Mundo*, ed. E.A. Moody (Cambridge, MA: The Medieval Academy of America, 2012), Liber I, Quaestio 18.

The flesh of the creature is replaced by mineral, energetic, or atmospheric bodies. Objects come into existence made of unknown materials with inscrutable functions, textures, sounds, tastes, and colours that cannot be described. The organisation of organisms becomes more and more alien, contradictory, and disharmonious, gradually extracting itself from any adaptive value: tangles of mouths, eyes, and tentacles, sentient clouds, electric currents traversed by affective motions, gelatinous clusters, plasmid spectra, 'shapeless congeries of protoplasmic bubbles, faintly self-luminous, and with myriads of temporary eyes forming and unforming as pustules of greenish light [...]'.[29]

This deformity and inaccessibility are *Imago Dei*, that is, in the 'image of God', since they repudiate all worldly attributes, making room for the supreme darkness of the unknown. The point of maximum propulsion has been reached:

> And when thou hast transcended thyself and all things in immeasurable and absolute purity of mind, thou shalt ascend to the superessential rays of divine shadows, leaving all behind and freed from the ties of all. [...] This fire [...] which he alone truly perceives who says, 'My soul rather chooseth hanging and my bones death' [Job 7:15]. He who chooses this death can see God because this is indubitably true [...]. Let us then die and pass over into darkness; let us impose silence on cares, concupiscence, and phantasms.[30]

At this dizzying height, the soul—having abandoned and surpassed all form and all matter—becomes Godlike, entering the heart of the Divine. Xeno-creaturality is reconjoined with xeno-divinity, each pole being denuded to the point of vanishing. In this glacial 'place' there is neither beginning nor end; neither here nor now; neither one nor many; neither before nor after....

---

29. H.P. Lovecraft, 'At the Mountains of Madness', in *The H.P. Lovecraft Omnibus 1: At the Mountains of Madness and Other Novels of Terror* (London: HarperCollins, 1999), 133.

30. St. Bonaventura, *The Mind's Road to God*, Ch. 7. §1–2.

The lover has merged with the beloved object, becoming one with nothingness. In dissolving, the mystic has defeated gravity, flouting its force and revealing its inessentiality: everyone and everything will fly one day, vanishing into the night. Triumph of anti-gravity: 'that devout / triumph on whose account I ever weep for my / sins and beat my breast [...] the triumph that plays ever / around the point that had overcome me'.[31]

Since there is no longer any friction, the ascent continues in absolute emptiness. If there is no return then there is no fulfilment, if there is no fulfilment then there is no return. 'Xenophilia is doubly unconditional. Lacking satisfaction conditions, it [...] does not represent a goal state and [...] cannot oppose a present state on the grounds that it fails to realize those goals.'[32] Being intrinsically unsatisfiable, love for the *Xenos* is founded on an absence of foundation: plummeting, never touching the bottom—indifferently, falling or rising in a hyper-alien silence.

Thus my mind, entirely lifted up, gazed fixedly,

immobile and intent, and became ever more

aflame to gaze.

In that Light one becomes such that it is

impossible ever to consent to turn away from it

toward any other sight.[33]

CK

31. D. Alighieri, *The Divine Comedy of Dante Alighieri: Paradiso*, tr. ed. R. M. Durling (Oxford: Oxford University Press, 2011), Canto 22, ll. 106–108, 441; Canto 30, ll. 10–11, 601.

32. Roden, 'Xenophilia'.

33. Alighieri, *Paradiso*, Canto 33, ll. 97–102, 665.

AFTERWORD: THE ASYMMETRY OF LOVE

Amy Ireland

> Systems cannot stop interacting with the world which lies outside
> of themselves, otherwise they would not be dynamic or alive. By the
> same token, it is precisely these engagements which ensure that
> homeostasis, perfect balance, or equilibrium, is only ever an ideal.
>
> Sadie Plant[1]

I. THE DISEASE OF THE ABSOLUTE

There are many ways to respond to the nihilism that is synonymous with
modernity but they tend to take two prevailing forms: fascism and despair.
Despair is the simpler of the two. The subject of despair sees the elimination
of transcendent sources of meaning as an irrecoverable loss. There is no way
back. But neither is there a way forward. With the future grasped from the
perspective of what it cannot contain, and the past accessible only through a
nostalgia that is as realistic about the impossibility of a return to former ways
of being as it is ardent for them, all that remains is perpetual immobilisation
in an unfulfilling present. The temporality of despair is characterised by this
inertia—a feeling of paralysis.

---

1.   S. Plant, *Zeros + Ones*, 160.

Fascism is more complex, and far more insidious. It emerges from the same paralysing sense of loss that characterises despair, but without possessing the latter's realism. Instead of facing the horror brought about by the evacuation of sense, value, and any guarantee of individual significance underwritten by some greater force (and perhaps even, as in Klaus Theweleit's famous study of the proto-Nazi Freikorps, an inadmissible *desire for passivity, femininity, and dissolution*),[2] it sublimates this horror, burying what it cannot bear to acknowledge beneath a mythology of power that reinstates the lost transcendent structure, only in a far more convoluted form. Fascism's deep sense of betrayal by the present is nursed by an inflated attachment to the past, often accompanied by theories of time and history that valorise eternity, cyclicality, or return. If despair does not end in suicide and is not overcome, it is liable to follow this path of sublimation into fascism.

In more or less overt ways, it is a passionate involvement in this problematic—how to respond to nihilism, to the feeling that there is nothing outside of oneself that can be relied upon to make sense of one's life, to modernity's 'black night of divine abandonment', without succumbing to either despair or fascism—that is the common thread running through the writings of the obscure Italian occultist collective the Gruppo di Nun. The predicament will be especially familiar to anyone engaged in contemporary online politics, but it also has a profound lineage in twentieth-century Italian history, not least as a defining moment in the personal biography of Julius Evola, one of Italy's most famous right-wing occultists and co-founder of the influential Gruppo di Ur (the esotericist group of the late 1920s which the name 'Gruppo di Nun' parodies).[3] In 'The Highest Form of Gnosis', the penultimate text in

2.   K. Theweleit, *Male Fantasies*, tr. S. Conway (Minneapolis: University of Minnesota Press, 2 vols, 1989).

3.   'The name Gruppo di Nun mirrors Evola's *Gruppo di Ur*, whose writings are a prime example of *alchemical ultra-fascism*. Ur, the upward triangle and rune of fire, representing human Will triumphing above the chaotic abyss of matter, was changed to *Nun*, deity of the primeval waters in Egyptian mythology and Kabbalistic sigil for the ocean of infinite recombination.' D. Breitling, 'Under the Sign of the Black Mark: Interview with Members of Gruppo di Nun', *Diffractions Collective*, 2019, <https://diffractionscollective.org/under-the-sign-of-the-black-mark-interview-with-members-of-gruppo-di-nun/>.

this anthology, 'EM', one of the members of the Gruppo di Nun (enemies of identity who we know only by their initials) narrates the event as follows:

> There is a pathetic story that Julius Evola tells in his biography. He recalls an extremely desperate time in his life in which he lost the will to live. He felt as if possessed by a very negative interpretation of Nietzsche, an interpretation that had come to him from an author who he first described, in order to distance himself from him, as 'Jewish'. The depressive reading of Nietzsche had spread through Evola's life like black bile, paralysing him to the point of being unable to be or do anything. His whole macho-Aryan pose collapsed miserably as the result of a confrontation with the words of a teenager.

The teenager in question was a student named Carlo Michelstaedter, who, the day after submitting an academic dissertation entitled *Persuasion and Rhetoric* to the University of Florence in 1910, committed suicide in his family home—an act that has been read by many as drawing the inevitable conclusion of the philosophy of despair elaborated in his dissertation.

The philosophical world view presented in *Persuasion and Rhetoric* proceeds, as the title suggests, from the division of reality into two parts. 'Rhetoric' names the intrinsically deceptive conventions of worldly, gregarious existence, the common field through which, in the wake of the death of God, socially contingent meanings and values are imposed on the individual, inhibiting them from expressing their internal singularity by forcing them into an illusory form of socially-determined being deprived of any access to truth. Rhetoric is characterised by lack and a fundamental, never-ending need to fill that lack—beginning with the biological necessities of food, water, and sleep, and extending into more complex forms of desire—which projects the individual into the future: so long as we are in a state of lack, we are condemned to live in time. 'Persuasion', on the other hand, names an ideal state of fulfilment, a total absence of lack that would bring the individual into coincidence with themselves, releasing them, in their singularity, from the hollow, worldly coercion of rhetoric, exchanging the contingent sophistry of society for access to eternity and eternal concepts, including absolute truth. But Michelstaedter concludes that persuasion is impossible to attain. Since lack is commensurate with time, short of transcending time itself there is no way to eliminate lack, and therefore living, desiring beings can never be truly persuaded. Human existence is characterised by this fundamental paradox. The only way to experience being fully is to die, but death extinguishes being. EM continues:

> The account of [Michelstaedter's] work in Evola's *The Path of Cinnabar* reads like a typical Lovecraftian story. We have the protagonist who comes across a terrifying text and, word by word, begins to understand the unthinkability of human existence. Finally, he accepts the idea that reality is more monstrous and icy than he could ever have thought. The terrible text appears as the pinnacle of a masochistic prosthetics, a machine that wounds the mind endlessly, that drives you toward a mortal apotheosis until you plunge into the bowels of Hell.

After his encounter with *Persuasion and Rhetoric,* Evola's despair is total. However, unlike the protagonists of Greek tragedy that inspired Michelstaedter's dissertation (figures whose human hubris sees them pitting themselves against the absolute—against time—and losing) it is his extravagant arrogance that spares him the fate of his confrère. For Michelstaedter, establishing a philosophical understanding of persuasion is a means to the end of grasping the paradox of human finitude and cultivating an understanding of reality as inherently tragic. If anything, it is a source of humiliation, not aspiration, hence EM's characterisation of it as 'a masochistic prosthetics [...] tracing the movements and exchanges of unconscious libidinal forces *without us*'. But Evola would come to see it differently. His characterisation of *Persuasion and Rhetoric* in *The Path of Cinnabar* as 'a purified, extreme theory of "being", internal self-sufficiency and autarchy' encapsulates the route he would take out of despair and into fascism, in so doing annulling all the subtleties of the paradox outlined by Michelstaedter.[4] For in his idiosyncratic reinterpretation of *Persuasion and Rhetoric*, persuasion would be cast as an *attainable* state, time and desire *could* be overcome, and direct access to the absolute was not the impossible fantasy of a lost metaphysical tradition, but a concrete goal that could be worked toward through disciplined occult training, ultimately facilitating a practitioner's ascension to the state of 'Absolute Individual'.[5] And Evola would not stop there (at the point where so many theories of intellectual intuition find their limit). His claim for access to the absolute would exceed simple knowledge of the absolute (despite his fidelity to philosophical idealism, he despised what he saw as an anaemic commitment to 'mere' epistemological transcendence in the philosophy of the Italian fascist heirs of Hegel such as his rival, Giovanni Gentile)—it would be fully and unabashedly ontological:[6] the self truly *becomes* absolute.

In the works dating from this early period, Evola's thinking is organised around a dichotomy between passive acceptance ('spontaneity') and active control ('domination')—gendered analogues of 'rhetoric' and 'persuasion' which stand at the extremes of a scale of spiritual power. An individual's spiritual virility, which is biologically expressed in sexual and racial characteristics, determines in advance which side of the spontaneity-domination spectrum they are liable to inhabit.[7] Accordingly, the path to the Absolute Individual, total domination, or 'freedom' (a synonym of 'domination' in Evola's terminology) is not open to everyone. Women—too passive and

---

4.   J. Evola, *The Path of Cinnabar*, tr. S. Knipe (London: Arktos, 2010), 10.

5.   For a discussion of the specificities of Evola's usage of this term, especially in relation to Italian Hegelianism, see P. Furlong, *Social and Political Thought of Julius Evola* (London and New York: Routledge, 2011), 25–28.

6.   'The I—I argued—cannot be defined as mere "thought", "representation" or "epistemological subject"; rather, the I is truth, action and will. All it took to shake the foundations of abstract Idealism was to place these values at the centre.' Evola, *The Path of Cinnabar*, 41–42. See also Furlong, *Social and Political Thought of Julius Evola*, 29–30.

7.   Although his misogyny, antisemitism, and white supremacism follow the most predictable contours, Evola always maintained that their source was 'spiritual' not biological.

too material—are disqualified, as are spiritually weak men, which includes those of 'non-Aryan' races, such as Michelstaedter. In the service of this theory, and in yet another idiosyncratic interpretation, Evola takes the key claim of Immanuel Kant's *Critique of Pure Reason*—that (in Evola's words) 'all things are mediated by an "I"'—as a moral tenet, understanding the individual as actively *responsible* for that mediation and therefore able to alter the world that is generated through it.[8] If for Kant the basic structure of empirical reality, being owed to a part of the mind that the mind cannot itself transcend, is set in advance as a feature of experience, organising the chaos of sensation into something consistent and cognitively tractable, for Evola the structure of empirical reality is understood as a constraint upon one's 'true will', which, in the Absolute Individual, effectively takes the place of the Kantian noumenon, grasped not as an extra-objective 'thing-in-itself' but as hypostasised human consciousness.[9] From this perspective, being subject to material suffering or natural forces and laws beyond one's control can only be a sign of impotence and spiritual deficit, for it signals that one has failed to personally take 'possession' of the portion of reality that makes one suffer and to 'nullify' it by 'absorbing' its causal power.[10]

8.   Evola, *The Path of Cinnabar*, 50.

9.   'To claim that an individual, as an "I" or self-sufficient (*autarches*) principle, cannot define himself as the *unconditioned* cause of representations (viz. of nature), does not imply that such representations are the product of an "other" (of things which are real and which exist in themselves). Rather, this condition merely suggests that the individual does not have complete control over his own actions. [...] Yet when will it be possible to truly affirm the Idealist principle that the "I" places all things? It will only be possible once the individual has transformed the dark passion of the world into a kind of freedom; that is to say: once the individual experiences his action of representation no longer as a form of spontaneity and coexistence of reality and possibility, but rather as a form of unconditioned, willed causation and *power*.' J. Evola, *Essays on Magical Idealism*, quoted in *The Path of Cinnabar*, 50.

10.   '[T]he [empirical] Ego must understand that everything that seems to have a reality independent of it is nothing but an illusion, caused by its own deficiency'; 'Just as fire can affirm the will of fuel to live and blaze, so the "I" which wishes to be sovereign unto itself has the power to absorb its own non-being [i.e. all that which it does not will or determine for itself] as the matter from which, alone, the splendour of an absolute life and of absolute actions might spring forth.' J. Evola, *Essays on Magical Idealism*, quoted in Furlong, *Social and Political Thought of Julius Evola*, 28, and Evola, *The Path of Cinnabar*, 47; see also 51. Power is important for Evola

This outlook allowed Evola to interpret Michelstaedter's suicide as a product of feminine passivity and racial infirmity, symptoms of spiritual weakness that had led the young Jewish philosopher to accept empirically constrained, passive extinction rather than striving for absolute, unconstrained, *willed* extinction. Michelstaedter's capitulation to despair misled him into carrying out what was ultimately an impotent act, for the individual who died in Michelstaedter's suicide was a mere puppet of the illusory world of rhetoric, suffering from 'a form of "ignorance" contrary to true freedom', not a fully persuaded Absolute Individual, true source and master of his own death.[11] But Evola was not weak like Michelstaedter. He would not 'surrender and drown in things'. He was one of the 'virile men', one of the 'heroic souls, awakened to disgust, to revolt' who 'dare[d] face the current and the under-tow' of material reality and would be led by an 'ever more firm, ever more unshakeable will' to the stable ground of the far shore of being, from whose ideal fortifications, in the company of other 'strong men', he would be able to control the world.[12] 'God does not exist', he maintained, '[t]he Ego must create him by making itself divine'.[13]

As the author of 'The Highest Form of Gnosis' summarises,

---

because in his system (but this structure will be immediately recognisable to anyone familiar with the tenets of Hermetic Kabbalah and the Tree of Life), matter is understood to be connected to thought on a spectrum corresponding to degrees of spiritual potency. The stronger the individual's exercise of spiritual power, the more unconditioned his act of thinking is, and the less beholden to external material determination he becomes. He thus climbs the ranks of determination to take the place of the absolute, yet apparently without relinquishing the characteristic aspects of his empirical self.

11.   Evola, *The Path of Cinnabar*, 16. As EM recounts in 'The Highest Form of Gnosis', this interpretative shift was sparked by an encounter with the Majjhima Nikaya, a scripture from the Theravada school of Buddhism. Evola continued to be influenced by ideas from Eastern religions including Buddhism and Daoism, while nonetheless rejecting what he perceived to be their endemic passivity and substituting a more 'Western'—that is, 'active'—approach to transcendence. Furlong, *Social and Political Thought of Julius Evola*, 26.

12.   Evola, *The Path of Cinnabar*, 51; Evola and the Ur Group, 'Knowledge of the Waters', in *Introduction to Magic*, 19.

13.   Evola, *Essays on Magical Idealism*, quoted in T. Sheehan, 'Myth and Violence: The Fascism of Julius Evola and Alain de Benoist', *Social Research* 48:1, 'On Violence: Paradoxes and Antinomies' (Spring 1981), 45–73: 52–53.

[o]nly a newly acquired fascist spirituality, with its humanist and supremacist dream of material acquiescence and subjective indestructibility, could put a stop to the madness of the metaphysical masochism that [Evola] had been facing.

All the real problems of modernity that Michelstaedter had attempted to confront in his thought—the absence of the gods, the loss of absolutes, the cruelty of time, the passivity of the subject in the thrall of blind material forces—were simply cast aside, and the subtle tragedy of *Persuasion and Rhetoric* was transformed into a paranoid theory of personal transcendence.

Evola would call his new philosophy—a deeply humanist voluntarism that hypostasises identity in a universe of disconcerting change—'Magical Idealism'.[14] It provided the theoretical support for the work of the Gruppo di Ur and, although Evola's plans to use the group's network of devotees to commandeer a level of magical influence over Mussolini capable of shifting the leader's populist political approach to one more in tune with his own beliefs never came to fruition, and the uncompromising elitism of his thinking prevented it from being taken up in any official form by Hitler's Nazi regime, it was nevertheless an important element in the establishment of fascist political culture in both Italy and Germany throughout the first half of the twentieth century and beyond.[15] The relationship of Evola's work to historical fascism is uncontroversial. But even more importantly for grasping what the Gruppo di Nun (along with other more mainstream commentators) has

14.   Evola detested Renaissance humanism because of its association with notions of democracy and reason, both of which he was vehemently opposed to, and insisted on calling his own thinking an 'inhumanism', despite its fidelity to idealism, and the fact that the path to self-deification it describes transposes the empirical self into the realm of the absolute with minimal alteration. The Gruppo di Nun's identification of it as a humanism relates to the group's broader analysis of the centrality of human thought and will in Western magic and the privilege these faculties are routinely granted over the inhuman effectivity of matter and number. This is not the first time a deeply humanist philosophy has tried to pass itself off as 'inhumanism'.
15.   See N. Goodrick-Clarke, 'Julius Evola and the Kali Yuga' in *Black Sun: Aryan Cults, Esoteric Nazism, and the Politics of Identity* (New York: NYU Press, 2001), 52–71.

identified as the contemporary return of fascism[16] and for understanding the context in which the texts in this anthology are intervening, it is an extremely clear-cut example of how fascism operates in the deeper, ontological sense that Evola was so intent on laying claim to.

II. THE LONG SHADOWS OF LIMITLESS MODERNITY

> [W]here will the revolution come from [...]? It is like death—where, when?
>
> Gilles Deleuze and Félix Guattari[17]

In *Anti-Oedipus*, Gilles Deleuze and Félix Guattari advance a theory of fascism based on an analysis of desire, drawn famously from an amalgam of the philosophies of Karl Marx and Sigmund Freud. As Michel Foucault writes in the preface to the book,

> the major enemy, the strategic adversary [of *Anti-Oedipus*] is fascism [...] and not only historical fascism, the fascism of Hitler and Mussolini—which was able to mobilize and use the desire of the masses so effectively—but also the fascism in us all, in our heads and in our everyday behaviour, the fascism that causes us to love power, to desire the very thing that dominates and exploits us.[18]

To be able to discern this second form of fascism—'the fascism in us all'—it is important to understand that Deleuze and Guattari's account of desire exceeds the petty dramas of individual needs and wants: it is

---

16. See Breitling, 'Under the Sign of the Black Mark: Interview with Members of Gruppo di Nun'.

17. G. Deleuze and F. Guattari, *Anti-Oedipus*, tr. R. Hurley, M. Seem, H.R. Lane (London: Penguin, 2009), 378.

18. Ibid., *xiii*.

an account of the production of reality itself (hence the terminology of 'desiring-production') in the tradition of critical philosophy inaugurated by Kant. It is this cosmogenic aspect of desiring-production that makes it relevant to the history of Western Hermeticism addressed by the Gruppo di Nun in *Revolutionary Demonology*. For Deleuze and Guattari, desire is immanent, material, impersonal, pre-human and—contrary to Michelstaedter and Evola's reading of desire as lack—positive. In its actualisation, it falls across a spectrum marked out by two poles of investment—'the paranoiac, reactionary, and fascisizing pole, and the schizoid revolutionary pole',

> one of which subordinates desiring-production to the formation of sovereignty and to the gregarious aggregate that results from it, while the other brings about the inverse subordination, overthrows the established power, and subjects the gregarious aggregate to the molecular multiplicities of the productions of desire [...] [t]he schizophrenic process is revolutionary, in the very sense that the paranoiac method is reactionary and fascist.[19]

The terms 'paranoid' and 'schizophrenic' delineate processes that structure and destructure desiring-production, producing and disassembling the actualised world rather than describing particular subjects or clinical diagnoses. In fact, the 'subject' as such is a paranoiac organisation of desiring-production, being the culmination of a series of material repressions that channel desire, turning it from a productive force into a reactive one (schizophrenia, in its clinical sense, denotes a breakdown of subjective unity, and it is this dimension of the original terminology that remains meaningful in Deleuze and Guattari's use of the word). In *Anti-Oedipus*, the fixed and bounded notion of the intentional human subject that, as civilised moderns, we tend to take ourselves to be, arises precisely through a depotentiation of desire's impersonal productive energy.

---

19.   Ibid., 366; 376.

Desire does not lack anything; it does not lack its object. It is, rather, the subject that is missing in desire, or desire that lacks a fixed subject; there is no fixed subject unless there is repression.[20]

Deleuze and Guattari lay out a very precise and complex schema (which follows the one developed by Kant in the *Critique of Pure Reason*) for desire's production of reality, but it suffices to grasp desiring-production in terms of the two poles mentioned above, without collapsing them into a dualism (since dualism is a concept that is viable only on the paranoid side of the division). The schizophrenic organisation of desiring-production functions under a logic of non-exclusive difference, non-identity, and parts that are not subsumed under wholes; it dissolves borders, breaks things down, opens new pathways, undoes repression, destabilises, fluidifies, and escapes. At its limit, schizophrenia coincides with death understood as the abstract motor of change and the source of all new forms of organisation. The paranoiac organisation of desire functions under a logic of exclusive difference, identity, and already constituted objects and subjects; it draws boundaries, creates hierarchies, seals off alternative routes, stabilises, congeals, and blocks escape. At its limit, paranoia coincides with fascism, it is the domain of conservation, centralisation, and the fortification of identity against the becoming that is synonymous with time—privileging 'interiority in place of a new relationship with the outside'.[21]

---

20. Or, to sloganise it, following Nick Land—'organisation is suppression' (an idea also dramatised in Land's mid-nineties writings as the 'Human Security System' with its 'pseudo-universal sedentary identity' and 'paranoid ideal of self-sufficiency'). Deleuze and Guattari, *Anti-Oedipus*, 26 [italics added]; N. Land, 'Organisation is Suppression', Interview with James Flint, *Wired Uk* 3:2 (1997); N. Land, 'Meltdown', in *Fanged Noumena*, 443.

21. Georges Bataille's explication of fascism via the word's Latin etymological root *fasces*, with its denotation of 'bundling' (and connotations of 'high office' and 'supreme power') in 'The Psychological Structure of Fascism' (another important text engaging fascism on an operational rather than purely historical or political level) is helpful, for fascism is understood here abstractly and across diverse domains as the fortification and rigidification of structure (identity, the body, the state)—as it is in Theweleit's *Male Fantasies*, read both as a particular study of the *Freikorpsmen* and a general study of 'irreducible human desire' (as Barbara Erenreich

Importantly, what distinguishes the two poles of desiring-production is not a moral judgement (morality already belongs to the paranoid pole) or a political distinction (socialists can be fascists too) but the critical differentiation introduced by Kant's transcendental philosophy in its effort to eliminate metaphysical error, or the conflation of produced objects with the conditions of their production. In 'Making it with Death', a text that deals with *Anti-Oedipus*'s deployment of the tools of transcendental critique in its approach to fascism, Nick Land, whose work (both early and late) is a consistent reference point for the Gruppo di Nun, explains this mechanism as follows:

> Critique operates by marking the difference between objects and their conditions, understanding metaphysics as the importation of procedures which are adapted to objects into a discussion of their constitutive principles.[22]

For Deleuze and Guattari, schizophrenic investments of desire align with conditions of production and paranoid investments of desire with objects of production, including the 'fixed subjects' mentioned above.[23] Schizophrenic conditions of production cannot be understood by means of concepts belonging to paranoiac objects of production, such as unity, duality, or identity, without falling into metaphysical error. This is no arbitrary decision on Deleuze and Guattari's part but the result of a recursive application of the critical method to the history of critical philosophy, whose operations,

---

suggests in her foreword to the book). Deleuze and Guattari, *Anti-Oedipus*, 270; G. Bataille, 'The Psychological Structure of Fascism', in *Visions of Excess: Selected Writings 1927–1939*, tr. A Stoekl (Minneapolis: University of Minnesota Press, 1985), 137–60. Bataille also singles out the key role of identity and the superior individual in the emergence of the fascist state—effectuating an abstract 'bundling' through which a prior impersonal 'revolutionary effervescence' is negated (see sections X–XI); K. Theweleit, *Male Fantasies*, vol. 1, xi–xii.

22.   N. Land, 'Making it with Death', in *Fanged Noumena*, 272.

23.   '[A]s a rule, the schizoid pole is potential in relation to the actual, paranoiac pole.' Deleuze and Guattari, *Anti-Oedipus*, 376.

originally understood to be the province of the thinking subject, are shown instead to be impersonal, material, and decentralised.[24] Through an analysis of the history of human social configurations, they go on to argue that modernity is synonymous with the operation of critique as an impersonal material process, retrospectively producing its necessity as part of a universal history that only goes one way—deeper into nihilism.[25] Among other things, this occasions a profound displacement of the human subject, whose true status as an object of production is revealed, dismantling the humanist pretensions of the Enlightenment and providing an ontological understanding of fascism—as a structuring coagulation based on repression.

This is consequential for Evola's Magical Idealism, and for the doctrines of Western Hermeticism more generally, not least because it structurally disbars the thinking subject from claiming any direct purchase (unmediated by matter) upon cosmogenesis, or any form of direct intervention in, let alone complete control over, reality.[26] For Evola, who explicitly situates his thought in the lineage of Kant, the inherent tendency of critique to diminish

24. Kant, they demonstrate, for all his brilliance, and against the impulse that drives his work, commits a metaphysical error when he transposes the empirical idea of subjective unity into his description of the conditions of the production of experience. (This error is the basis for what Deleuze and Guattari refer to as an illegitimate use of the syntheses that produce reality, which 'relate[s] use to a hypothetical meaning and re-establish[es] a kind of transcendence', Deleuze and Guattari, *Anti-Oedipus*, 109). Marx and Freud, along with the other great materialist philosopher of the nineteenth century, Friedrich Nietzsche, are important to the critical project laid out in *Anti-Oedipus* because they remind us of conditions of production that operate prior to the unity of the subject and the logic of identity that grounds its apprehension of itself: economic relations, the unconscious, and physiology respectively. Following their lead, Deleuze and Guattari replace the idealism of Kant, for whom (as Evola noted) reality is mediated by the thinking subject, with an account of reality production driven by an impersonal material unconscious ('in reality the unconscious belongs to the realm of physics') that cordons both thought and the subject off on the paranoiac side of the object—as the *products* of material syntheses (Deleuze and Guattari, *Anti-Oedipus*, 283).
25. 'The "history of nihilism" just [...] being an alternative vocabulary for the same processes that we can examine as philosophical critique.' N. Land, 'The Concept of Accelerationism, Sesssion 2' (lecture, The New Centre for Research & Practice, March 12, 2017).
26. Let alone an individual human thinker with specific characteristics—e.g. male and 'Aryan' (a very obvious example of metaphysical error, even more so when these are understood as 'spiritual' qualities).

the causal power of the subject is unacceptable, even in the muted tones of his Idealist contemporaries for whom 'the individual does not endure: it gives way; it does not rule things, but melts within them'. The impossibility of acknowledging personal vulnerability, even as a universal attribute of the subject, leads to a predictable diagnosis: 'This is the path of decadence.'[27]

The equation of modernity and nihilism with decadence, a feature of much contemporary right-wing thought, nonetheless accords with Deleuze and Guattari's prognosis. And Evola's philosophical solution to the predicament, like every other theory of self-deification—magical, fascist, rationalist, or transhumanist—can be understood through their analysis of human desire as a mere symptom of a deeper movement of materially driven immanence. In every such theory we find a paranoid reaction to modernity's generalised immanentisation of structure which, as exemplified in Evola's development of the philosophy of the Absolute Individual in response to Michelstaedter's tragic vision of existence, cures itself of its depression through illusion, misattributing the order of causes and effects, primary and secondary processes, and locating causal power in the objects of production (including the human subject), or tracing attributes from the level of these products onto the processes that produce them. Far from launching an escape, fascist desires to exit modernity are themselves already circumscribed by modernity. The desire to overcome nihilism through transcendence is absolutely, predictably, modern.

But despair and suicide are not solutions either. Even though young suicides predominate amongst their influences, the Gruppo di Nun challenges us to see 'the world in its a-human grace without giving up our own lives, at least for a moment'; to know, during those difficult hours 'when one realises that one is immersed in a dense darkness, so thick that it seems to preclude

---

27.　At this point in his thinking, what makes it 'decadent' appears to be nothing more than an arbitrary and illegitimate (because external to the operation of critique itself) moral judgement. Evola himself does admit, while congratulating himself for his 'boldness', that 'the system [he] outlined in *Phenomenology* [of the Absolute Individual] might have been accused of being based, at least to some extent, on arbitrary choices'. Evola, *The Path of Cinnabar*, 43–44; 58.

any return to the light', 'moments of mourning, despair, or depression', 'moments suspended over the chasm of madness' when 'life seems to have lost all meaning' and the world 'which had until then revolved like a planet around the sun of an I or a We, shows itself to be no more than a collection of fragments from which, like a collage, it had emerged' that 'there is always more than *one* world and that, even from the same fragments, it is possible to construct totally different worlds'. The writings and rituals comprising this collection can be read as an attempt to furnish its readers with the tools required for just such an immense and difficult task. Because it is easy to commit suicide, and easier still to become a fascist. Contrary to what Evola thought, the path of fortification, domination, and control is the weak path. Only the strong can let go and live. Fluidity, acceptance, adaptability—these are all attributes of strength. A desire for death, whether of oneself or of others, is not the same as an exaltation of death as a great generative motor, invalidating every eternity and plunging all stable forms into the 'boundless liquid expanse of indefinite recombination'. Between the intentional subject and the 'inverted wisdom' proffered by the Gruppo di Nun, aeons of ossifying repression intervene. But all is not lost:

> If only we could [...] see our desires for what *they really are*, then we would finally feel in touch with a universe penetrated by an infinite love of its own dissolution.

Standing beneath a disconnected electricity pylon—inorganic Christ, cyborg figure of post-industrial humanity, a travesty of the crucifixion—the author of 'The Highest Form of Gnosis' elaborates a ritual for tuning into this counterintuitive perspective on reality. Plotting the coordinates provided in the text's footnotes reveals a triangle of evocation surrounding Lake Varese in the northern outskirts of Milan, to be deployed, we are told, in summoning not only the disaffected voices of the landscape and culture of the Gruppo di Nun's native Italy (a blighted land stalked by demons which operates metonymically throughout *Revolutionary Demonology* as a symbol of impurity, plurality, and anti-absolutism, fulfilling its vocation as the site of a great fallen empire and guardian of the decaying ruins of two of the West's most virulent mythologies of redemption, Renaissance Humanism and Roman Catholicism) but also voices of a less consummately human provenance, to let their black gnosis flow through us like haunted transmissions through a spirit box.

III. THE DOWNWARD ASCENT

> In reality, man is passive.
>
> Guido Morselli[28]

> Revolution is not duty, but surrender.
>
> Nick Land[29]

The Gruppo di Nun's reading of Michelstaedter is almost as idiosyncratic as Evola's, but in a completely opposite manner. For it is precisely Michelstaedter's acceptance of the tragic nature of existence—interpreted by Evola as weakness—in which they find succour, and which comes to ground the unique theorisation of masochism advanced in *Revolutionary Demonology*. Far from being a guide to self-deification, EM insists, *Persuasion and Rhetoric*

is a book that truly seems like an alien artefact, and one that resists all forms of categorisation and temporal analysis. It is clearly the work of an angst-ridden teenager, angry at the world and at himself, locked in his isolated room writing clumsy anathemas; but at the same time, paradoxically, it is a rigorous

---

28. G. Morselli, *Dissipatio H.G.* (New York: New York Review of Books, 2020), 71.
29. Land, 'Making it with Death', 287.

treatise on a higher form of black physics, a deeper and more disturbing form of entropy. It is an essay written in a language that is a pidgin of dead and living languages schizophrenically blended together, addressing a deeper gnosis of the fundamental laws of nature.

Running entirely counter to Evola's paranoiac investments, masochism names an orientation toward existence that treats an acceptance of the diminishment of control over reality in the face of the 'fundamental laws of nature'[30] not as a concession to be lamented, but as a *revelation*. A relief, brought about by the dissipation of an illusion so solid and prodigious it has sustained the weightiest edifices of human thought, which overflows into an experience of cosmic ecstasy rivalling that of the most devoted ascetic. 'We have been illuminated by suffering' will become a kind of mantra that resonates throughout the Gruppo di Nun's writings—whether in the context of a retelling of creation myths in which the price of cosmogenesis is the compromised integrity of an ancient chthonic monster, more often than not depicted as female and representing primordial chaos or unstructured matter, violently dismembered by 'some male solar deity syncretised with the figure of the King', whose screams resound endlessly through the whole of creation, or as the conclusion of a harrowing personal account of the nausea and sensory torment that accompany chronic migraine; in the wordless discipline of the bodybuilder or the transports of various heretics and saints, such as Christina the Astonishing, who, having died numerous times, is repeatedly forced by God to return to the earth and suffer the company of a humanity she despises, or Teresa of Ávila, who employs the same effusive vocabulary in her descriptions of religious rapture as she does in her accounts of paroxysmal sickness.

---

30. The Gruppo di Nun have a complex and nuanced understanding of what is meant by 'nature' which should not be confused with the conservative use of 'nature' or the 'natural' to justify the maintenance of a status quo. See 'Dogma', 'Catastrophic Astrology', 'Spectral Materialism', 'Gothic Insurrection', 'Gothic (A)theology', and 'Mater Dolorosa' in this volume.

What is perceived in these moments of illumination—revealed not by the brilliance of an Apollonian sun but the refraction of an Artemisian moon— what is celebrated, even, is the 'wound' at the heart of matter. An originary, material volatility whose unconditioned and effervescent creativity has, since the dawn of time, been channelled, constrained, solidified, stratified, organised, and repressed through a sustained series of congelations to form stars and planets, the geological stratifications of Earth, the evolutionary developments of organic life, human civilisation, language, reason, the notion of the autonomous subject, and all the triumphs and the terrors of the human mind. From this process of accumulative extrusion and rigidifi- cation—which the Gruppo di Nun, following the cryptogenealogical path opened up by Daniel Barker,[31] understands as a 'continuous propagation of traumas', both phylogenetic and ontogenetic, material and conceptual—the human emerges 'not so much as the apex of a developmental process, but rather as the ultimate receptacle for universal suffering'. Far from being gods, we are merely the residue of the progressive depotentiation of initial cosmic possibility, built out of catastrophes and doomed, along with the rest of the universe, to terminal dissolution. Pain, therefore, operates as a trans-catastrophic vector that can be used to travel masochistically back in time,[32] regressing through the succession of encrustations upon which the stability of the forms and ideas that make up what we take to be ourselves and the world is founded, to make contact with the 'Prima Materia of the ocean of Nun'—'black primordial magma', 'liquid darkness', cradle and grave of all things.

As CK reminds us in 'Cultivating Darkness',

> [o]ur fragile partiality emanates from chaos—matter itself is this chaos and
> this hidden inscrutability—but multiplicity and lawlessness, hidden in the
> innermost core of things, also vibrate in the human soul. However frustrating,

---

31. See 'Barker Speaks', in Ccru, *Writings 1997–2003*, 155–62.
32. Ibid. On pain and chronotaxis, see also Moynihan, *Spinal Catastrophism*.

insubstantial, insane, or laughable all of this may be, there is only this fatality, this concordance between the unravelling of the real and the dissolution of the world. And if there were any teleology, it would only be the passage from a vague foreboding of doom to a scream full of horror.

Here we are firmly in the nightmare of Magical Idealism's rigid, unyielding, and immaterial *I*, with its paranoid objective of 'bind[ing] and freez[ing] the Waters' of this chaotic and senseless materiality and of 'rescuing' from it 'something stable, impassive' and 'immortal'.[33] Yet, like the migraine sufferer in 'Mater Dolorosa' who suddenly understands, at the peak of her misery, as if it has come to her in a vision, that '*bodies* are unstable', rather than recoiling at this horror and seeking to exert their control over this instability, the masochist seeks out experiences that expose them to the ephemeral materiality of the world—its indifference, its senselessness, its inexorable entropic destiny—only in order to love it more furiously. Hence the para-doxical motif of the 'downward ascent': the highest form of gnosis lies in the deepest machinations of matter. What we really want, what *she* wants to realise in us—Apophis, Nibiru, Tiamat, Nemesis, Malkuth, the Infernal Mother, *Stilla Maris,* Virgin of Sorrows, Our Lady of Tears, Femboy Remus, the Black Goddess, the Whore of Babylon, the matter that screams in our blood...chaotic and multiplicitous *Nun* the Uncreator, in her many guises—is not stasis, disembodiment, transcendence, and a guarantee of eternal iden-tity and power, but *transformation*. A fluidity emblematised by the great iron ocean that interminably churns at the centre of the earth, a remnant of the status of the globe in its entirety before its ancient ebullience was smothered by the cooling crust. Through the counterintuitive nature of their art, the masochist seeks to accommodate an inversion that will vent the psychic and material pressure built up around this primordial wound, perforating the solidity of the illusions that press upon it, to attain an 'anti-gravity' that might propel them toward that 'enigmatic alien attractor' that calls from the

---

33.   Evola and the Ur Group, 'Knowledge of the Waters', 19, 18.

darkness of the sidereal void. This is the insight revealed in the subversion of the Thelemic formula 'Every Man and Woman is a Star' that names the ritual with which the book begins: 'Every Worm Trampled is a Star'—it is our suffering that makes us glow.

But the 'spark of anti-gravity' that each 'living form bears within itself' cannot be released through a mental act, whether that involves an expansion or diminishment of the powers of the conscious mind. In this respect, the Gruppo di Nun's notion of masochism also operates as a critique of 'the meditative experiences commonly sought in initiatic traditions' whose purpose is to bring about 'states of absolute concentration that obliterate individual consciousness and elevate it to a state of consciousness that we might call cosmic or universal'. A practice indispensable to the magical doctrines of self-deification which Evola and his collaborators in the Gruppo di Ur rehashed and which the texts in this book call ceaselessly into question, along with the longstanding insistence on coding matter as feminine and consciousness as masculine, with the latter consistently posited as the privileged term. For the masochist's ecstasy, whether obtained through Barkerean geotraumatic regression, Sparean Atavistic Resurgence, or Saturnalian revelry in the queer clubs of Remoria, is always embodied and 'radically feminine'. Opposed in every way to Evola's solipsistic philosophy of mental 'domination' and control, it denotes a material practise of anti-mastery, a discipline of release and letting go.

Consequently, in the apocryphal 'Lifting the Absolute', penned by the pseudonymous 'Bronze Age Collapse' (catastrophic Nemesis to the Sun of erstwhile alt-right internet phenomenon and bodybuilder Bronze Age Pervert), the practice of weightlifting is presented as a means not of transcending matter, but of reconnecting the body to a primary material dynamism that has been lost through millennia of reactive inertia, symbolised by the dumbbells that the bodybuilder lifts, in so doing propelling themselves, with each repetition, away from the sclerotic torpor of God and back through the body to the centre of the earth, melting themselves down in a rite of cosmic devolution consecrated by fire, sweat, and iron: 'What a bizarre turn of events for philosophy, for the body to become the voice of the spirit and the source of all wisdom!'

The role granted to matter as the terminus and goal of the masochist's magical and devotional labour is contrary to the path laid out by the bulk of Western esoteric systems, for which matter is precisely what is to be sloughed off in order to ascend to a purely mental dimension that coincides with the consciousness responsible for inaugurating the cosmos. Following the lead of Ccru,[34] the Gruppo di Nun rejects this hierarchical organisation of being, as diagrammed in the Kabbalistic Tree of Life, where an immaterial unified mind unfolds into an increasingly multiple and material world, its initial purity progressively debased in the process, with the Tree being typically interpreted as a map to be traversed in the reverse direction by the magical practitioner or alchemist as they extract themselves from the contingency of the material world and work toward the completion of the 'Great Work'.[35] Instead, the cosmos of the Gruppo di Nun, 'like a golem self-assembled from mud, is born and extinguished in the materiality of the processes that produce it', which are 'essentially devoid of human intentionality'.

The Kabbalistic hierarchy of emanation is questioned with particular intensity by LT in 'Mater Dolorosa', via the relationship between the highest and lowest feminine sefirot, Binah and Malkuth, whose conspiratorial dance of rupture and conjunction in the *Zohar*'s description of reality's unfolding betrays an esoteric resistance to its straightforward arrangement on a spectrum that runs from immaterial mind to embodied matter. The complex interactions between these two sefirot reveal a tendency

---

34. See 'Part 8: Pandemonium', in Ccru, *Writings: 1997–2003*, 239–553.

35. 'This focus on the human mind, and its enhancement through practices such as concentration and meditation, often results in the celebration of consciousness as a God, even when the individual self is annihilated. In our view, proposing the existence of an anthropomorphic and immortal ultra-consciousness, accessible only to the few through an esoteric path of illumination, is not only delirious, but inherently fascist.' Breitling, 'Under the Sign of the Black Mark: Interview with Members of Gruppo di Nun'.

to self-organisation and nonlinearity native to the feminine aspect of the Kabbalah that is concealed by an otherwise exoteric linearity, in which the feminine is characterised merely 'as a passive and receptive aspect of the process of emanating divine light'. LT identifies the repression of this independently active, schizophrenising, non-hierarchic nonlinearity by a dependently active, paranoiac, hierarchic linearity as a consistent feature in the doctrines of the Right Hand Path, whose system, as the Gruppo di Nun asserts in 'Dogma', although founded on a contingent and insidious humanist hallucination that functions to impose and maintain 'a highly organisational and hierarchical force aimed at establishing a pyramid with Man on top, be it an absolute monarchy legitimised by God, a Nazi-fascist dictatorship, a white ethnostate, or a meritocratic society dominated by the figure of the cisgender heterosexual white male', is simultaneously presented as the sole, necessary, and universal truth of the cosmos.[36]

The Gruppo di Nun counter the doctrinal supremacy of the emanationist hierarchy reinforced in the diagram of the Tree of Life with the 'tri-triangular seal', a 'decapitated' reconfiguration of the original decimal structure from which the highest sefira, Kether ('the Crown') has been removed.[37] Once emancipated from the tyranny of this immaterial sovereign, a second diagram can be discerned within the ruins of the Tree of Life. The remaining nine sefirot arranged in three sets of three, interpreted statically, compose three triangles of evocation (the triangle being the shape traditionally used for summoning demons), with each, as we are told in 'Mater Dolorosa', relating to one of the three 'apocalyptic female aspects'—'the Dragon', 'the Celestial Virgin', and 'the great Babylon falling in flames'—which when deployed in concert with the ritual text of 'Every Worm Trampled is a Star' function as an evocation of the Dismembered Mother Tiamat—the Great Mother of creation, but now decoupled from the masculine power that is supposed to mould her flesh

---

36.   For the Gruppo di Nun's explanation of their usage of the traditional magical distinction between the 'Right Hand Path' and 'Left Hand Path' see page 14 in this volume.

37.   See page 2 in this volume.

into form, and therefore, via an appropriation of Jung that affirms rather than condemns independent 'unripe' female sexuality, an avatar of 'non-heterosexual or non-conforming womanhood, of the woman who evades the reproductive patriarchal order, refusing to take on her role as Great Mother and dialectical counterpart to male consciousness'. Interpreted dynamically, with the first sefira 'Ammit, The Devourer' in the position of Binah, and the ninth sefira 'Tiamat, The Worm' in the position of Malkuth, the nine sefirot together form a 'sinister spiral', a 'circumference without centre', a 'divergent series from the heart of which issues forth a vast and boundless chasm'. In this model, the mundane sexual dimorphism and obligatory heterosexuality upon which, almost without exception, every Western magical system is based, are refused and replaced with various economies of non-reproductive desire—lesbian, virginal, sodomitic, xenophilic, inorganic, mitotic (*Revolutionary Demonology* contains at least one text devoted to each)—revealing a 'monstrous, headless machine which advances irreversibly' on its own terms, without the intervention of some primordial form-giving masculine counterpart, 'suffocating the structure that generated it'.[38]

For the Gruppo di Nun, dismantling the heterosexual reproductive economy that subtends Western esotericism is part of larger onslaught directed at the idealist dogmas of symmetry, stasis, and equilibrium that sustain the latter's doctrines. As LT points out in 'Catastrophic Astrology', heterosexual reproduction, despite its superficial heterogeneity, is an enforcer, not only of the banal homogeneity of the self, but also of the 'human' as an eternal form—reifying, through the idea of genetic inheritance, the resistance to

---

38.   The heterosexual reproductive model of cosmogenesis is another example of metaphysical error: 'But what is even more interesting to us is the social and political outcome of this arbitrary cosmology that results in the establishment of what we may define as *cosmological sexism*: gender is not only a set of more or less reasonable social rules, but it is elevated to an inescapable axiom underlying reality, that poses polarization as a boundary condition for the existence of the universe.' Breitling, 'Under the Sign of the Black Mark: Interview with Members of Gruppo di Nun'.

change that any system in equilibrium seeks to maintain, and mobilising this reification in a way that is structurally analogous to religious doctrines of personal redemption:

> In my nightly terrors, I had often considered my own disintegration, dissecting in every possible way the paradoxical insanity of being an individual, and then being no more; but there was something strangely reassuring about the idea of dying as a part of the universal cycle of Nature, as if in an eternal wildlife documentary where death is perfectly compensated by new life and equilibrium is forever preserved. I was never truly Catholic. I was raised not to believe in any God, but there was something religious about the way I was taught to approach Nature as a redeeming force of heterosexual preservation: the sun sets only to rise again; we die, only to leave room for our offspring to thrive and carry on our legacy. As a cisgender girl approaching puberty, I could finally access salvation by consecrating myself to the natural cycle of heterosexual reproduction.

Economies of non-reproductive desire are demonic economies—'the demonic' indexing for the Gruppo di Nun the multiplicity of forces that act on the human from a position alien to it, transforming it from a conservative system perpetually seeking to maintain equlibrium to a dissipative system open to the transformative potential of its outside; 'a dimension which is external to the order built by humans but which, at the same time, is capable of violently breaking into this order, upsetting its fundamental axioms'.[39] LT's reverie ends not with a vow to uphold the heterosexual perpetuation of the same that promises salvation, but with an affirmation of demonic love for Apophis, an asteroid which shares its name with the Egyptian serpent-god of the Netherworld, and which, at the time, was understood to be on a deadly collision course with Earth.

---

39.   Ibid.

Far from reassuring us of a comforting symmetry between the microcosm of 'Man' and the macrocosm of the universe, the Gruppo di Nun maintains that the relationship between ourselves and this demonic outside is disconcertingly *asymmetrical*. For why would the deep machinations of the universe reflect empirical structures already familiar to us or conform to the repudiation of our personal and very human fears? Why would the conditions of the production of objects reflect specific features of those objects? What insane anthropocentric hubris lies behind the Hermetic maxim 'As Above, So Below'?

The asymmetrical cosmology of the Gruppo di Nun can be summed up in a formula from 'Every Worm Trampled is a Star': 'Order descends into chaos. Light fades into darkness. No structure is eternal'. The beginning and the end of the universe do not resemble one another, and the processes that generate the world are not identical to the world. This is the 'black physics' intuited by Michelstaedter and consolidated in the second law of thermodynamics, which tells us that

> [n]ot only is it not possible to convert energy without losing it as 'background noise' into the universe—everything that happens, any phenomenon that takes place in any corner of the cosmos, is a process in disequilibrium. Everything rushes in a specific direction; nothing is reversible; under no circumstances can we return.

Entropy is fundamental to the occult system of the Gruppo di Nun, not least because it disproves the human fantasy of order without chaos or the preservation of structure over and against the blind flux of material dissolution that draws the universe inexorably toward heat death. Yet its counterintuitive nature can make it difficult to countenance—just as modernity produces the paranoid-fascist illusion of identity, stability, power, and control, entropy produces the illusion of equilibrium:

We can explain our attachment to the concept of equilibrium in accordance with our nature as limited living systems: we require an internal order to be maintained to guarantee our survival and the functioning of our machines; the amazement we experience before our organic organisation is a deceptive feeling that conceals a misunderstanding of the true cost of our existence. We want to believe in conservation because, faced with the evidence of our inevitable disintegration, we seek a theory that makes life less futile, but above all less unnecessary; a universe in disequilibrium confronts us with the realisation that we are but a spontaneous and frantic proliferation of molecular machines that burn, consume, multiply and die, in an ineluctable and meaningless dance.

The fantasy of perpetual equilibrium is paranoia translated into energetic terms. Like paranoia, it constitutes itself through a repression of transform-ative potential. Perhaps, then, it is not surprising that the Gruppo di Nun understands its consecration in the doctrines of the Right Hand Path as part of a deliberate ideological strategy in a long running occult war between the 'the radical immanentism of a materialist neo-magic'—for which the cosmos is asymmetrical and equilibrium is therefore a local, secondary, and ephemeral effect of a deeper entropic law of uncreation, maintained through an open and unrepressed relationship with its outside—and the 'absolute idealism of an esoteric fascist tradition'—for which the cosmos is symmetrical, and equilibrium is therefore posited as a universal, primary, and constant feature of reality, maintained through a repressed and disavowed relationship with its outside:

[a] closed, self-subsistent cybernetic system that maintains perfect equilib-rium is a dead system (i.e. it ceases to be a system); or else it contains *hidden mechanisms* that place it in a condition of absolute dependency upon that same *outside* from which it desperately seeks to emancipate itself.

Because of this asymmetry, the various figures of inversion and reversal that appear throughout *Revolutionary Demonology* are 'revolutionary' in a way that might not at first be apparent. The inversion of evolutionary history in the masochist's practice of regression and the bodybuilder's devotional return to matter; the inversion of light and knowledge explored in 'Solarisation' which, via their excess, yield darkness and unknowing; the inversion of 'phallic' Rome in a sprawling, sunken Remoria, celebrated by VM as 'the city that would have been born if, in the ancient fratricidal legend about the origins of Rome, Remus had won instead of Romulus'; the inversion of civilisation and the atomised individual in the faceless barbarian hordes, 'wild myriads, born of chaos', that 'Gothic Insurrection' prophesies will one day be the harbingers of a new and inhuman world; the reverse philosopher's stone that has the alchemist crashing backwards through levels of successive sublimation toward the Black Sun of primordial *nigredo*, or even an inverted Tarot that terminates with the Fool, symbol of a world 'founded on an absence of foundation: plummeting, never touching the bottom'—all of these are 'non-reciprocal' inversions. Inversions based on asymmetry that unveil a repressed substrate of an existing regime rather than inaugurating a substitute regime, equivalent in status but opposed in content to the original. They are demonic in the sense that in each, contact is made with the outside of the system in order to open it up to transformation. The thermodynamic description of the relationship between Rome and Remoria exhibits the asymmetrical mechanism clearly: '[i]f the Rome of Romulus is the city in which energy is put to good use so as to continually fertilise and reproduce what already is, Remus's Remoria must be the city of expenditure, of *dépense*'. Rome is not the opposite of Remoria, but its repression.

Non-reciprocal inversion is a principle whose real world political application does not require great stretches of imagination to comprehend.[40] It is, moreover, very different to the figures of inversion that those versed in

---

40. Magic *is* politics in the sense that, at its most esoteric levels, it is always dealing with questions of the production of reality.

the Western magical tradition will already be familiar with—a necessary innovation, as the Gruppo di Nun will maintain, since any inversion based on symmetry is ultimately ineffectual when mobilised tactically in the occult war against the paranoid hetero-patriarchal hegemony of the Right Hand Path that they see themselves embroiled in:

> The principal mistake committed, more or less deliberately, by the vast majority of those who tried to trace a Left Hand Path in opposition to that indicated for centuries by the Hermetic tradition, was that of doing no more than working toward a reversal of the dogmas of the Right Hand Path, evidently ignoring that a system endowed with total symmetry remains, by definition, identical to itself whichever way it is turned.

> [Hence, the] Hermetic Kabbalah is appropriately armoured against any attempt at sabotage from within. Under no condition will it ever be sufficient to invert any symbol proposed by the Right Hand Path—from the Tree of Life itself to crosses and pentagrams—in order to obtain something radically different from its original meaning.

'Every Worm Trampled is a Star' is dedicated to 'our sisters of the Left Hand Path' and the Gruppo di Nun consistently present themselves as allies of this typically subversive and unorthodox strand of magic on the condition that its relation to the Right Hand Path is not understood as one of simple symmetrical inversion:

> The only way to trace a path toward an alternative esotericism is to definitively break the symmetry of the Hermetic Kabbalah, proposing a new system based upon entirely different symbols and connections.

The figure that comes to define the abyssal asymmetry of the Gruppo di Nun's entropic cosmos in *Revolutionary Demonology* is love. This is not the mundane love of the 'the BDSM romantic comedy' of subjects and objects that keeps us trapped within familiar categories of identity and modes of social interaction—forms of love constrained by the hetero-patriarchal economy of equilibrium and symmetry. It is not the immaterial love of religious ecstasy whose price is the repudiation of matter and the denigration of the flesh. It is not the countervailed love of magical traditions such as Thelema, which seeks to balance the decentralised passivity love symbolises in its system by placing it in a dualistic relationship with a centralised and active will.[41] Love, for the Gruppo di Nun, is far more difficult, obscure, and encompassing. They define it simply as 'the thermodynamic property of bodies that attracts them to their death'—a '[p]rimordial hunger' that is 'the cryptic and telic structure of reality itself' and the enigmatic answer to the questions they pose at the end of 'Dogma':

How can we reach a darkness so radically and frighteningly alien to everything we know? How can we think of approaching its black fire without being destroyed?

It names simultaneously that blind and insatiable material striving that is at the heart of Michelstaedter's tragic vision of existence (and which drove Evola to the brink of a despair that he could only overcome through fascism), and an orientation toward dissolution that not only accepts it as a primary feature of reality but is also able to access, by relinquishing anthropocentric fantasies of the centrality of human 'will', a cosmic perspective from which the irredeemably entropic character of the universe can be understood in all its spontaneous, autonomous, and unsentimental richness.[42] In the words of

---

41. See above, 282n3.

42. It is important to note, in passing (as this could easily be the subject of another essay of equivalent length) that despite the centrality of entropy to their thinking, the Gruppo di Nun do not assume a linear-progressive model of time. In fact, they understand linear time as a ramification of the 'absurd' circular model their critical approach to equilibrium attempts to dislodge: 'The relevance of equilibrium in the magical tradition is related to the idea of absolute *reversibility*,

their beloved Georges Bataille, '[t]here can be anguish only from a personal, *particular* point of view that is radically opposed to the *general* point of view based on the exuberance of living matter as a whole.'[43]

The predicament we began with—how to respond to the nihilism of modernity without succumbing to despair or constructing a paranoid fantasy of control whose function as a shield against the terror of divine abandonment, impotence, and personal insignificance can never be fully avowed—is resolved, for the Gruppo di Nun, through a recalibration of the relationship between the intentional subject, the world, and 'the iron laws of thermodynamics' that indefatiguably assemble and disassemble them. What Michelstaedter and Evola understood in negative terms as lack is celebrated as a positive, joyous, and effusive force of cosmic uncreation and recombination. Because of love's asymmetrical primacy over the subjects and objects it actualises and de-actualises—as *effects* not *causes* of cosmogenesis—their passivity is an ontological fact. Acknowledging this passivity, accepting the spontaneity of existence[44] and being capable of grasping it as a strength, in turn opens one up to the positive virtuality of a self-determining matter:

---

that is, the notion that the past is entirely preserved in the future, and the future completely contained in the past, forming a never-ending circle in perpetual motion, where the active principle (*Will*) and the passive principle (*Love*) are eternally chasing each other. This duality is only resolved in God (*consciousness*), that can be thought as the static *point within the circle* in which this motion converges. This view of the cosmos as an equilibrium of polarities is rooted in our cultural substratum to the point where it is perceived as *natural* and, therefore, sacred and immutable. We believe, instead, that this notion of equilibrium conveys a clear political agenda, and that, far from being a perfect *theory of everything*, it contains arbitrary—and even absurd— assumptions. The absurdity of circular cosmology is, put simply, that it relies on perpetual motion, and thus denies the evidence of time as a material drive towards disintegration. This is expressed in the patriarchal project of *progress* as conservation and accumulation, which, being absolutely unsustainable, can only be realized through time sorcery.' Breitling, 'Under the Sign of the Black Mark: Interview with Members of Gruppo di Nun'.

43.   G. Bataille, *The Accursed Share*, tr. R. Hurley (New York: Zone Books, 2 vols., 1991), vol. 1, 39.

44.   Evola's technical definition of 'spontaneity' as 'non-self-centredness' or an absence of intentional subjecthood ('leaving one's internal throne empty') which he identifies as 'ultimately the principle of nature' is shared by the Gruppo di Nun, who assert, for instance, in 'Dogma' that '[t]he universe is by definition spontaneous; the spontaneity of things is independent of our will'.

Love is the door that allows us to reconcile ourselves with darkness, provided that we understand its true meaning, and that we do not make the mistake of subjecting it to our individual consciousness, transforming it into a play of mirrors. Confronted with a thermodynamic universe, we understand that every moment of our existence is the spontaneous fruit of a wonderful proliferation to which we belong entirely.

Love, therefore, is an 'already accomplished anti-politics', a politics without an image of the subject or the world. And nihilism, far from being an adversary, is the motor of love. For it is only through the consummate destruction of transcendent values and meanings, and the definitive elimination of the need for validation from some external or divine authority, that new values and meanings—new subjects and new worlds—are able to come into being. Nun's entropic embrace keeps us safe, protecting us from the tyranny of sedimented regimes of power (the 'historical fascism' that does not cease to haunt our social configurations), and releasing us from the stranglehold of our own accumulated repressions (the 'fascism in us all, in our heads and in our everyday behaviour').[45] Since love is opposed to conservation, not as a contrary operation but as what conservation represses, there is no equivalent countervailing force—no active 'masculine' will—able to balance or constrain its devotional labour of infinite uncreation. Nun reigns alone, nourished by her own intrinsic multiplicity.

However, while Evola sees it as something to be overcome through 'domination', the Gruppo di Nun, in line with their rejection of the fantasy of equilibrium that underwrites the plausibility of Evola's Absolute Individual, understand 'spontaneity' as a necessary component of an inexorable and living rite that, whether we are aware of it or not, we are all participants in. Here they quote Nicola Masciandaro: '[T]he verbal root of spontaneity, PIE *spend- (to make an offering, perform a rite, to engage oneself by a ritual act), contains this sense of sacrifice and self-offering, just as we speak of the spontaneous as something "surrendered to", as to a whim. The spontaneity of authentic transformation is also thus a species of death, of surrendering to the expiration of what is untenable.' Evola, *The Path of Cinnabar*, 54, 44; Masciandaro, *On the Darkness of the Will*, 34.

45.   Deleuze and Guattari, *Anti-Oedipus*, xiii.

∇

The Gruppo di Nun disbanded only a short time after the period of intense and sustained collaborative effort that furnished these texts. Whether in relation to the publication of these translations or to other matters, all our attempts to reach them have been met with silence. But before having succumbed to the entropy they loved so fiercely, they succeeded in their aim of 'tracing a path toward an alternative esotericism', questioning the fundamental premises of the Western magical tradition, reconceiving the way that difference and reciprocity are typically understood within its doctrines, and offering a model of cosmogenesis based on an entirely different logic to that of the heterosexual desire that has for centuries inhibited the ability of magical practitioners to really and truly 'traffic with the outside'. In the wake of this work, strange new occultisms based on alternative models of desire are given space to flourish—queer, alien, inorganic—bound by a love that knows nothing of subjects or objects, only a hunger so tremendous that it will not be sated until it has devoured time itself.

If a single message could be distilled from *Revolutionary Demonology* it would be that there is always another world hidden in this one. A claim whose guarantee does not lie in the redemptive promise of a new dawn but in the black incandescence of the long shadows of limitless modernity—a darkness that reveals all the monsters that hide in the light. Like every city that 'conceals within the folds of its geography a latent Remoria that pushes for the inversion to take place', we too contain the repressed doubles of ourselves: alien vistas to be revealed through the masochistic discipline of giving in and letting go—for 'only while we fall inexorably into our dissolution can we fulfil our destiny and shine'.

For Nine.

Alighieri, Dante. *The Divine Comedy of Dante Alighieri: Inferno*, tr., ed. R.M. Durling. Oxford: Oxford University Press, 1996.

────── *The Divine Comedy of Dante Alighieri: Paradiso*, Tr., ed. R. M. Durling. Oxford: Oxford University Press, 2011.

Angela of Foligno. *Angela of Foligno's Memorial*, tr. J. Cirgnano. C. Mazzoni. Cambridge: D.S. Brewer, 1999.

Anonymous. '99942 Apophis 2004 MN4', https://web.archive.org/ web/20200602220236/http://www.99942-apophis.com/>

────── 'The Tower'. *Vast Abrupt*. <https://vastabrupt.com/2018/06/12/ the-tower/>.

Aquinas, Thomas. *On Evil*, tr. R. Regan, ed. B. Davies. Oxford: Oxford University Press, 2003.

Artaud, Antonin. *The Theatre and its Double*, tr. M.C. Richards. New York: Grove Press, 1958.

────── *The Death of Satan and Other Mystical Writings*. London: Calder & Boyars, 1974.

────── *Heliogabalus or, The Crowned Anarchist*, tr. A. Lykiard. London: Creation Books, 2003.

Augustine. *Earlier Writings*, tr., ed. J.H.S. Burleigh. Louisville, London: Westminster John Knox Press, 2006.

Barad, Karen. *Meeting the Universe Halfway*. Durham, NC: Duke University Press, 2007.

Bartolomei Romagnoli, Allessandro. 'Christina l'Ammirabile'. *Scrittrici Mistiche Europee*. Vol. 1, ed. A. Bartolomei Romagnoli, A. Degl'Innocenti and F. Santi. Firenze: Sismel, 2015.

————— 'Christina l'Ammirabile', *Nuovo Dizionario di Mistica,* ed. L. Borriello, E. Caruana, M. Rosaria Del Genio, R. Di Muro. Vatican: Libreria Editrice Vaticana, 2016.

Bataille, Georges. *Visions of Excess: Selected Writings 1927–1939,* tr. A Stoekl. Minneapolis: University of Minnesota Press, 1985.

————— *Erotism,* tr. M. Dalwood. San Francisco: City Lights, 1986.

————— *Guilty,* tr. B. Boone. Venice, CA: The Lapis Press, 1988.

————— *The Accursed Share,* tr. R. Hurley. New York: Zone, 2 vols., 1991.

Batygin, Konstantin, and Michael. E. Brown. 'Evidence for a Distant Giant Planet in the Solar System'. *The Astronomical Journal* 151:22 (2016), 1–12.

Benatar, David. *Better Never to Have Been.* Oxford: Oxford University Press, 2006.

Benjamin, Walter. *Selected Writings Volume 4, 1938–1940,* ed. H. Eiland and M.W. Jennings. Cambridge, MA: Harvard University Press, 2003.

Berger, Edmund. 'Waveforms: Art and the Revolutionary Transformation in the Age of Blockchain', *ŠUM* 10:2 (2018), <http://sumrevija.si/en/eng-sum10-2-edmund-berger-waveforms-art-and-the-revolutionary-transformation-in-the-age-of-blockchain/>.

Bergson, Henri. *The Two Sources of Morality and Religion,* tr. R. Ashley Audra and C. Bereton. London: MacMillan, 1935.

Bernard of Clairvaux. *De Diligendo Deo.* Vancouver: Eremitical Press, 2010.

Bey, Hakim. *T.A.Z.: The Temporary Autonomous Zone, Ontological Anarchy, Poetic Terrorism.* Brooklyn, NY: Autonomedia, 1985.

Blau, Herbert. *The Dubious Spectacle: Extremities of Theater 1976–2000.* Minneapolis: University of Minnesota Press, 2002.

Boito, Arrigo. *Opere.* Rome: Garzanti, 1979.

Boltzmann, Ludwig. *Theoretical Physics and Philosophical Problems,* tr. P. Foulkes. Ed. B. McGuinness. Dordrecht and Boston: D. Reidel, 1974.

Bonaventura, Saint. *The Mind's Road to God*. Boston: Wyatt North, 2020.

Bostrom, Nick. 'Existential Risk Prevention as Global Priority'. *Global Policy* 4:1 (2013).

Brassier, Ray. *Nihil Unbound: Enlightenment and Extinction*. Basingstoke: Palgrave, 2007.

Breitling, Dustin. 'Under the Sign of the Black Mark: Interview with Members of Gruppo di Nun'. *Diffractions Collective*, 2019. <https://diffractionscol-lective.org/under-the-sign-of-the-black-mark-interview-with-members-of-gruppo-di-nun/>.

Bronze Age Collapse, *The Search for Absolute Fitness: Plato as a Body-builder*. Agharta, 1991.

Buridani, Iohannis. *Quaestiones super Libris quattuor De Caelo et Mundo*, ed. E.A. Moody. Cambridge, MA: The Medieval Academy of America, 2012.

Caillois, Roger. *The Edge of Surrealism: A Roger Caillois Reader*, tr. C. Frank, C. Naish, ed. C. Frank. Durham, NC and London: Duke University Press, 2003.

Carli, Alberto. *Paolo Gorini. La fiaba del mago di Lodi*. Rome: Interlinea, 2009.

Carroll, Peter J. *Liber Null*. Newburyport, MA: Red Wheel Weiser, 1987.

Ccru, *Writings 1997–2003*. Falmouth: Urbanomic, 2017.

Crowley, Aleister. *Liber 333: The Book of Lies, Falsely So-Called* Ilfracombe: Haydn Press, 1952.

—— *Magick Without Tears*. Ed. I. Regardie. St. Paul, MN: Llewellyn, 1973.

—— with V.B. Neuburg and M. Desti. *The Vision and The Voice with Commentary and Other Papers*. York, ME: Samuel Weiser, 1998.

Davis, Marc, Piet Hut and Richard A. Muller. 'Extinction of Species by Periodic Comet Showers'. *Nature* 308 (1984), 715–17.

Deleuze, Gilles. *Nietzsche and Philosophy*. New York: Columbia University Press, 2006.

—— *Masochism: Coldness and Cruelty*. New York: Zone, 1989.

—— and F. Guattari. *Anti-Oedipus*, tr. R. Hurley, M. Seem, H.R. Lane. London: Penguin, 2009.

———— and F. Guattari. *A Thousand Plateaus*, tr. B. Massumi. Minneapolis: Minnesota University Press, 1991.

Derrida, Jacques. *Specters of Marx: The State of the Debt, the Work of Mourning and the New International*, tr. P. Kamuf. London and New York: Routledge Classics, 2006.

Dimech, Alkistis, and Peter Grey. *The Brazen Vessel*. London: Scarlet Imprint, 2019.

Eckhart, Meister. *The Complete Mystical Works of Meister Eckhart*, tr., ed. M. O'C. Walshe. Chestnut Ridge, NY: Crossroad, 2009.

Eliade, Mircea. *Rites and Symbols of Initiation: The Mysteries of Birth and Rebirth*, tr. W.R. Trask. New York: Harper & Row, 1965.

Empedocles. *The Texts of Early Greek Philosophy: The Complete Fragments and Selected Testimonies of the Major Presocratics*, tr., ed. D.W. Graham. Cambridge: Cambridge University Press, 2010.

Emo, Andrea. *Supremazia e maledizione*. Rome: Raffaello Cortina, 1998.

Evola, Julius. *The Path of Cinnabar*, tr. S. Knipe. London: Arktos, 2010.

———— and the Ur Group. *Introduction to Magic: Rituals and Practical Techniques for the Magus*, tr. G. Stucco. Ed. M. Moynihan. Rochester, VT: Inner Traditions, 2001.

Faulkner, R.O. 'The Bremner-Rhind Papyrus IV', *Journal of Egyptian Archaeology* 24:1 (1938), 41–53.

Federici, Silvia. *Caliban and the Witch*. Brooklyn, NY: Autonomedia, 2004.

Ferenczi, Sandór. *Thalassa: A Theory of Genitality*, tr. H.A. Bunker. New York: Norton, 1968.

Fisher, Mark. 'Downcast Angel: Interview with Burial'. *The Wire* 286 (December 2007).

———— *Ghosts of My Life: Writings on Depression, Hauntology and Lost Futures*. Winchester: Zero, 2014.

———— *Capitalist Realism: Is There No Alternative?* Winchester: Zero, 2009.

———— *K-Punk: The Collected and Unpublished Writings of Mark Fisher (2004–2016)*. Ed. D Ambrose. London: Repeater, 2018.

Foligno, Angela da. *L'Autobiografia e gli Scritti della Beata Angela da Foligno.* Castello: Il Solco, 1932.

Fortune, Dion. *The Mystical Qabalah.* York Beach, ME: Samuel Weiser, 1999.

Frass, Elytron. 'Alt Economy of Inner Night'. *Vast Abrupt* (2019). <https://vastabrupt.com/2019/10/21/alt-economy-of-inner-night/>.

Freud, Sigmund. *Totem and Taboo*, tr. J. Strachey. Routledge: London and New York, 2004.

Furlong, Paul. *Social and Political Thought of Julius Evola.* London and New York: Routledge, 2011.

Galilei, Galileo. *Sidereus Nuncius.* Oklahoma City: Byzantinum, 2004

Galloway, Alexander R. 'Warm Pride'. *Culture and Communication.* 29 October 2014. <http://cultureandcommunication.org/galloway/warm-pride>.

Garton, Vincent. 'Leviathan Rots'. *Urbanomic Documents.* 2017, <https://www.urbanomic.com/document/leviathan-rots>.

—— 'Catholicism and the Gravity of Horror'. *Jacobite.* 2018. <http://jacobitemag.com/2018/07/05/catholicism-and-the-gravity-of-horror>.

—— 'The Limit of Modernity at the Horizon of Myth'. *Cyclonograph II.* 2018. <https://vincentgarton.com/2018/07/23/the-limit-of-modernity-at-the-horizon-of-myth/>.

Goodrick-Clarke, Nicholas. *Black Sun: Aryan Cults, Esoteric Nazism, and the Politics of Identity.* New York: NYU Press, 2001.

Grant, Kenneth. 'Austin Osman Spare: An Introduction to His Psycho-Magical Philosophy'. *Carfax 4: Austin Osman Spare* (1960).

—— 'Austin Osman Spare'. *Encyclopedia of the Unexplained: Magic, Occultism and Parapsychology*, ed. R. Cavendish, 224. New York: McGraw-Hill, 1974.

Griško, Miroslav. 'Operation Eukaryotic Cell'. 2018. <https://www.academia.edu/35500410/Operation_Eukaryotic_Cell_>.

Guariento, Tommaso. 'Dalla Parte Del Caos, Per Distruggere Il Biofascismo'. *Not.* 2018. <http://not.neroeditions.com/caos-vs-biofascism>.

Harman, Graham. *Weird Realism: Lovecraft and Philosophy*. Winchester: Zero, 2012.

Heisenberg, Werner. *Quantum Theory and Measurement*, ed. J. A. Wheeler and W. H. Zurek. Princeton, NJ: Princeton University Press, 1983.

—— *Reality and its Order*, tr. M.B. Rumscheidt, N. Lukens, and I. Heisenberg, ed. K. Kleinknecht. Cham: Springer, 2019.

Heraclitus. *The Texts of Early Greek Philosophy: The Complete Fragments and Selected Testimonies of the Major Presocratics*, tr., ed. D.W. Graham. Cambridge: Cambridge University Press, 2010.

Hildegard of Bingen. *Scivias*, tr. Mother C. Hart, J. Bishop. Mahwah, NJ and New York: Paulist Press, 1990.

Hobbes, Thomas. *Leviathan*, ed. C. Macpherson. London: Penguin, 1980.

Hunt-Hendrix, Hunter. 'Transcendental Black Metal'. *Hideous Gnosis: Black Metal Theory Symposium*, ed. N. Masciandaro, 53–65. CreateSpace, 2010.

Idel, Moshe. *Primeval Evil in Kabbalah: Totality, Perfection, Perfectibility*. Brooklyn, NY: Ktav, 2020.

Ireland, Amy. 'Black Circuit: Code for the Numbers to Come'. *e-flux* 80 (2017). <https://www.e-flux.com/journal/80/100016/black-circuit-code-for-the-numbers-to-come/>.

—— 'The Poememenon: Form as Occult Technology'. *Urbanomic Documents*. 2017. <https://www.urbanomic.com/document/poememenon>.

—— 'Alien Rhythms'. *oAZ*. 2019. <zinzrinz.blogspot.com/2019/04/alien-rhythms.html>.

Jaeger, Werner. *Paideia: The Ideals of Greek Culture*, tr. G. Highet. New York and Oxford: Oxford University Press, 1939.

John of the Cross. 'Ascent of Mount Carmel by Saint John of the Cross'. *The Collected Works of St. John of the Cross*, tr. K. Kavanaugh and O. Rodriguez. Washington DC: Institute of Carmelite Studies, 1991.

Johnson, L.W., and M.L. Wolbarsht. 'Mercury Poisoning: A Probable Cause of Isaac Newton's Physical and Mental Ills'. *Notes Rec. R. Soc. Lond* 34 (1979), 1–9.

Kierkegaard, Søren. *Fear and Trembling*, tr. A. Hannay. London: Penguin Classics, 1985.

Klossowski, Pierre. *Diana at Her Bath and The Women of Rome*, tr. S. Sartarelli. New York: Marsilio, 1998.

Kondepudi, Dilip, and Ilya Prigogine. *Modern Thermodynamics: From Heat Engines to Dissipative Structures*. Hoboken, NJ: Wiley, 2014.

Konior, Bogna. 'Unlearning Habitual Cosmologies: Reading Stanisław Lem at the Event Horizon'. *Dispatches from The Institute of Incoherent Geography* 1:4 (2019), 39–46.

Kristeva, Julia. *Black Sun: Depression and Melancholia*. New York: Columbia University Press, 1992.

Laitman, Michael (ed.), *The Zohar*. Toronto: Laitman Kabbalah Publishers, 2009.

Land, Nick. *The Thirst for Annihilation*. London: Routledge, 1992.

——— 'Organisation is Suppression'. Interview with James Flint. *Wired Uk* 3:2 (1997).

——— *Fanged Noumena: Collected Writings 1987-2007*. Falmouth: Urbanomic, 2011.

——— *Reignition: Nick Land's Writings (2011–)*. 4 Vols. <https://github.com/cyborg-nomade/reignition>.

——— *Phyl-Undhu, Abstract Horror, Exterminator*. Shanghai: Time-Spiral, 2014.

——— 'The Concept of Accelerationism, Sesssion 2' (lecture, The New Centre for Research & Practice, March 12, 2017).

——— 'Disintegration', *Jacobite* (2019), <https://jacobitemag.com/2019/07/15/disintegration/>.

Lem, Stanislav. *Solaris*, tr. J. Kilmartin and S. Cox. London: Faber, 1970.

Leopardi, Giacomo. *Zibaldone*, tr. K. Baldwin et al., ed. M. Caesar. New York: Farrar, Strauss and Giroux, 2015.

———*Saggio sopra gli errori popolari degli antichi*. Firenze: Le Monnier, 1846.

—— 'Wild Broom (XXXIV)'. *The Canti*, tr. A.S. Kline, *Poetry in Translation*. 2003. <https://www.poetryintranslation.com/PITBR/Italian/Leopardi. php>.

Levi, Carlo. *Christ Stopped at Eboli*, tr. F. Frenaye. New York: Time, 1947.

Lévi, Éliphas. *The Doctrine and Ritual of High Magic: A New Translation*, tr. J.M. Greer and M.A. Mikituk. New York: TarcherPerigree, 2018.

Levi, Primo. *The Periodic Table*, tr. R. Rosenthal. New York: Schocken, 1984.

Lieder, N. 'Re: Planet X/12th Planet Cover-Up Mechanism'. *ZetaTalk*. 1998. <http://www.zetatalk.com/usenet/use00561.htm>.

Ligotti, Thomas. *The Conspiracy Against the Human Race: A Contrivance of Horror*. London: Penguin, 2018.

Lindsay, Joan. *Picnic at Hanging Rock*. London: Vintage, 2013.

Lovecraft, H.P. *The Doom that Came to Sarnath*. New York: Ballantine, 1971.

—— *The H.P. Lovecraft Omnibus 1: At the Mountains of Madness and Other Novels of Terror*. London: HarperCollins, 1999.

—— *The H.P. Lovecraft Omnibus 3: The Haunter of the Dark and Other Tales*. London: HarperCollins, 2000.

Lunn, Arnold. 'Alpine Mysticism and Cold Philosophy'. *For Hilaire Belloc: Essays in Honour of His 72nd Birthday*, ed. D. Woodruff. London: Sheed & Ward, 1942.

Maas, Anthony. 'The Name of Mary'. *The Catholic Encyclopedia*. New York: Robert Appleton Company, 1912.

Mackay, Robin. 'A Brief History of Geotrauma'. 2011. <https://readthis.wtf/ writing/a-brief-history-of-geotrauma/>.

Marcaccioli Castiglioni, Anna. *Streghe e roghi nel ducato di Milano. Processi per stregoneria a Venegono Superiore nel 1520*. Rome: Selene, 1999.

Marcellinus, Ammianus. *Roman History*, tr. J. C. Rolfe. Cambridge, MA: Loeb, 3 vols, 1986.

Marx, Karl. *Capital: A Critique of Political Economy*, tr. S. Moore and E. Aveling. New York: Random House, 1906.

Masciandaro, Nicola. *On the Darkness of the Will*. Milan: Mimesis International, 2018.

———— 'Laughing In(side) the Face of Evil: Notes on *Mandy*'. *The Whim*, 2018. <http://thewhim.blogspot.com/2018/09/laughing-inside-face-of-evil-notes-on.html>.

Mathers, S.L. MacGregor, and Aleister Crowley. *The Lesser Key of Solomon*. Bristol: Mockingbird Press, 2016.

Mattioli, Valerio. 'Il medioevo digitale'. *Il Tascabile*. 2018. <http://www.iltascabile.com/linguaggi/il-medioevo-digitale>.

———— *Remoria. La città invertita*. Rome: minimum fax, 2019.

McDermott, Rachel Fell. *Singing to the Goddess: Poems to Kālī and Umā from Bengal*. Oxford: Oxford University Press, 2001.

McSweeney, Joyelle. *The Necropastoral: Poetry, Media, Occults*. Ann Arbor, MI: University of Michigan Press 2015.

Meillassoux, Quentin. *After Finitude: An Essay on the Necessity of Contingency*, tr. R. Brassier. London and New York: Continuum, 2008.

Metcalf, Stephen. 'Introduction: "Even When the Heart Bleeds"'. F. Nietzsche, *Hammer of the Gods: Apocalyptic Texts for the Criminally Insane*, tr., ed. S. Metcalf. Sun Vision Press, 2012.

Metzinger, Thomas. *Being No One: The Self-Model Theory of Subjectivity*. Cambridge, MA: MIT Press, 2003.

Michelstaedter, Carlo. *Persuasion and Rhetoric*, tr. R.S. Valentino, C.S. Blum, and D.J. Depew. New Haven, CT and London: Yale University Press, 2004.

Mishima, Yukio. *Sun and Steel*. New York: Kodansha America, 1970.

Mohaghegh, Jason Bahbak. *Omnicide*. Falmouth and New York: Urbanomic/Sequence, 2019.

Morselli, Guido. *Contro-passato prossimo* (Rome: Adelphi, 1987).

———— *Dissipatio H.G.* New York: New York Review of Books, 2020.

Moynihan, Thomas. *Spinal Catastrophism: A Secret History*. Falmouth: Urbanomic, 2020.

nix. 'Gender Acceleration: A Blackpaper'. *Vast Abrupt.* 2018. <https://vas-tabrupt.com/2018/10/31/gender-acceleration/>.

Negarestani, Reza. 'The Corpse Bride: Thinking with Nigredo', *Collapse IV: Concept Horror,* ed. R. Mackay and D. Veal. Falmouth: Urbanomic, 2008.

―――― *Cyclonopedia: Complicity with Anonymous Materials.* Melbourne: re.press, 2008.

Neumann, Erich. *The Great Mother.* Princeton, NJ: Princeton University Press, 1963.

Nietzsche, Friedrich. *Untimely Meditations*, tr. R.J. Hollingdale, ed. D. Breazeale. Cambridge: Cambridge University Press, 1997.

―――― *Daybreak: Thoughts on the Prejudices of Morality*, tr. R.J. Hollingdale. Cambridge: Cambridge University Press, 1997.

―――― *The Anti-Christ, Ecce Homo, Twilight of the Idols and Other Writings*, tr. J. Norman. ed. A. Ridley and J. Norman. Cambridge: Cambridge University Press, 2005.

Otto, Rudolf. *The Idea of the Holy*, tr. J.W. Harvey. Oxford: Oxford University Press, 1958.

Parinetto, Luciano. 'Bruno pro nobis'. *Giordano Bruno, La magia e le ligatures,* 11–12. Rome: Mimesis, 2000.

Parsons, Jack. 'The Book of Babalon'. *Hermetic Library.* <https://hermetic.com/parsons/the-book-of-babalon>.

Pauli, Wolfgang. 'The Influence of Archetypal Ideas on the Scientific Theories of Kepler'. *Writings on Physics and Philosophy*, tr. P. Silz. ed. C.P. Enz and K. von Meyenn. Berlin and Heidelberg: Springer, 1994.

Petrarch, 'The Ascent of Mount Ventoux'. *Selections from the Canzoniere and Other Works*, tr., ed. M. Musa. Oxford: Oxford University Press, 1999.

Plant, Sadie. *Zeros + Ones: Digital Women and the New Technoculture.* London: Fourth Estate, 1998.

Prigogine, Ilya, and Gregoire Nicolis. *Self-Organization in Non-Equilibrium Systems.* Hoboken, NJ: Wiley, 1977.

Pseudo-Dionysus, *The Complete Works*, tr. C. Luibheid. New York and Mahwah, NJ: Paulist Press, 1987.

Radcliffe, Ann. 'On the Supernatural in Poetry'. *The New Monthly Magazine* 7 (1826), 145–52.

Reik, Theodor. *Masochism In Modern Man*. New York: Farrar and Rinehart, 1941.

Rimbaud, Arthur. *Complete Works*. New York: Harper Collins, 1967.

Roden, David. 'Xenophilia'. *Enemy Industry*. 2019. <http://enemyindustry.wordpress.com/2019/05/02/x-phi-or-alienation-is-not-correlation>.

Ruhs, August. Endorsement. F. Hecker, *Inspection II* (CD). Editions Mego/Urbanomic, eMego 268, 2019.

Sacks, Oliver. *Migraine*. London: Picador, 1995.

Safranski, Rudiger. *Schopenhauer and the Wild Years of Philosophy*. Cambridge, MA: Harvard University Press, 1990.

'Satyr' (Sigurd Wongraven). 'Interview with Quorthon', *Nordic Vision* 5 (Winter 1996). <https://bathory.clan.su/publ/3-1-0-19>.

Scholem, Gershom. *On the Kabbalah and Its Symbolism*, tr. R. Manheim. New York: Schocken Books, 1969.

Schopenhauer, Arthur. *The World as Will and Representation*, tr. E.F.J. Payne. New York: Dover, 2 vols, 1958.

—— *Manuscript Remains, Volume 1: Early Manuscripts (1804–1818)*, tr. E.J.F. Payne. Ed. A. Hubscher. London: Bloomsbury, 1988.

Schrödinger, Erwin. 'What is an Elementary Particle?'. *Annual Report of the Board of Regents of The Smithsonian Institution* (1950), 183–96.

—— 'Are there Quantum Jumps?: Part II', *British Journal For the Philosophy of Science* 3 (1952), 233–42.

Sheehan, Thomas. 'Myth and Violence: The Fascism of Julius Evola and Alain de Benoist', *Social Research* 48:1, 'On Violence: Paradoxes and Antinomies' (Spring 1981), 45–73.

Sitchin, Zecharia. *The Twelfth Planet*. New York: Harper, 1976.

Solomon, Andrew. *The Noonday Demon: An Anatomy of Depression*. New York: Scribner, 2001.

Spare, Austin Osman. *Ethos: The Magical Writings of Austin Osman Spare*. Thame: I-H-O Books, 2001.

Stirner, Max. *The Ego and Its Own*, tr. S. Byington. Cambridge: Cambridge University Press, 1995.

Suso, Enrico. *Libretto dell'Eterna Sapienza*. Rome: Paoline, 1992.

Teresa of Ávila, *The Book of Her Life*, tr. K. Kavanaugh and O. Rodriguez. Indianapolis: Hackett, 2008.

Thacker, Eugene. *In the Dust of this Planet*. Winchester: Zero, 2011.

────── *Infinite Resignation*. London: Repeater, 2018.

Theweleit, Klaus. *Male Fantasies*, tr. S. Conway. Minneapolis: University of Minnesota Press, 2 vols, 1989.

Thomas of Cantimpere. *The Life of Christina the Astonishing*, tr. M.H. King. Toronto: Peregrina Publishing, 1999.

Thoreau, Henry David. 'Slavery in Massachusetts'. *The Writings of Henry David Thoreau, Journal, Volume 8: 1854*, ed. S. H. Petrulionis. Princeton, NJ: Princeton University Press, 1981.

Tomba, Massimiliano. *Insurgent Universality: An Alternative Legacy of Modernity*. Oxford: Oxford University Press, 2019.

Valentino, Basilio. *Azoth*. Rome: Edizioni Mediterranee, 1988.

Ventura, Raffaele Alberto. *Teoria della classe disagiata*. Rome: minimum fax, 2018.

Vittorini, Elio. *Conversations in Sicily*. New York: New Directions, 2000.

Whitmire, Daniel P., and A.A. Jackson. 'Are Periodic Mass Extinctions Driven by a Distant Solar Companion?'. *Nature* 308 (1984), 713–15.

Wittgenstein, Ludwig. *Culture and Value: A Selection from the Posthumous Remains*, tr. P. Winch, eds. G.H. von Wright, H. Nyman. Oxford: Blackwell, 1998.

Woodard, Ben. *Slime Dynamics. Generation, Mutation, and the Creep of Life*. Winchester: Zero, 2012.

Yarvin, Curtis. *Unqualified Reservations*, <http://www.unqualified-reserva-
tions.org/>. *See also* Moldbug, Mencius.

Zolla, Elémire. *Le Meraviglie della Natura. Introduzione all'alchimia*. Rome:
Marsilio, 1997.

FILMOGRAPHY

Aster, Ari, dir. *Hereditary. 2018.*

Canevari, Cesar, dir. *Matalo!* [*Kill Him*]. 1970.

Carpenter, John, dir. *In the Mouth of Madness.* 1994.

—— *Halloween.* 1978.

Cosmatos, Panos, dir. *Mandy.* 2018.

De Seta, Vittorio, dir. *I dimenticati* [*The Forgotten*]. *1959.*

Di Gianni, Luigi, Gianfranco Mingozzi, Vittorio De Seta, and Cecilia Mangini, dirs. *Magia lucana* [*Magic from Lucania*]. 1958.

Fulci, Lucio, dir. *Non si sevizia un paperino* [*Don't Torture a Duckling*]. 1972.

Green, David Gordon, dir. *Halloween.* 2018.

Mangini, Cecilia, dir. *Stendalì: Suonano ancora. 1960.*

Mingozzi, Gian Franco, dir. *La Taranta* [*Tarantula*]. 1962.

Mirnau, F.W., dir. *Nosferatu.* 1922.

Pasolini, Pier Paolo, dir. *Salò or the 120 Days of Sodom,* 1975.

Questi, Giulio, dir. *Se sei vivo spara* [*Django Kill... If You Live, Shoot!*]. 1967.

—— *Arcana.* 1972.

Rondi, Brunello, dir. *Il demonio* [*The Demon*]. 1963.

Rossellini, Roberto, dir. *Stromboli terra di Dio* [*Stromboli, Land of God*]. 1950.

Visconti, Luchino, dir. *La terra trema* [*The Earth Trembles*]. 1948.

Von Trier, Lars, dir. *Melancholia.* 2011.

DISCOGRAPHY

Ain Soph. *Ars Regia*. Nekrophile Records, 1986.

Anibaldi, Leo. *Cannibald*. ACV, 1992.

———— *Muta*. ACV, 1993.

Bathory. 'Baptised in Fire and Ice'. *Hammerheart*. Noise Records, 1990.

———— 'Blood and Iron'. *Twilight of the Gods*. Black Mark Production, 1991.

Canzoniere Del Lazio. *Lassa Stà La Me Creatura*. Intingo, 1974.

Chevelle. 'Send the Pain Below'. *Wonder What's Next*. Epic Records, 2002.

Coil. *Horse Rotorvator*. Force & Form, 1986

Dark Polo Gang. *Full Metal Dark*. 777, 2015.

Darkthrone. 'Transilvanian Hunger'. *Transilvanian Hunger*. Peaceville Records, 1994.

Death in June. 'Death of the West'. *Burial*. Leprosy Discs, 1984.

Easy Going. *Easy Going*. Banana Records, 1978.

Gel & Metal Carter (Truceklan). *I più corrotti*. Vibrarecords, 2006.

Goblin. *Profondo Rosso*. Cinevox Records, 1975.

———— *Suspiria*. Cinevox Records, 1976.

Hecker, Florian. *Inspection II*. Editions Mego/Urbanomic, 2019.

Lil Peep. 'Witchblades'. *Castles 2*. Self-published, 2017.

———— 'Cry Alone'. *Come Over When You're Sober*. Columbia, 2018.

Lomax, Alan. *Diego Carpitella—Southern Italy and the Islands*. Columbia Masterworks, 1957.

Lory D. *Antisystem*. RCA, 1993.

———— *Sounds Never Seen 1990–1999*. Rephlex, 2003.

Noyz Narcos (TruceKlan). *Non dormire*. Traffik Records, 2005.

Pierce The Veil. 'Today I Saw the Whole World'. *Misadventures*. Fearless, 2016.

Sense Fracture. 'Crime as Poetry'. *Forever*. Haunter Records, 2019.

Sick Luke. *Instrumentals*. Honiro, 2013.

The Sound. 'New Dark Age'. *The Lions Mouth*. Korova, 1981.

TruceKlan. *Ministero dell'Inferno*. Propaganda Records, 2008